The Judiciary,
Civil Liberties and
Human Rights

Steven Foster

Edinburgh University Press

© Steven Foster, 2006

Edinburgh University Press Ltd
22 George Square, Edinburgh

Typeset in 11/13pt Monotype Baskerville by
Servis Filmsetting Ltd, Manchester, and
printed and bound in Great Britain by
Antony Rowe Ltd, Chippenham, Wilts

A CIP record for this book is available from the British Library

ISBN-10 0 7486 2262 4 (paperback)
ISBN-13 978 0 7486 2262 7 (paperback)

The right of Steven Foster to be identified as author of this work has been
asserted in accordance with the Copyright, Designs and Patents Act 1988.

Published with the support of the Edinburgh University Scholarly Publishing
Initiatives Fund.

Civil Liberties and Human Rights

University of Plymouth Library

Books in the Politics Study Guides series

Contents

Boxes

Tables

Preface

The aim of this book is to guide students (and their teachers) through an increasingly important if somewhat inaccessible area of contemporary politics. While it was written with the needs of those studying British government in mind, it is very much my hope that those whose studies take them into the associated areas of comparative British–American politics and English public law will find much to interest them.

Part of the problem facing anyone following courses on the judiciary and civil liberties is knowing where the law ends and politics begins. Identifying this point is by no means easy. Uncovering the meaning of the law is invariably a complex and time-consuming task and one which, when completed, leaves little room for distinctively political analyses. More than anything else, it is this issue – retaining the prominence of politics in the face of what has become a 'flood tide' of primary statutes and leading cases – which has proved the most taxing. I can only hope that I have struck an appropriate balance.

The production of this book would not have been possible without the advice and support of a number of people. My students (past and present) at the Manchester Grammar School are deserving of special mention, not least because of their collective ability to remind me that the acquisition of knowledge must always lead somewhere. I would also like to record an enduring thanks to my colleagues in the Politics Department at MGS – Rod Martin, Richard Kelly and Neil Smith – for years of fellowship in the common struggle. A debt of gratitude is owed to the Series Editor, Duncan Watts, both for the many suggestions which have made this book considerably better than it would have been otherwise, and a seemingly inexhaustible supply of tolerance and goodwill. On that note, the long-suffering staff at Edinburgh University Press, most especially Nicola Ramsey, have shown me levels of kindness and consideration far greater than I ever deserved.

Finally, this preface would not be complete without recording the love and regard in which his partner for the last nineteen years – Dr Lynn Perry – is held by the author. The completion of *The Judiciary,*

Civil Liberties and Human Rights occurred in circumstances where my attention and priorities should have lain elsewhere. That Lynn accepted this without complaint, quietly getting on with the near-impossible task of balancing her own extensive professional commitments with the demands of our daughter, Kathryn, makes me more grateful than she can know. She will also understand better than anyone else why I have dedicated this book to the memory of Dora and Julie, whose thoughts on its contents would, I suspect, have given me pause for thought.

Introduction

This book is effectively divided into two parts. Part I, which comprises the first four chapters, focuses on a variety of conceptual and historical issues broadly concerned with the protection of rights. The subject matter is orientated very much to the politics of the United Kingdom. However, where comparisons are appropriate, I have made every effort to include references to the United States. The principal issues that dominate Part I are as follows:

- The meaning of the terms civil liberties and human rights
- The several ways in which the state might seek to protect them
- The arguments for and against the incorporation of the European Convention on Human Rights into British law
- The judiciary's role within the liberal democratic tradition in protecting fundamental liberties
- The nature of judicial reasoning together with a supplementary analysis of how the judiciary's independence and reputation might be guaranteed
- The reasons why, despite the constitutional emphasis on judicial neutrality and independence, senior judges have come in for increasing criticism in recent years, criticism that is very much linked to demands for greater executive power.

The aim in Part II is to use the materials included in the first four chapters as the background to one of the most important and controversial aspects of contemporary politics. This is the tendency of governments across the Western world, but especially in Britain and the US, to favour increasingly authoritarian responses to what they see as challenges to their power and legitimacy. To amplify this point, I have chosen to concentrate on recent legislative enactments – the Prevention of Terrorism Act 2005 in the UK and, in America, the USA/Patriot Act being two prominent examples – which have provoked considerable political interest. However, there is much more to what follows than a descriptive analysis of the relevant areas of public policy, important and revealing though this is. The principal sub-theme of Part II is to identify and consider the *patterns* formed by law and order legislation passed over the last twenty years or so. In particular, these include:

- The determination of the executive branch of the state to increase its ability to act on its own discretion, that is, without reference to the other two branches, especially the judiciary.
- The manner in which highly specific threats give rise to laws with a wide application, so wide in fact that many who subsequently find their liberties restricted were not those originally targeted
- The tendency which sees the most extraordinary measure become the basis on which subsequent additions to a particular body of law are constructed
- The implications of this 'drip-drip' effect on government power for the state of liberty.

Rather than attempt to cover every relevant area of public law, I have opted to illustrate these points via three case studies: public order policing, covert surveillance and anti-terrorism. These have the advantages of contrast and topicality. Further, by restricting their number, a better opportunity is created to examine *in detail* what it is about these laws that has caused so much outrage among civil libertarians. Consequently, a designated section of each chapter is devoted to an extensive discussion of their concerns.

At the same time, it is important to bear in mind that, precisely because civil libertarians can stand so easily on the moral high ground, there is a risk that their arguments acquire a superficial attractiveness. In other words, the ease with which they appeal to our liberal instincts should not distract us from the complexities of law and order policy-making. Like it or not, ministers in a liberal democracy are in an unenviable position on this issue. Not only are they forced to co-operate with regimes who do not share their own values; they also know only too well that a principled stance in keeping with the liberal tradition could all too easily result in an electoral backlash if voters believe, however unfairly, that their personal safety has been compromised. In the last analysis, ministers are forced to take ultimate responsibility for breaches in security and, in consequence, they demand the discretionary powers to act according to their own assessments of risk.

That said, it is rare, despite populist temptations to the contrary, to hear ministers in liberal democracies completely dismiss the importance of civil liberties. As a result, they tend to defend their policies by emphasising the themes of 'necessity', 'proportionality' and 'balance'. This suggests that erosions of civil liberties are justified by events and by the fact that they do no more than is strictly necessary to ensure that such threats are countered. In addition, ministers are very keen to highlight the various safeguards that are in place to guard against abuse. This is, in short, a detailed defence and the three main chapters of Part II (Chapters 5, 6 and 7) each devote a lengthy section to it. Those readers who wish to maximise their marks in examinations must aim to incorporate at least some aspects of this 'official' viewpoint into their answers.

On a final note, any reader unaccustomed to the law may be a little surprised by the detail in which the relevant statutes are examined. I make no apology for this. The relationship between statutory provisions and civil liberties is a complex one. If we entertain any hope of understanding this, the law must be properly deconstructed to uncover both its meaning and the legal principles that lie at the heart of the ensuing debate.

CHAPTER 1

Liberty and Rights

Contents

Overview

This chapter aims to introduce the reader to the politics of liberty and rights. Many of the issues it explores are intrinsically important. However, the reader is advised that it also raises a number of themes that figure throughout the remainder of the book, chief of which is the likely impact of human rights legislation on both public policy and the constitutional role of the judiciary.

Key issues to be covered in this chapter

- The language of liberty and rights
- 'Classical' civil liberties and socio-economic rights
- The debate over the protection of rights

Liberty, civil liberties and human rights

As is the case with so many terms that find their way into everyday usage, what one might call the 'language' of rights is highly contested. An attempt to address this problem has been made by David Feldman (2000) who advises that we begin by distinguishing between five basic concepts.

The first of these is *liberty*. For Feldman, this is the core value for liberals the world over, who regard liberty (freedom) as a key ingredient in human happiness. Liberty can exist only when both citizens and the state accept certain responsibilities. For example, citizens must avoid using their liberty in ways which, accidentally or otherwise, harm the interests of others. Secondly, government must establish how best to regulate liberty, both in the interests of equality (that is, that one person's exercise of freedom does not intrude unreasonably on that of others) and public order. Liberty, to re-use the old phrase, must not become licence.

The fact that liberty implicitly demands some form of government intervention explains the significance of the next three terms in Feldman's lexicon: *liberties, civil liberties* and *fundamental liberties*. The need for regulation forces government to consider which aspects of liberty – which *liberties* – are especially valuable. This issue presses particularly hard on the liberal democratic state, which should place great significance on those liberties that facilitate participation in public affairs (Ewing and Gearty 2000). These liberties are classified as *civil liberties*. The concept of *fundamental liberties* is a further derivation on this theme, these being absolutely essential to the individual living in a state that aspires to be both liberal and democratic. Such governments are under a powerful obligation to uncover the best means of protecting them, something which may involve according them special legal status in a charter (or Bill) of rights.

Feldman concludes his analysis by arguing that, in the course of the twentieth century, a variety of bodies – the United Nations and the Council of Europe are two examples – sought to incorporate the concept of fundamental liberties into international law. In turn, this has given rise to the idea of universal *human rights*. Those who draft international treaties of this type do so in the hope that all states will endeavour to protect them.

Classical civil liberties and socio-economic rights

The first attempts at drafting charters of rights focused exclusively on what are called 'classical' liberties. A particularly important example of this type is the United States Bill of Rights. This term referred initially to the first ten amendments to the US Constitution. A second series of amendments – the 'Second Bill of Rights' – followed the conclusion of the American Civil War in 1865, with further

Box 1.1 Deconstructing the US Bill of Rights

The First Amendment
This captures the six basic ideas on which 'a politically tolerant democracy' is to be constructed. These are:

- No established (that is, state-supported) religion
- The free exercise of religious beliefs
- The freedom of speech
- A free press
- The freedom of assembly
- The right to petition for redress of grievances.

The Second to Tenth Amendments
These add a more extensive list of civil liberties that are designed to offer additional protection to the six core values outlined in the First. The list below gives a variety of *selected* examples.

- The right to keep and bear arms
- No compulsory quartering of troops on citizens' properties
- No unreasonable searches and seizures of property
- The necessity of a specified warrant showing probable cause
- The need for a Grand Jury indictment in cases of serious crime
- A provision of double jeopardy to guard against repeat prosecutions
- A provision preventing self-incrimination
- No deprivation of life, liberty and property without due process of law
- No taking of property by an official for private use
- No taking of property for public use without just compensation
- The right to an impartial criminal jury trial
- A provision that all trials be both speedy and public.

amendments on two occasions in the twentieth century. The original Bill of Rights captures the essence of liberalism in its classical phase, when liberals were overwhelmingly concerned with the question of how best to create 'a proper functioning . . . [and] politically tolerant democracy' (Neuborne 1996: 84).

Leading American jurist (legal scholar) Bill Neuborne has deconstructed the original Bill of Rights into a set of no fewer than thirty-one ideas, each enforceable in law. You can gain a sense of this from Box 1.1. The first point to note is how the values underpinning the first amendment present the state as the *primary* threat to liberty. Second, and partly as a result, the Bill of Rights leaves 'the economic and social arena to the free play of democratic judgment' (Neuborne 1996: 84). The framers of the Bill of Rights took the view that economic and social rights were not fundamental to the construction of their ideal commonwealth. They also felt that the levels of material support the individual might expect – with all the implications this has for taxation and the disposal of private property – were destined to change from generation to generation. As a result, it is left to governments to decide such questions, not the courts. This thinking has stood the test of time. Over 150 years later, the Council of Europe also avoided the inclusion of socio-economic rights in its own Convention.

Social and economic rights

Today the classical tradition is regularly criticised for excluding economic and social rights. Thanks to the influence of social and Christian democracy, early liberal attitudes to the state have been superceded by a widespread acceptance that the latter is in the best position to provide certain 'social' goods. One of the first charters to include such goods is the UN *Covenant on Economic, Social and Cultural Rights* which:

> enshrines a wide range of social justice rights, including the right of everyone to the highest attainable standard of health; the right to adequate housing and a right 'to the continuous improvement of living standards'.

According to Professor Geraldine van Bueren (2004), the incorporation of the UN Covenant into domestic law offers a variety of advantages:

- Firstly, it would create a new framework for government policy. Ministers would be compelled to test their social policies against Covenant rights in a process that would be more objective and exacting than is currently the case.
- Secondly, transparency and accountability in policy-making would increase. In particular, the onus would be on government to justify before the courts alleged failures to meet its obligations.
- This should prove particularly useful to those groups – she gives the example of the poor housing experienced by British residents of Pakistani and Bangladeshi origin – who have suffered decades of disadvantage.

The growing influence of social rights campaigners is also reflected in the decision of the European Union to include social and economic rights in its *Charter of Fundamental Rights*.[1] This recognises that the ability to access the classical civil and political liberties depends on having equal access to the rights listed in Box 1.2. Whether this feeling has penetrated Whitehall is, of course, another matter. Government

---

Box 1.2 Chapter IV of the EU Charter of Fundamental Rights

Chapter IV Solidarity

Article 27	Workers' right to information and consultation within the undertaking
Article 28	Right to collective bargaining and action
Article 29	Right of access to placement services
Article 30	Protection in the event of unjustified dismissal
Article 31	Fair and just working conditions
Article 32	Prohibition of child labour and protection of young people at work
Article 33	Legal protection of the family and the reconciliation of family and professional life
Article 34	Entitlement to social security and social assistance
Article 35	Access to health care
Article 36	Access to services of general economic interest
Article 37	Environmental protection
Article 38	Consumer protection

Source: Ewing and Dale-Risk 2004: 111–112.

in the UK has been reluctant to depart from the traditional view that economic and social policy is a matter for Parliament. Tony Blair's rearguard action against adding the *Charter of Fundamental Rights* to the proposed EU Constitution suggests that it will be some time yet before official attitudes begin to change.

The Diceyan tradition

The substantive content of any list of fundamental liberties is destined to be debated for as long as men and women retain an interest in politics. However, for the most part, the politics of human rights has centred on a different question: how best should they be *protected*? The US Constitution has set the standard for those who believe that this should be done via a process of legal entrenchment. From the first, the US Bill of Rights was established as a form of a 'higher law' which could be amended only with the greatest difficulty. Further, thanks to the famous ruling of Chief Justice Marshall in *Marbury* v. *Madison* (1803), in the USA it is the court, not the legislature, which ultimately determines the meaning of the law. The importance of Marshall's judgement cannot be underestimated. Its effect was to reinterpret Article III of the Constitution in a way which granted the courts the power to review not just the actions of federal and state governments but also the laws passed by any legislative body. As a result, even Acts of Congress can be tested against the Bill of Rights to confirm their constitutionality (legal validity). If a court – but especially the Supreme Court – comes to the view that a particular action or law offends against the Constitution, it can be declared null and void, the popular term for which is 'struck down'.

A. V. Dicey and the British tradition

By contrast, politicians in the United Kingdom historically dismissed entrenchment as, at best, unnecessary and, at worst, dangerously unreliable. No one made this case with greater force than Albert Venn Dicey. Writing at the turn of the nineteenth and twentieth centuries, Dicey remains one of Britain's most influential jurists.[2] He is especially famous for his assault on continental polities which he accused of popularising the dangerous nonsense that rights could be best protected by designated charters. His scepticism was based on the fact that such documents represent a mere ideal, one that is not necessarily immersed in a country's political and legal traditions. Instead, Dicey insisted that the only successful method of protecting individual freedom was that stumbled upon by the British: a tradition which combines **parliamentary sovereignty** with respect for the **rule of law**.

The cornerstone of Dicey's constitutional ideal is unconditional parliamentary sovereignty. This manifests itself in three ways:

- Primarily, because Parliament is the supreme source of legal authority, the government is ultimately dependent upon it for its own powers. Ministers cannot pass and enact their own laws in defiance of Parliament's will.
- Secondly, thanks to attendant constitutional conventions such as ministerial responsibility, Parliament can compel ministers to account for unconstitutional behaviour and, where necessary, withdraw its confidence.
- Thirdly, and most importantly, Parliament itself is subject to recall from the electorate. No later than five years after it first sits, each Parliament must be dissolved to give the voters a chance to express their views on its conduct.[3] Any member who fails to meet the expectations of her electorate could find herself replaced. It is this knowledge, that what the electorate gives it can withdraw, that ensures Parliament's vigilance. It is not in the interests of MPs to allow government to ride roughshod over the rights and freedoms enjoyed by their electors.

The second check on executive power is via the courts and their determination to maintain the rule of law. For Dicey, the rule of law is an all-important constitutional principle. It contains the following ingredients:

- The actions of government must be authorised in law; ministers cannot act lawfully on the basis of powers they have simply invented for themselves. In effect, they must find authority in the **common law** (law created by the courts) or statute law (law created by Parliament).
- Further, the government cannot draw on a special reservoir of discretionary powers to which only it has access.

- Finally, the ordinary law applies just as much to ministers and their officials as it does to private citizens. Consequently, not only do they have the same obligations under the law, but any cases involving the government must be also heard in the ordinary courts.[4]

The rule of law places a special emphasis on the constitutional role of the courts. Unlike the USA, the British courts are ultimately subordinate to Parliament. That, after all, is the essence of parliamentary sovereignty. However, according to Dicey, this did not mean that the courts were powerless in defence of individual freedom. On the contrary, it was the primary duty of the court to establish whether government actually possessed the powers it claimed. Further, when doing so, the courts were expected to apply the presumptions that formed the common law tradition (see Box 1.3). Chief of these was the idea of 'negative' freedom. An individual seeking to defend himself did not have to convince the court that he actually possessed the freedom he claimed. It was assumed that he possessed it anyway. In addition, if the government wished to remove or restrict the freedom to act in a particular way, it would first have to prove it possessed the legal powers to do so. If it could not, it would have to persuade Parliament to grant it clear and explicit approval. Under no other circumstances would the courts accept the erosion of personal freedoms.

In addition, nothing in Dicey's conception precludes Parliament from creating specific positive rights. In recent years, beginning with the Race Relations Act 1965, Parliament has adopted this technique to counter deep-seated tendencies to discriminate against certain groups. It is true, of course, that such rights cannot be entrenched: what Parliament creates, it can repeal. However, a minister advocating the repeal of an established positive right is faced with the same dilemma as ministers seeking to nullify negative ones. He is compelled to argue his case in Parliament and accept the political consequences should his explanations fail to convince.

Defective Dicey

Whatever the merits of Dicey's analysis, it suffers from one rather glaring defect: it is shaped too much by constitutional practice during the mid-Victorian era. Later writers such as Sir Ivor Jennings felt that Dicey's constitution was designed to protect private property from the

Box 1.3 Freedom and the common law tradition

Presumption that all conduct was legal unless expressly prohibited
This famous presumption established the British tradition of 'negative' liberty. As Michael Zander (1998: 18) puts it: 'The traditional approach to civil liberties in Britain is that the citizen is free to do what is not prohibited by law.'

Presumption against the alteration of common law rights
Judges would only contemplate this if legislation was unequivocally clear on the common law rights to be removed or modified, and the circumstances in which this should happen (see Slapper and Kelly 2004: 209–10). This reaffirms the principle that the British can behave as they please unless and until they are told otherwise.

Presumption against the retrospective effect of new law
The concept of retrospective effect refers to a law that applies both 'backwards' and 'forwards'. In the case of criminal law, conduct which was perfectly legal when it took place suddenly becomes illegal and exposes erstwhile innocent individuals to criminal prosecution. Again, because it is the supreme legislative body, Parliament can pass laws with retrospective effect.[5] The courts, however, will apply such laws only when Parliament has expressly declared its intention. Further, as was the case with the War Crimes Act 1991, ministers may expect fierce judicial criticism when they attempt to do so.

Presumption against deprivation of liberty
Once again, the courts have taken the view that Parliament does not intend a person to be deprived of his liberty. As Lord Scarman in *R v. Secretary of State for the Home Department, ex parte Khawaja* (1983) stated, 'if Parliament intends to exclude effective judicial review of the exercise of a power in restraint of liberty, it must make its meaning crystal clear' (quoted in Slapper and Kelly 2004: 209)

claims of social justice. There is much truth in this. However, from our perspective, other consequences stemming from Dicey's hidebound perspective are more important still. In particular, in the years after World War One many of the assumptions he made both about Parliament and the judiciary as defenders of liberty were progressively undermined by events.

Parliament, for example, has shown a consistent willingness to grant ministers ever-wider discretionary powers. This process began when Dicey himself was alive, much to the old liberal's deep irritation. At first the motor of change was the emerging welfare state. Ministers sought a variety of powers to regulate the behaviour of factory owners, private landlords and those responsible for running the public services. However, in more recent years Parliament's willingness to empower government to act as it pleases has touched upon the most sensitive civil and political liberties. This has been especially so since the passage of the original Prevention of Terrorism Act in November 1974, a statute which heralded the arrival of a new era of authoritarianism in law and order legislation (see Box 1.4). More worrying from a civil libertarian's perspective is the fact that, in its eagerness to please the executive, Parliament has been particularly disinterested in the freedoms of the most vulnerable minorities (Travis and Dyer 2000).

The reasons for parliamentary compliance in the face of government demands for greater power are long and complex. The impact of modern electioneering on the culture and organisation of political parties is undoubtedly important. So, too, are changes within government, especially the centralisation of power around the person of the Prime Minister. In this respect, Margaret Thatcher's domination of British government between 1979 and 1990 demonstrated just how extensive Prime Ministerial control can become.

The result is that, by the mid-1990s, the UK's stock of liberty had been reduced to a residue. Fuelled by a succession of statutes, government power had grown at a robust pace. Moreover, Parliament has been most unwilling to create positive statutory remedies to counter it.[6] Further, despite their various presumptions in favour of liberty, the common law courts have been quite helpless in the face of this onslaught. It is worth adding, however, that certain authors have argued that, far from fighting a rearguard action, the senior judiciary has actually assisted government in its plans to impose greater restraints on the individual (Ewing and Gearty 1990 and 2000).

Consequently, by the 1990s a major campaign had developed, demanding that Parliament break with the Diceyan tradition and introduce a general Bill of Rights. Despite one or two misgivings, those who favoured such a reform tended to support the idea of

Box 1.4 The growth of law and order legislation

The following statutes have all had a significant impact on civil liberties in the United Kingdom

- The Prevention of Terrorism Acts 1974, 1976, 1984, 1989 and 1996
- The Police and Criminal Evidence Act 1984
- The Interception of Communications Act 1985
- The Public Order Act 1986
- The Security Service Acts 1989 and 1996
- The Criminal Justice and Public Order Act 1994
- The Intelligence Services Act 1994
- The Criminal Procedure and Investigations Act 1996
- The Police Act 1997
- The Crime and Disorder Act 1998
- The Criminal Justice (Prevention of Terrorism Act) 1998
- The Youth Justice and Criminal Evidence Act 1999
- The Terrorism Act 2000
- The Regulation of Investigatory Powers Act 2000
- The Football (Supporters) Act 2000
- The Criminal Justice and Police Act 2001
- The Anti-Terrorism, Crime and Security Act 2001
- The Proceeds of Crime Act 2002
- The Sexual Offenders Act 2003
- The Anti-Social Behaviour Act 2003
- The Criminal Justice Act 2003
- The Serious Organised Crime and Police Act 2005
- The Prevention of Terrorism Act 2005

incorporating an existing **charter of rights** – the European Convention – into UK law for this purpose. The nature of this charter and the supposed advantages its incorporation would confer is the subject of the next section.

A Bill of Rights for the United Kingdom?

One of the stranger episodes in post-war British history was the decision of March 1951 to ratify the *European Convention for the Protection of Rights and Fundamental Freedoms*, better known as the European Convention on Human Rights (see Box 1.5). The oddity of the decision

Box 1.5 The European Convention for the Protection of Fundamental Rights and Freedoms

The Convention was drawn up by the Council of Europe. This body was established in 1948 to achieve greater unity between the nation states and peoples of Europe. In light of the dramatic collapse of liberal democratic values during the 1920s and 1930s, one of the first tasks the Council set itself was the re-creation of 'a common heritage of political traditions, ideals, freedom and the rule of law' as the basis of a new European identity. In addition, the Council was heavily influenced by the *Universal Declaration of Human Rights* proclaimed by the UN General Assembly on 10 December 1948. The product of two years of deliberations, the Convention was duly signed by fifteen governments in Rome in November 1950. It came into effect three years later. By 1998, in keeping with the tradition that the Convention should be a 'living' charter, twelve additional documents (or Protocols) had been added.

However, much more important than the substantive content (which was not particularly original) was the manner in which these rights were to be enforced. The preamble made clear the Council's view that the human rights of Europeans would be protected much more effectively via what it called 'collective enforcement'. To that effect, an elaborate system of institutions centring on a Commission and Court was set up. It would be these bodies, rather than national legal systems, which would interpret and enforce Convention rights. The significance of this innovation is best seen in light of another, namely the desire that individuals could bring actions against their own governments. At first, not everyone was happy about this arrangement. However, throughout the following decades a movement in favour of individual petition gathered pace, with British citizens being accorded this right in 1965.

A key organisational change was made via Protocol Eleven which replaced the original Articles 19–56 with a new set numbered 19–51. The main consequence was that the original and separate Commission and Court were both scrapped and replaced with a single, full-time Court. The new arrangements came into effect on 1 November 1998. One of the main criticisms of the old arrangements was that they led to unnecessary delays. A typical case might drag on for five years before a final ruling was made. Protocol Eleven is designed to streamline the process of adjudication offering more effective remedies to complainants.

stems from the fact that, immediately after ratifying this Convention, ministers declared that UK citizens would have no need of it. The Convention, it seemed, was for the unfortunate residents of foreign countries, where, to echo the lament of Mr Podsnap, constitutional and political tradition was less favourably disposed to individual freedom.

As you will have gathered from the previous section, over time this defence became ever harder to make. With hindsight, the decision of the Wilson government to allow individual petitions in 1965 gave impetus to the case for change. Since this point the UK government has been regularly forced to explain why it is in breach of the very rights it pledged itself to protect. In addition, the reformers' cause was assisted by various other developments. One of these was the changing nature of judicial opinion. In his famous 1974 Hamlyn Lectures, Lord Scarman became the first senior judge to declare for a domestic Bill of Rights. By the 1990s, however, he and his colleagues had come to play the 'leading part' in the campaign for change (Bradley and Ewing 2003: 416). This was important. Without judicial support, the case for a domestic Bill of Rights would have lacked political credibility.

At the same time, it is arguable that sections of public opinion were becoming more receptive to the idea of legally entrenched rights. Social historians have pointed to the steady shift in popular attitudes to authority, notably the decline of deference to the views of the 'officer class'. The creation of the post-war welfare state played a central part in this process. Jeffrey Jowell (2003) has noted that, as more and more individuals sensed their dependency on the state, so they became more assertive in the face of what they saw as bureaucratic intransigence.[7] Equally, the 1960s saw the emergence of a wide variety of new social movements for whom the idea of entrenched human rights represented a means of countering centuries of discrimination and disadvantage. The fact that the language of rights figured so prominently in the American civil rights movement is not without its significance.

That a Bill of Rights might prove popular with the electorate was not lost on the leadership of the Labour party, especially in the aftermath of its 1992 general election defeat. The nature of British politics is such that political change ultimately depends upon the support of at least one of the two main parties. In this respect, the decisive breakthrough occurred in March 1993 when the Labour party leader, the late John Smith, delivered his lecture 'A Citizen's Democracy'. In a bold move, Smith committed his party to the incorporation of the European Convention into UK law. Not everyone was overjoyed at this. There is much in the British socialist tradition which remains deeply suspicious of charters of rights. In part, this reflects the tension between collectivist and individualist ideologies. Collectivists much prefer to talk about individual responsibility and duty. They also tend to think of charters of rights as promoting selfishness and irresponsibility. It is important to remember that the history of both the Labour party and the trade union movement is dominated by attempts, often unsuccessful, to force slum landlords and unscrupulous employers to behave humanely in their dealings with others. The very last thing British socialists wanted in the post-Thatcher era was a new legal mechanism to help owners of property evade their civic responsibilities.

The second source of suspicion is that a charter of rights has the potential to change the relationship between Parliament and the courts. One of the main reasons why British socialism rejected the politics of revolution in favour of gradualist reform was the realisation that parliamentary sovereignty could be used by a Labour government to force through desired social reforms. Though the courts might resist this process, providing such legislation was carefully drafted and implemented with a will, even the most obdurate judge would be compelled to enforce progressive policies in his court. The idea that a charter of rights, no matter how well intentioned, could provide a conservative judiciary with a weapon to block social reform is anathema to more traditionalist Labour politicians.

Despite Smith's premature death in May 1994, his successor determined to maintain this commitment. Sentiment may have had something to do with this. However, Tony Blair also had sound *political* reasons for doing so. Labour had seen all too clearly how the activities of the trade unions and other groups with which it was associated had been curtailed during the Thatcher-Major years, and were inclined to prevent this happening again (Travis and Dyer 2000). More importantly, for some time Labour had been trying to weaken its association with collectivist values, something which many in the party believed had made it vulnerable to Margaret Thatcher's populist economic policies. Support for a Bill of Rights was a partial corrective for this. It was a sign that Labour, too, cared about individuals and, further, that there was much more to its programme than concern over unemployment and the state of the public services. Finally, it is possible that behind Labour's proposals for a Bill of Rights was a hidden motivation. This is hinted at by Helen Fenwick (2000), who suggests that the principal political purpose of such a charter may prove to be the political cover it gives to a Labour government which has shown itself to be every bit as authoritarian in matters of 'law and order 'as its Conservative predecessors.

The case for change
Those who favoured a domestic Bill of Rights were able to marshall an impressive array of evidence to support their campaign. For the reasons explored in the previous section, the Diceyan view of the UK constitution could no longer be supported. If further proof was needed, it lies in the fact that the European Court of Human Rights (ECtHR) consistently found the UK guilty of violating Convention rights. By the end of 1997, of the ninety-eight cases defended by the UK, the Court ruled in no fewer than fifty that the UK government had breached at least one Convention article. Nor was it the case that the defeats experienced by the UK were of a technical or marginal nature. As Box 1.6 demonstrates, many touched upon issues of profound constitutional importance and, in doing so, called into question the integrity of British justice.

Such statistics also drew attention to the adequacy or otherwise of the domestic mechanisms for redressing grievances. On this point, a particularly influential thesis was developed by Professor Michael Zander who has famously described a domestic Bill of Rights as 'an extra string to the citizen's bow'. In other words, it offered an alternative and potentially more effective means of constructing successful legal arguments when bringing actions against the government. A third justification suggested that the refusal to adopt a domestic Bill of Rights was wholly illogical, since the UK continued to endorse both the Convention and the right of its residents to petition the ECtHR. This being so, it was unfathomable why government continually denied its citizens the ability to enforce the same rights in their own, national courts. This was even more so when using the ECtHR was

Box 1.6   The case of *V(enables) and T(hompson)* v. *the UK*

An indication of the impact the ECtHR can have on UK politics can be found in the case of two children who had been found guilty in November 1993 of the murder of a two-year-old boy from Liverpool, Jamie Bulger. The case remains one of the most controversial in the history of English criminal justice. The age of the victim was itself shocking. However, what really transfixed the public was that his murderers were both only ten when they lured him away from his mother on 12 February 1993.

Upon their conviction for murder, the boys were given mandatory life sentences, with the trial judge recommending that they both serve a minimum tariff of eight years before being considered for parole.[9] The Lord Chief Justice subsequently raised this to ten years. However, legal controversy erupted when the Conservative Home Secretary, Michael Howard, raised their tariffs a second time by another five years. The boys' lawyers appealed against this decision on the grounds that Howard had taken into account highly prejudicial material – namely a 278,000 signature petition along with a further 20,000 'coupons' collected by the *Sun* newspaper – while failing in his statutory duty to consider the welfare of the boys.

On 12 June 1997 the House of Lords ruled in favour of the boys and immediately quashed the fifteen-year tariff. However, that was by no means the end of the matter. Lawyers acting for the complainants then petitioned the ECtHR on two further grounds, both of which concerned alleged violations of their clients' rights under Article Six of the Convention: the right to a fair trial or hearing. Firstly, they sought a ruling on whether a politician – the Home Secretary – should have the power to set a tariff at all. Michael Howard's conduct up to this point had been highly questionable, leading many to suspect that his stance on such a notorious case was influenced by his determination to wrest control of the law and order agenda from the Labour Opposition. Secondly, they also sought the opinion of the Court over whether or not the original trial itself at Preston Crown Court was fair. Media reports at the time questioned whether the boys really understood what was going on. They were often asleep at key points and were certainly unable to advise their legal teams.

The ECtHR delivered its judgement on 16 December 1999. Finding in favour of the complainants on both counts, the Court effectively told the government that key parts of the criminal justice system were incompatible with the UK's obligations under the Convention. Either the government would have to reform them in a way acceptable to the Court, or risk further legal defeats in Strasbourg. Statutory changes duly followed.

both long and expensive[8] and, worse, led to the UK being perpetually embarrassed in the international arena.

Finally, reformers hoped that a Bill of Rights would have a transforming effect on the entire culture of politics and administration in the UK. Though it may take years for this to happen, the constant exposure to human rights issues could make those in positions of authority more conscious of the expectations of those with whom they deal. If nothing else, fear of legal defeat might act as a powerful corrective to the inevitable arrogance that accompanies power.

Conservative objections to a domestic Bill of Rights

It would be quite wrong, however, to imagine that these arguments impressed conservative critics. The Conservative party itself had a number of objections on both constitutional and ideological grounds (Zander 1998: 20). Taking the constitutional arguments first, it is undeniable that a domestic Bill of Rights involves a major break with constitutional tradition. While Conservatives are not opposed to constitutional reform per se, they are deeply sceptical about its efficacy. The default position of the party is that constitutional reform should be only contemplated in unusual circumstances or where existing arrangements have clearly broken down.

Lying behind Conservative scepticism is the intuitive belief that constitutional reform suffers from an innate flaw: it sacrifices the known for the unknown. Unlike both liberals and socialists, Conservatives question the ability of human beings to produce effective solutions where these depart from the accumulated wisdom that is tradition. Constitutional reform risks unforeseen consequences and invariably creates more problems than it solves. This can be seen in the decision of the House of Lords to outlaw the indefinite detention of foreign nationals without trial under the Anti-Terrorism, Crime and Security Act 2001. As a result of its defeat, the government replaced detention orders with a new set of control orders,[10] far more draconian in impact and more extensive in scope. The irony, of course, is that had ministers not been constrained by human rights legislation, such an authoritarian response would have been quite unnecessary (Thomson 2005).

However, the principal Conservative objection is concerned less with ironies than with the capacity of a Bill of Rights to destabilise the UK constitution as a whole. No matter how such a document is incorporated into law, its immediate consequence is that the senior judiciary will be called upon to pass judgement on matters which, in the past, were regarded as properly falling to either government or Parliament. The likely result was not lost on Lord McCluskey. In his 1987 Reith Lectures he argued that ministers will inevitably respond by trying to ensure that the 'right' judges are promoted to the country's leading courts: the House of Lords, the Court of Appeal and, in Scotland, the High Court of Justiciary and the Court of Session. Ministerial interference with the appointments process would eventually bring UK practice dangerously close to that of the United States, where appointments to the senior federal courts are closely contested and often bitterly divisive. McCluskey left his audience in no doubt that he viewed this as a retrograde development that would seriously compromise public faith in the integrity of judges (Zander 1998: 20).

In addition, Conservatives have also raised objections over the very nature of human rights charters. For example, Conservatives argue that the experience of the UK at the hands of the ECtHR demonstrates that a Bill of Rights is too easily exploited by criminals and other undesirables to justify or gain redress for conduct that the overwhelming majority find absolutely objectionable. This was especially so in a series of cases involving Irish Republicanism, notably *Brogan* v. *United Kingdom* (1988) and the hugely controversial *McGann, Farell and Savage* v. *United Kingdom* (1995).[11]

Irritation with the ECtHR was akin to an open wound in the party the last time it found itself in government. However, Conservatives have continued to criticise human rights legislation in Opposition. A further objection was raised by David Davies, to the effect that such documents are too often used to create 'spurious' rights which are out of kilter with both normal expectations and domestic traditions. For example, Conservative peers condemned the Human Rights Bill as it proceeded through Parliament on the grounds that one of its effects might be to compel the Church of England to marry same-sex couples in defiance of traditional teaching (*The Guardian*, 17 February 1998). Similarly, in August 2004 both Davies and Michael Howard launched an attack on Britain's 'rights-based' culture, which they held responsible for the growing obsessions with compensation and the over-protection of children (White 2004). While a rather oblique attack on a Bill of Rights per se, it is nonetheless consistent with Conservative scepticism that such measures are more trouble than they are worth. This theme is taken up by Tim Lawson Cruttenden (2004) who has argued that the real nature of Conservative objections stems from the fact that the very language of rights runs counter to traditional Tory dogma: responsibility, self-discipline and strong government. If true, such objections are, in part, eerily reminiscent of those of Labour's traditionalists.

Conclusion

The politics of rights are central to the liberal democratic tradition. However, you will have seen from this chapter that opinion differs on how rights should be best protected, or even whether their value has been overstated. Eventually, Parliament was persuaded that, despite Conservative arguments to the contrary, human rights in the United Kingdom would benefit from a separate charter or Bill. However, two important questions remained to be answered. The first of these was what might be included in such a document? Would the European Convention suffice, or was it in need of amendment? Secondly, and more importantly, given the nature of parliamentary sovereignty how could it be entrenched without provoking a constitutional crisis? The answers arrived at are the subject of Chapter 2.

••

✔ What you should have learnt from reading this chapter

• A basic understanding of the language of rights, including the distinction between civil liberties and economic and social rights.

• A more detailed understanding of the British tradition of protecting freedom, how this tradition contrasts with that of the United States and why over the last four decades this tradition has come under intense criticism.

• An insight into the nature of the European Convention of Human Rights and the arguments of those who both supported and opposed its introduction into UK law.

Glossary of key terms

Charter of rights A list of fundamental liberties associated with the idea of entrenchment. This argues that human rights are best protected through special constitutional arrangements.
Classical civil liberties Those freedoms associated with the emerging liberal democracies of the eighteenth century.
Common law Law developed by the courts, rather than the legislature.
Parliamentary sovereignty The tradition in the United Kingdom that law passed by Parliament supersedes all other forms of law, including that made by the courts.
Rule of law A fundamental value in any liberal democracy which states that society should be organised around laws, not the wishes of individual rulers.

Likely examination questions

What are civil liberties?

Outline two civil liberties.

What is the rule of law?

Helpful websites

www.charter88.org.uk   Charter 88

www.humanrights.coe.int   Council of Europe

www.europarl.org.uk   European Parliament

Suggestions for further reading

An excellent overview of the history of civil liberties in the United Kingdom is David Feldman, 'Civil Liberties' in Vernon Bogdanor (ed.), *The British Constitution in the Twentieth Century* (Oxford: Oxford University Press), 2003. A Scottish perspective on the same themes can be found in Chapter 1 of K. D. Ewing and Ken Dale-Risk, *Human Rights in Scotland* (Edinburgh: Thomson–W. Green), 2004. For those of you who wish to read more about the history of the American Bill of Rights, Chapter 3 of Edward Ashbee, *US Politics Today* (Manchester: Manchester University Press), 2004, is an excellent place to begin.

Notes

1. This was proclaimed at the meeting of the European Council in Nice on 7 December 2000.
2. Despite opinions such as Lord Cooper in *MacCormick* v. *Lord Advocate*

(1953), the Scottish courts never attempted to develop a distinctive stance on human rights issues (Ewing and Dale-Risk 2004).

3. There is a provision for this rule to be suspended, though both Houses must agree. This has happened on one occasion since 1911 when the law was last changed. A dissolution of Parliament was due in 1940. However, given the wartime emergency, the 1935 Parliament decided to remain in existence.

4. On this point, Dicey was famously sceptical of the French system of administrative law, a system which not only granted ministers wide discretionary powers but also enabled disputes over the use of these powers to be heard in separate administrative courts. Dicey was opposed to granting government broad powers to act on its own initiative since he saw in these the erosion of individual liberty. However, he regarded special hearings in separate courts as even more inimical to the rule of law, not least because he saw them as secretive and open to ministerial manipulation.

5. Recent examples include the War Damage Act 1965, the War Crimes Act 1991 and s. 75 of the Criminal Justice Act 2003.

6. A possible exception to this is the Police and Criminal Evidence Act 1984, which sought to balance increases in police powers with better statutory safeguards for suspects.

7. A cause célèbre in this respect was the scandal of a land sale in the early 1950s – the Crichel Down affair – in which the rights of the original owners had been totally disregarded by officials at the Ministry of Agriculture.

8. Though figures do vary, it has been suggested that the typical wait for a decision was five years at an average cost of £30,000.

9. Contrary to popular belief, this did not mean that the two boys would be released automatically at the end of the eight-year period. Rather, eight years would have to lapse before the boys could petition the Parole Board for early release.

10. The power to issue such orders was created under the Prevention of Terrorism Act 2005.

11. The latter, more popularly known as the 'Death on the Rock' case, was brought by the relatives of three suspected IRA terrorists killed by the SAS in an ambush on the island of Gibraltar. In a complex ruling, the ECtHR found that the UK had violated their rights to life under Article 2 by failing to retain sufficient operational control over its special

forces team. That the ruling was made by the slimmest margins – ten votes to nine – and the level of compensation awarded unusually low, did nothing to assuage Conservative anger, with many Tory backbenchers calling for the withdrawal of the UK's signature from the Convention.

CHAPTER 2

Human Rights Legislation

Contents

Overview

This chapter continues the narrative begun in Chapter 1. However, whereas its predecessor concentrated on the theoretical debate over the protection of rights, culminating in a discussion of the value of the European Convention, Chapter 2 has more practical concerns. First of these is to explain the precise nature of the Human Rights Act 1998, a statute which has become more rather than less controversial since it finally came into force across the United Kingdom in October 2000. In addition, it considers the wider impact of this Act for the judiciary in the United Kingdom, especially the all-important question of its relations with the executive.

Key issues to be covered in this chapter

- The Human Rights Act 1998
- Human rights in Scotland
- An alternative perspective on human rights in the UK
- An initial comment on the judiciary's role in protecting human rights in both the UK and USA

The Human Rights Act 1998

Despite opposition from both within and without, the Blair government insisted on honouring its election pledge to incorporate the European Convention into UK law. The subsequent enactment of the Human Rights Act 1998[1] duly brought the UK more closely into alignment with the USA and most European countries. For the purposes of the Act, the Convention rights incorporated into UK law are laid out in Box 2.1. Of the original fourteen Articles, Parliament refused to incorporate Article 2 (the right to life) and Article 13 (the right to enjoy an effective remedy). Ministers successfully argued that these particular provisions were already covered elsewhere in UK law. Their inclusion, therefore, would have been superfluous. While this might be true of Article 2, it is far less certain that the provisions of Article 13 are equally well catered for. If so, this suggests a certain defensiveness among ministers, very possibly in respect of the remedies available to those who believe their right to privacy under Article 8 has been unlawfully interfered with. The implications of this will be discussed in more detail in Chapter 6 below.

The key features of the Human Rights Act
As far as the individual complainant is concerned, the key features of the Act are set out below:

- Under s. 6 it is unlawful for any public authority, or any other body fulfilling a public function, to act in a way which is incompatible with the Convention rights specified in Box 2.1.
- This means that, under s. 7, an actual or potential victim of such conduct can bring proceedings before a court in the hope that the latter will order the authority to review or possibly even reverse its decision.
- Further, and also under s. 7, a person may use the Convention rights to defend herself against charges brought by the government. Typically, this will involve a criminal prosecution, though other types of action could also be covered. For example, a person charged with a public order offence might argue that his conduct was justified because of the rights granted by Articles 9, 10 and 11.

Box 2.1 The Convention rights incorporated into UK law

Article	Substantive Content	Type
3	Freedom from torture and other forms of behaviour which are degrading or inhuman	Unconditional
4	Freedom from slavery and forced labour	Unconditional
5	The right to liberty and security of the person	Conditional
6	The right to a fair hearing or trial	Conditional
7	Freedom from retrospective criminal laws	Conditional
8	The right to respect for a person's private and family life, home and correspondence	Conditional
9	Freedom of thought, conscience and religion	Conditional
10	Freedom of expression	Conditional
11	Freedom of peaceful assembly and association, a freedom which extends to forming and joining a trade union	Conditional
12	The right to marry and found a family	Conditional
14	Prohibition of discrimination	Unconditional
Protocol 1		
1	The right to peaceful enjoyment of one's possessions	Conditional
2	The right to an education	Conditional
3	The right to participate in a free election via a secret ballot	Conditional
Protocol 6		
1	Abolition of the death penalty	Conditional
2	Preservation of the death penalty in times of war	Conditional

- The Act also offers additional and highly specific advantages to anyone whose case involves freedom of expression (but especially journalistic, literary and artistic materials) and the exercise by a religious organisation of freedom of thought, conscience and religion. Under ss. 12–13, a court must have particular regard to these rights when considering its ruling.

- More generally, the Act compels the courts to take note of the jurisprudence of the ECtHR (s. 2(1)). As a result, the concepts they must use to assess the legality of official action under judicial review will have to change in a way that should benefit the individual complainant.
- Providing the court does not exceed its powers when doing so, under s. 8 it can order the offending authority to make such remedy or relief as it deems appropriate.

The Act also imposes a duty on the courts that, where it has to interpret the meaning of a law passed by Parliament, it must do so in such a way to render the law compatible with the Convention. If it cannot do so, the following arrangements apply:

- If the law is a form of secondary legislation it becomes invalid, unless the secondary law is brought into being in order to give effect to a primary one.
- This is particularly important for laws passed by the Scottish Parliament, since these are all secondary laws for the purposes of the Act.
- If the law is primary legislation – and the court is sufficiently senior[2] – it can issue a **declaration of incompatibility** under s. 4. This places Parliament 'on notice' that the Act contravenes a **Convention right**, the clear implication being that new primary legislation should be introduced to remedy this.
- However, in the event that the minister concerned believes that the situation warrants it, a special 'fast track' procedure was created under s. 10 to bring about a change in the law much more quickly.

The strengths of the Human Rights Act
Does the Human Rights Act fulfil the aspirations of those who have long campaigned for a UK Bill of Rights? Supporters of the Act argue that its real value emerges against the following criteria:

- Will it enhance access to the courts?
- Will it make it easier for complainants to prove their cases?
- Will it compel ministers and other public officials to take human rights issues more seriously?

I shall take each of these in turn.

Access to justice

As can be seen from the previous section, the Act creates two new opportunities to bring actions against public authorities. However, what is equally important is the manner in which it does this.

Firstly, the rights incorporated are designed to cover everyone living in the United Kingdom. In the past, when Parliament created positive rights, it tended to focus on the needs of very particular groups. In addition, it did this with a certain reluctance and only after years of intensive lobbying, something which was not lost on the judiciary who tended to apply these laws in a less-than-liberal attitude. In particular, the courts have been keen to restrict the number of people who can use these laws to seek redress. However, this option is less available to the courts when hearing a *human* rights case.

The second advantage is that the wording of the Articles establishes a far more comprehensive range of positive rights than UK citizens have ever possessed in domestic law and, more importantly, does so using language that is deliberately open-textured. As a result, complainants have considerably greater flexibility in constructing cases under the Human Rights Act. This does not guarantee them success. Far from it. What it does mean, however, is that they have a better chance than before of bringing an arguable case before the courts.

Adjudication

These points suggest that the Human Rights Act will significantly increase access to the courts as a means of redress. However, supporters go further and suggest that, in cases brought under the Act, they enjoy a greater likelihood of gaining a favourable decision once there. This point is best illustrated via a comparison with the pre-existing arrangements for judicial review.

During the last century, judicial review emerged as the principal means of using the courts to correct what the individual believed to be abuse of power by a *public* body.[3] However, in large part thanks to Lord Greene's ruling in *Associated Provincial Picture Houses* v. *Wednesbury Corporation* (1948), severe and self-imposed limits were placed on the ability of the courts to review government decisions. In a later case – *Council for the Civil Service Unions* v. *Minister for the Civil Service* (1985), also known as the GCHQ case – Lord Nolan reinterpreted Lord Greene's formulation to mean that a decision could be reviewed only when the court was satisfied:

- That the decision was either illegal (the official did not have the authority to act as he did), or;
- That it was improper (it offended the principle of natural justice), or, finally;
- That it was irregular (it was not taken according to the correct procedures).

Put more succinctly, if it could be established that the official did indeed have the power to act as he did, and, further, had followed the correct procedures, the only circumstance when a court would intervene was if the decision was *so unreasonable that no other person acting in that position could have arrived at it.* In short, that he had taken leave of his senses.

The unsatisfactory nature of this situation was pointed out by Lord Nolan in the GCHQ case. It is noteworthy that, in his reformulation, he attempted to add a fourth criterion for judging the validity of official decisions: **proportionality**. Here, Lord Nolan argued that the likely benefits of a decision have to be offset against their adverse consequences. The implication is that, if the latter outweigh the former, the decision should not stand. This was an important departure. The concept of proportionality demands a far more critical response from the courts. In essence, it asks judges to consider not whether the decision lies within an acceptable range of options, but whether the intended outcome is sufficiently meritous that it justifies the loss suffered by the complainant. The ECtHR had long since employed the concept of proportionality and the associated idea of necessity in its decision-making. As a result, the Convention consistently offered 'greater scope for the protection of rights than the . . . concepts employed in judicial review' (Barnett 2004: 525). Thanks to the Human Rights Act, UK courts can at last use precisely these concepts when dealing with complaints brought under the Convention.

In *R v. A (Complainant's Sexual History)* (2000), the House of Lords laid down the following guidelines to help lower courts interpret the legal meaning of proportionality and necessity. The first question to ask is whether the provision in question interfered with a Convention right? If so, the court then has to decide whether the interference is justified. This is where the doctrines of proportionality and necessity are so important. They demand that three further questions be asked:

- Was the objective sufficiently important as to justify limiting a fundamental right?
- Were the measures adopted rationally connected to the objective?
- Were the measures which interfered with the right or freedom no more than necessary to accomplish it?

If the answer to any of these questions is negative, then it follows that the breach cannot be justified.

A human rights culture
The final strength of the Human Rights Act 1998 lies in its likely impact on Parliament and government. Despite the inability of the courts to strike down primary legislation, the Act places ministers and parliamentarians under an unusual degree of pressure to consider human rights issues when developing legislation. The quality of pre-legislative scrutiny will be enhanced both by the statutory duty imposed on ministers by s. 19 of the Act to declare whether their Bills comply with the Convention and the work of the new Joint Committee on Human Rights under the chairmanship of Lord Norton.

However, supporters of the Act also point out that the senior courts can also exert considerable pressure on both government and Parliament where they believe that the process of legislative scrutiny has failed to protect Convention rights. While it is self-evidently the case that declarations of incompatibility fall short of the power available to the US courts to strike down primary legislation, their overall impact should not be underestimated. In the first place 'an Act of Parliament which carries a declaration of incompatibility is likely to be badly wounded' (Bradley and Ewing 2003: 419) with all this implies for the credibility of the government. Secondly, if the same government refuses to respond to a declaration, a number of practical problems will ensue. These will bear with particular heaviness on public authorities. On the one hand, ministers might insist that the latter continue to apply the contested law on pain of action for failing to fulfil a legal duty. On the other, the relevant authorities will be loath to enforce a law which will expose them to further legal action and almost certain defeat. Such a situation would be not only embarrassing to all concerned; since the successful but frustrated complainants would be almost certainly advised to take their case to Strasbourg, the matter could all too easily result in a further defeat in the ECtHR. Under such circumstances, it is unthinkable that a government would refuse to comply when put on notice by the courts (Bradley and Ewing, ibid.).

Human rights in Scotland

Fearing a constitutional clash with the UK Parliament, the Scottish courts never attempted to develop a distinctive stance on human rights. However, the idea that Scotland automatically falls into line with the rest of the UK on this issue is now a thing of the past. One of the more noticeable features of the devolution process is that government in Scotland may well find itself leading the way in the development of a **human rights culture** across the UK.

Human rights and the Scotland Act 1998
The main reason for this is that the Convention rights are more deeply entrenched in Scotland than is the case in the UK as a whole. This stems from s. 29 of the Scotland Act 1998. Under this provision, it is unlawful for the Scottish Parliament to pass a law which falls outside that body's legislative competence, *a concept which includes any measure deemed incompatible with Convention rights*. More importantly, a very detailed set of procedures has been put in place to ensure that breaches do not occur.

- Both the relevant member of the Scottish executive and the Presiding Officer must declare their opinion that the proposed legislation complies with the Convention.
- Further, the Presiding Officer cannot submit a Bill which has passed its parliamentary stages for Royal Assent if either the Attorney-General, Lord Advocate or Advocate General has referred the Bill to the Judicial Committee of the Privy Council and the result of that reference is as yet unknown.
- This is a major departure from UK practice. More importantly still, if the Judicial Committee rules that the Bill does not comply

with Convention rights, under s. 32(2) of the Scotland Act the Presiding Officer must refrain from seeking Royal Assent unless and until the Bill has been suitably amended.

- As a result, the Judicial Committee has a power over Scottish legislation which is not replicated in any court in respect of UK legislation.
- Finally, Scottish ministers are forbidden by s. 57(2) of the Scotland Act from making subordinate legislation which is incompatible with the Convention, unless they are required to do so under a statute passed by the UK Parliament.

There are also two remedies available for challenging the legality of the Acts of the Scottish Parliament or the actions of the Scottish executive. Under Schedule 6 of the Scotland Act this can be done by a court or, alternatively, by the Advocate General or Lord Advocate after receiving information from a court, on the grounds that a 'devolution issue' is involved. In essence, this means that, despite initial appearances, doubts exist that a provision really does comply with the Convention. Secondly, an individual can bring a complaint under the Convention to an ordinary Scottish court on grounds described in the previous section. To remind you, because Acts of the Scottish Parliament are classed as secondary legislation for the purposes of the Human Rights Act 1998, they can be struck down by the courts. However, in their analysis Ewing and Dale-Risk (2004: 41) suggest that this is most unlikely. One: under s. 101 of the Scotland Act Scotland's courts have the same obligation to interpret all legislation so that it complies with Convention rights. Two: the amount of pre-legislative scrutiny ought to ensure that potential breaches of the Convention are spotted and rectified.

A Human Rights Commission for Scotland

A second factor which has encouraged the view that human rights may be better protected north of the border is that the Scottish executive has shown notable enthusiasm for a Human Rights Commission. This is in marked contrast with the attitude of the Blair government, which was much-criticised for ruling out such a body for the UK.

A Human Rights Commission for Scotland would have a role similar to that of the various Commissions established under equal opportunities, race relations and disability discrimination legislation. It would monitor, advise, spread good practice and, where necessary, assist individuals in bringing cases to court. The hope is, however, that, if it successfully completes its other tasks, the last item in the list will become superfluous. At the time of writing, after two consultation exercises, the Scottish executive was still committed to a Commission.

Human rights in the United Kingdom: an alternative perspective

It might be all too tempting to conclude from the above that the Human Rights Act, especially when viewed alongside the Scotland Act, is destined to have a profound impact on British politics. However, before conservatives begin to fear the worst, it is worth remembering that considerable scepticism exists over the capacity of the Act to bring about really significant change. Indeed, the openly optimistic assessment of the Act above can be countered on three main grounds.

Omissions and conditions
Firstly, the Human Rights Act is not necessarily the most 'user-friendly' of documents.

- As mentioned above, the Convention is an example of an older type of charter: it singularly fails to make any provision for social and economic rights. This includes specific provision to outlaw discriminatory practices in employment, housing and access to public services.
- Secondly, it omits Article 13 which, as I have mentioned, may restrict a person's ability to seek effective redress under certain circumstances.
- Thirdly, it should be noted from Box 2.2 that few of the rights listed are unconditional. The others are all comprehensively qualified in certain ways.

According to lawyer Tim Lawson Cruttenden (2004) the significance of these qualifications is invariably missed by the Act's supporters and critics alike. In keeping with the overall style of the Act, the qualifications are themselves very broadly worded. This leaves

---

Box 2.2 Qualifications on Convention rights

A Convention right can be lawfully suppressed on the following grounds:

• That the government's conduct is in accordance with the law, normally that laid down in statute
• That it is necessary in a democratic society
• That it is in the interests of national security, public safety or economic well-being
• That it helps prevent crime and public disorder
• That it helps protect public health and morals
• Finally, that it helps protect the rights and freedoms of others.

Lawson Cruttenden to conclude, somewhat provocatively, that any competent lawyer defending a public authority against alleged breach of Articles 5 onwards 'could drive a coach and horses through the Act'. If so, and public authorities can successfully demonstrate that a condition applies, justifying interference with Convention rights will prove far easier than many had hoped or feared.

Derogations, reservations and declarations
Aside from the conditional nature of most Articles, the Human Rights Act also enables ministers to legitimately breach Convention rights under a variety of additional circumstances. The first of these is by entering a derogation. Strictly speaking, to derogate is to evade a right or obligation. Article 15 of the Convention grants a signatory state the power to do this in times of war or a public emergency which threatens the life of the nation as a whole. The exceptions to this concern Article 2, where a derogation can only be entered during wartime, and Articles 3, 4 and 7 where a derogation is never permitted. Article 15 is replicated in s. 14 of the Human Rights Act. The UK government has entered a derogation twice, both in respect of the treatment of terrorist suspects. Until February 2001, when the introduction of provisions under the Terrorism Act 2000 rendered it unnecessary, the UK had entered a derogation under Article 15 which allowed police officers to detain terror suspects for up to seven days. The legality of this had been rejected by the ECtHR in *Brogan*

v. *United Kingdom* (1988) as a violation of rights under Article 5(3).[4] More famously, the government entered a derogation to protect various provisions under Part IV of the Anti-Terrorism, Crime and Security Act 2001 which allowed the indefinite detention of foreign nationals suspected of being or supporting terrorists. What is interesting in both these cases is that the courts have tended to define the term 'public emergency' in a way which gives the UK government considerable discretion when entering derogations on this ground.[5]

A reservation is a statement made when signing a treaty which either excludes or modifies certain provisions as they apply to that particular state. The power to make a reservation is included in Article 64 of the Convention and is reproduced in s. 15 of the Act. The UK has made one reservation to date. Public authorities are excused their duties under Article 2 of the First Protocol.

However, by far the most interesting aspect of the Act was the manner in which it sought to reconcile the traditional model of judicial subordination to Parliament with the liberal aim of encouraging the judiciary to counter what Fenwick (2000: 8) calls 'the effects of over-centralisation of power'. As we saw above, rather than giving judges the power to check the statutory erosion of liberty, instead the Act enables the courts to apply what one might call moral pressure on ministers to amend laws which breach Convention rights. This is the purpose of the declaration of incompatibility. However, under s. 4(6) it is clear that such declarations are neither binding on Parliament, nor do they affect the continued validity of any provision to which they apply.

Supporters of the Act can make sound arguments that ministers will nearly always introduce amending legislation. However, Barnett (2004: 535) makes the point that they are not legally obliged to do so. As a result, there remains a distinct 'possibility that governments of differing political persuasions may react with greater or lesser enthusiasm to declarations of incompatibility'. In other words, a sufficiently united and motivated government may prefer to engage in a 'standoff' with the courts, rather than concede to a declaration of incompatibility. In such a scenario, the judiciary will be presented with an intolerable dilemma. How far will they be prepared to go when standing up to the declared will of the legislature? To do so would run counter to some of the deepest instincts of many judges.

There is, in addition, another possibility, one which can be illustrated through the following example. As mentioned above, in November 2001 the Blair government entered a derogation to enable it to implement Part IV of the Anti-Terrorism, Crime and Security Act 2001. Though the validity of the derogation was approved by the Court of Appeal on 25 October 2002, this decision was reversed by the House of Lords in *A and Others* v. *Secretary of State for the Home Department* (2004). However, far from deterring the government, it simply reintroduced these measures in other guises via the Prevention of Terrorism Act 2005. The notion that governments may simply circumvent adverse judgements under the Human Rights Act might run counter to the spirit of the law. Yet, as the above example illustrates, it is both permissible and all too possible.

The doctrine of deference (the margin of appreciation)
The third ground for doubting the transformative power of the Act concerns the tendency of the judiciary to adopt a more defensive posture in its dealings with government, something which can be seen in the emerging **doctrine of deference**. This is based on a concept developed by the ECtHR known as the **margin of appreciation**. The latter is part of international law and, as such, is not applied by the domestic courts. However, there is clear evidence that UK courts have developed the doctrine of deference to take its place. In essence, this doctrine means that, after completing their deliberations, the courts will set aside their own views and defer to the expressed views of either the government or Parliament.

The justification for this doctrine is part pragmatism and part principle. On occasion, a judge might decide that they lack either the expertise or the contextual information to challenge the opinion of the other branches of state. This is typically so when the matter before them concerns one of the central functions of government, such as national security. Alternatively, and this applies particularly when Parliament has made its view very clear, judges might feel that to oppose Parliament will compromise the concept of the separation of powers. In particular, they will want to avoid any accusation that they have disregarded policy approved by Parliament by substituting their own view instead. That judges take their responsibilities imposed by the separation of powers very seriously can be seen in Lord Woolf's ruling in *R* v. *Lambert* (2001) where he argued that the courts should always pay a degree of deference to parliamentary opinion as to the precise meaning of the public interest.

Clearly, much is going to depend on what Lord Woolf meant when he talked of a 'degree' of deference. As Hilaire Barnett notes (2004: 531), there is a very fine line to be drawn in human rights cases. However, if the courts become too swayed by the idea of obligatory deference, they could end by 'failing adequately to protect human rights – the duty which has been conferred on the judges by the Human Rights Act'. This is endorsed by Helen Fenwick (2000) who has written of three possible 'models' of judicial decision-making under the Act, only one of which – the 'activist' – is likely to afford the individual proper protection. The tone of both authors suggests that they have strong doubts that Britain's judges will adopt such an approach. I shall have much more to say about the consequences of this below.

Conclusion: human rights legislation and the judiciary

This chapter is shaped primarily around the following learning objectives. However, as I pointed out in my short introduction, above all others it is also designed to draw out a number of secondary themes which link together the entire study. On this note, we are reminded that the impact of the Human Rights Act for civil liberties in the UK will depend ultimately upon a very complex set of relations between judges, ministers and parliamentarians. The importance of an assertive judiciary, active in defence of individual freedom, is central to the liberal democratic tradition. It forms the basis of Article III of the US Constitution and is absolutely pivotal in Chief Justice Marshall's interpretation of this provision in *Marbury* v. *Madison*. Equally, it lies at the heart of Dicey's observations on the rule of law. Yet, you will have gained a sense that a number of academic and political observers question whether the judiciary is capable of fulfilling this role. These criticisms pre-date the Human Rights Act, but have become more noticeable since its enactment. Whether or not such fears are justified is the dominant theme of Chapter 4. However, a more immediate question is, given the inevitable tendency of judges to be the subject of adverse comment, what measures have been taken to preserve their integrity? This issue, which involves the study of judicial independence and neutrality, is the subject of the next chapter.

....

✓ What you should have learnt from reading this chapter

- A detailed analysis of the Human Rights Act 1998 together with the Scotland Act of the same year.

- An awareness of the ways in which the Human Rights Act's advocates believe it will improve the protection of civil liberties in the UK and, equally importantly, the views of those who question not its desirability but its capacity to bring about the desired changes.

- An insight into the ways in which the fate of such legislation may come to depend upon the responses of the judiciary.

🔍 Glossary of key terms

Convention right One of the rights listed in the European Convention on Human Rights which is now protected under the Human Rights Act 1998.
Declaration of incompatibility A device which a court must deploy if it cannot interpret primary legislation in a way which makes it compatible with a protected Convention right.
Doctrine of deference The legal theory that the courts owe a duty to defer to the executive and Parliament wherever fundamental matters of state are involved.
Human rights culture The desired impact of human rights legislation on the values and working practices of anyone involved in policy-making and implementation.
Proportionality The key test for assessing whether a breach of Convention rights is justified by the goal it seeks to attain.

? Likely examination questions

What is the constitutional significance of the Human Rights Act?

How might the Human Rights Act enhance the protection of civil liberties?

Why are conservative thinkers so sceptical over the value of the Human Rights Act?

Helpful websites

www.cre.gov.uk   Commission for Racial Equality

www.conservatives.com   Conservative party

www.labour.org.uk   Labour party

www.libdems.org.uk   Liberal Democrats

www.snp.org   Scottish Nationalist party

Suggestions for further reading

The relationship between the Human Rights Act and the British constitution is covered in some detail in Lord Lester of Herne Hill and Lydia Clapinska, 'Human Rights and the British Constitution' in Jeffrey Jowell and Dawn Oliver (eds), *The Changing Constitution* (Oxford: Oxford University Press), 2004. An alternative source is Chapter 6 of Dawn Oliver, *Constitutional Reform in the United Kingdom* (Oxford: Oxford University Press), 2003. Once again, Ewing and Dale-Risk, *Human Rights in Scotland* (Edinburgh: Thomson–W. Green), 2004 gives an excellent account of the development of human rights law in Scotland at Chapters 2 and 3.

Notes

1.   Enacted on 9 November 1998, this piece of legislation did not come into force until 2 October 2000.
2.   This term includes the House of Lords; the Privy Council; in Scotland, the Court of Justiciary (when acting as the final court of appeal in criminal cases) and the Court of Session; in England, Wales and Northern Ireland, the High Court and the Court of Appeal.
3.   Judicial review cannot be used in what are called private law cases; for example, a dispute between a shop owner and a customer. A variety of alternative legal remedies exist in such cases, some of which are provided by Parliament, others by the common law of contract and tort (or negligence).
4.   It is worth adding that the Court subsequently accepted the validity of the derogation itself in *Brannigan* v. *United Kingdom* (1993).
5.   See the ECtHR's ruling in *Brannigan* v. *United Kingdom* (1993) and the Court of Appeal in *A and Others* v. *Secretary of State for the Home Department* (2002).

CHAPTER 3

Judges and Judging

Contents

Overview

The point of departure for this chapter is that the act of judging is a highly contentious one. When deciding the meaning of the law, judges have demonstrated an alarming tendency to disagree. According to the traditional *declaratory theory of law*, this should not happen. That it does provokes both controversy and an obvious temptation for the parties involved to secure the appointment of judges favourably disposed towards them. The fact that all too often government has an interest in legal proceedings further exposes the position of senior judges.

As a result, measures are needed to assure the public of the independence and impartiality of the judiciary. The purpose of Chapter 3 is to explain what these are.

Key issues to be covered in this chapter

- The declaratory theory of law
- The flawed nature of judicial decision-making
- The doctrine of judicial independence and its different manifestations in England, Scotland and the USA
- The doctrine of impartiality (or neutrality)

The declaratory theory of law

A common image of a judge is that of an ill-tempered, somewhat crusty old gentleman whose role is akin to that of an umpire in a sporting contest. His task is to ensure that both sides – the complainant and the defendant – observe the rules, before briefing the jury as to how they might go about their business of deciding the case.

It is an impression which, while not exactly false, is incomplete. This is because popular attitudes are heavily shaped by the criminal trial, which does indeed restrict the role of the judge in the way described above. Yet, in those cases with which this book is concerned, the role of the judiciary is far more complex. Unlike the criminal trial, the judge (or judges) not only hear legal arguments, they also decide the case itself. Secondly, in order to reach their decisions, they are often compelled to engage in a highly complex intellectual exercise, where they are called upon to uncover the meaning of the law (construction) before applying it to the the case before them (interpretation).

Yet, despite these complexities, those who practise the law still claim a moral superiority for their methods of decision-making relative to other branches of the so-called 'human sciences'. Part of this stems from the consensus among senior judges of their subordinate constitutional position. The courts will defer to the stated will of Parliament, while allowing government a wide margin of discretion when carrying out its tasks. Much more important, however, is the manner in which

---

Box 3.1 The main bodies of law in the UK

In common law systems, there are basically two sources of substantive law:

- Those which have emerged as a result of rulings made by the courts themselves *when deciding actual cases*. This is known as common law, that is law made in the ordinary, 'common', courts.
- Secondly, those which have emerged from a legislative body with primary powers, known as statutes.

In the absence of a relevant statute, a court will refer to the common law.

judges arrive at their conclusions; a process which, if one accepts this view, **is notable for its unusual degree of objectivity**. This can be seen in the common law doctrine of *stare decisis*, or **binding precedent**. This means that, when the case is to be determined by common as opposed to **statute law**, a judge must seek for a precedent on which to base his ruling. Where this has been established by a higher court, the judge must follow it. In theory, this doctrine offers certain advantages. Firstly, each new generation is encouraged to consider the accumulated wisdom of preceding ones. Secondly, as a result, the common law will begin to acquire a high degree of both consistency and objectivity. Thanks to this doctrine, common law judges simply cannot do what they want, even when they feel it to be right.

Similarly, the courts have also developed rules to assist them in the task of interpreting statutes. The most important of these is the literal rule, a very strict rule designed to ensure that statutes are given a meaning as close as possible to Parliament's intention. However, where this proves impossible, a judge might decide to use either the golden or possibly mischief rule to aid construction.

The purpose of these rules is to ensure that judicial decisions are largely devoid of personal prejudice. This is so even in the 'hard cases' where the meaning of the law is initially uncertain. In turn, this has given rise to the **declaratory theory of law**. This idea suggests that the law already covers every possible legal problem, including those which are yet unknown. Using their esoteric knowledge, judges simply apply the rules of legal reasoning so as to uncover what has always existed. While a little mystical – some might say fanciful – the declaratory theory nonetheless expresses a very important sentiment. Judges merely uncover the law; they do not create it.

The inherent flaws of judicial reasoning

The declaratory theory of law has been effectively challenged by a host of legal scholars. Despite the emphasis on the objective nature of judicial decision-making, these critics insist that judges are far more creative in developing the law than the traditional view would ever concede. So creative, it is suggested, that there is a real danger of bias – whether intended or otherwise – influencing their judgements.

Box 3.2 The rules of statutory interpretation

The Literal Rule
This traditional rule suggests that, when interpreting statutes, judges should give words their literal (that is dictionary) meaning, even when to do so might risk an undesirable or even an unjust outcome. The rule is based on the premise that, if Parliament has erred in enacting an ill-considered provision, it is Parliament's business, not that of the court's, to remedy it.

The Golden Rule
This is a derivation of the previous rule and is designed to give judges some flexibility so as to avoid an obviously absurd outcome; one which the court cannot imagine Parliament would have intended. The most famous exposition of the golden rule is that of Lord Blackburn in *River Wear Commissioners* v. *Adamson* (1877) who warned his colleagues that it should be used only when a genuine difficulty bars the use of the literal rule. Lord Blackburn was right to be concerned because using the golden rule does involve the court substituting its view of what Parliament should have said for what it was Parliament did in fact say.

The Mischief Rule
This is a very ancient rule dating from *Heydon's Case* (1584). The mischief rule asks judges to consider the 'mischief' (that is the wrong) that the common law did not deal with and which the statute was intended to remedy. It also asks that the court considers Parliament's motives when deciding to adopt the particular remedy of its choice. It was also established in the famous case of *Pepper* v. *Hart* (1993) that, in the context of applying the mischief rule, the court could use the record of parliamentary debates, or Hansard, as an aid to answering these questions.

Source: Slapper and Kelly 2004: 194–205.

One important explanation for this is the law's dependency on language. This would not be a problem if the precise meaning of words – both singly and in combination – was beyond dispute. However, day-to-day experience tells us that this is rarely the case. Language is open to competing interpretations: it is open-textured. Further, the more complex the ideas language tries to convey, the more open-textured it becomes. This is a general problem faced by anyone who has to make sense of language. In the case of judges, it is compounded by others which are more specific to what one might call the 'language of the law'.

The elusive nature of the common law

The common law doctrine of binding precedent may be clear in the abstract. Unfortunately, it does not always guide judges on how it might best be used in individual cases. There are a variety of reasons for this. Part of the problem stems from the sheer number of cases available. There are now so many that precedents have to be ranked, some being regarded as more important than others.

Yet, before the court can even decide which precedent to apply it must first undertake two demanding tasks. No two cases are identical. The issue facing the court is whether two cases are *analogous*: that is, that the same legal issues apply to both. However, in order to do this, the court must determine what these issues are. In theory, this can be done by identifying what is known as the *ratio decidendi* of the earlier case. The *ratio* consists of those arguments which are central to the earlier ruling. Other arguments – those which are incidental to *ratio* – are classified as *obiter dicta* and should not, under normal circumstances, be considered as important. If, after all this, the judge then decides that the case before them is analogous to the earlier one, they can then use the *ratio* to reach a decision.

However, as anyone who has enjoyed the dubious pleasure of reading through a law report for the first time will attest, deciding whether the essential facts of two cases are analogous and distinguishing between what is the *ratio* of a judgement and what is *obiter* is far from easy. We can only trust that, guided by the arguments of well-qualified counsel for each side, they will use their knowledge and experience to come to legally correct conclusions. More pertinently, however, we cannot guarantee that different judges, acting with similar levels of skill and integrity, will arrive at the same decision. The latter may feel that another case offers a more appropriate analogy. Alternatively, they may decide that different aspects of the judgement in question form its *ratio*. The result is expressed in the subheading above: the common law has an elusive quality, one which is as much a source of divergence among judges as consensus.

The complexities of statutory interpretation

Statutory interpretation presents the judiciary with a second set of problems. This is particularly relevant to human rights cases where statutes now play the decisive part. The initial difficulty, once again, is a linguistic one, the details of which are laid out in Box 3.3 below:

A vast array of difficulties present themselves as judges go about these tasks. These have been neatly summarised by White and Willock (1999). Some of these are virtually identical to the problems discussed in the previous section, in that the meaning of statutes can be also highly unclear when applied to the particularities of a case. This might be the result of poor drafting, especially where ministers become too heavily involved. Equally, it might be the result of the legislature's failure to spot ambiguities and uncertainties, or, for that matter, government's refusal to listen to sound advice. A third problem stems from the fact that statute law has become increasingly difficult to read as new provisions are 'bolted' on to existing ones with seemingly scant regard to intelligibility.

The difficulties in interpreting statutes have encouraged the courts to develop the rules laid out in Box 3.2 above. Yet, the very fact that the golden and mischief rules exist suggests that the courts desire a degree of flexibility in order to ensure that justice is done. However, the precise circumstances when the court should depart from the literal rule will be inevitably a matter for the individual judge.

Box 3.3 Construing, interpreting and applying statutes

This is a multi-stage task. How difficult it might prove will depend upon both the statute and the facts of the case before the court.

- Despite the tradition in the United Kingdom that legislation be written in as exact a manner as possible, it is unthinkable that a statutory provision could ever be written in such a way that its meaning is clear in all circumstances.
- As a result, legislation must be 'applied' to the facts of the case.
- Before this can happen, however, the court must first 'construe' it to determine the legal rule it creates.
- Finally, where its legal meaning is unclear, it must interpret it so that it makes sense given the facts of a particular case.

A further complication has emerged since the passage of the Human Rights Act 1998. It can be argued that this area of law is especially likely to produce a large number of hard cases, both because of the vagueness of the Human Rights Act and the highly contentious nature of the cases themselves. In addition, as we saw in the previous chapter, Parliament has now created another 'rule' which obliges the court to interpret statutes in a way which is compatible with the protected Convention rights. This was designed to reduce the occasions when the courts declared statutes incompatible with the Convention. However, one adverse consequence is that judges may find themselves having to interpret legislation in ways which involve dramatic linguistic contortions. This can only encourage judicial creativity and heighten controversy over the 'political' nature of their decision-making.

Judicial independence in England and Wales

In the previous section it was established that the difficulties facing judges are such that they often become far more active, or creative, participants in developing the law than constitutional theory might prefer. This has profound implications for the business of selecting and appointing them. If they were all likely to agree on the law's meaning, who each judge was would not matter. That they are not might encourage those with the capacity to do so to influence the composition of the judiciary in a way which suits their interests. This is especially so in the age of human rights when the potential for clashes between the courts and the executive has notably increased.

In short, the judiciary is in need of some constitutional protection, one form of which is the doctrine of **judicial independence**. An essential feature of the rule of law is that those who bring a case before the courts must be confident that the presiding judge is not under any undue pressure to decide it in a particular way. It has the following elements:

* Judicial immunity from suit
* Constitutional restrictions which limit public criticisms of individual judges

- Security of tenure
- An objective appointments process

I shall briefly explore each of these in turn.

Immunity from suit and protection from political criticism
Particularly in the course of the last century, various rules emerged
which limited judicial exposure to legal action and political criticism.
One of these is judicial immunity from suit. This effectively prevents
judges being sued. It applies to any act which either falls under their
jurisdiction, that is, a judge's professional duties, or which the judge
concerned reasonably believes to do so. Judges are also granted
protection in the law of defamation.

The importance of such provisions is self-evident. If judges are
liable for huge financial losses each time they make a judgement, the
chances of independent rulings disappear into the ether. In *Sirros* v.
Moore (1975), Lord Denning highlighted the connection between
immunity and independence when he remarked that a judge 'should
not have to turn the pages of his books with trembling fingers, asking
himself: "If I do this, shall I be liable in damages?"' (Bailey et al. 2002:
280). However, while it offers judges tremendous protection from
private actions for damages, if proven, deliberate misconduct can
result in a criminal conviction and subsequent removal from office on
grounds of misbehaviour.

By contrast, the laws governing political criticism of judges are
less certain. On the one hand, attempts by the media and politicians
to intimidate individual judges are clearly unacceptable. Judicial
independence would be severely undermined if judges were subject
to tirades of abuse whenever their rulings provoked the outrage of
one well-connected group or another. On the other, however, any
rule which seeks to protect judges from public criticism per se must
consider certain qualifying factors. One of these is the freedom of
expression. A second is the obligation of the media to report on
matters of public interest. Thirdly, there is the issue of parliamentary
privilege. MPs and peers have constitutional duties to represent the
interests of the nation as a whole. They cannot fulfil these if they
themselves are unfairly hampered in what they can say and whom
they can criticise.

Clearly, there is a balance to be struck. Taking the media first, 'scurrilous abuse' of judges is an offence which may result in a prosecution for contempt. In the years before World War Two the courts were keen on developing this aspect of the law; so much so that media freedoms suffered as a result. However, more recently the higher courts have compromised. Qualifications to the law on contempt were made in the case of *R v. Metropolitan Police Commissioner, ex parte Blackburn (No 2)* (1968). Here, Lord Justice Salmon ruled that even a vigorous criticism of a court does not amount to contempt 'provided it keeps within the bounds of reasonable courtesy and good faith' (Bailey et al. 2002: 265). In other words, journalists, editors and their publishers must avoid unnecessary abuse and act honestly. Where they do so, the law is unlikely to punish them.

In similar vein, Parliament has also developed rules to keep criticism of the judiciary within reasonable bounds.

- Any matter which is sub judice (before the courts) normally must not be discussed.
- There are certain exceptions to this, for example where a ministerial decision is in question or where, in the opinion of the chairperson, a matter of national importance is at stake.
- Further, other than when an address for a judge's removal is being debated, parliamentarians must refrain from casting aspersions on a judge's motives or character.

The important aspect about these rules is that Parliament has its own disciplinary system to ensure compliance. Matters are more complex, though, when a parliamentarian makes a statement attacking a judge outside Parliament. This is particularly so when the person concerned is a member of the executive, especially the Cabinet. Bailey et al. (2002: 279) note that 'Members of the executive are . . . expected to refrain from attacking judges, unless provoked.' The latter is, of course, an important qualification, not least because of the increasing tendency for judges themselves to speak out in public on matters of policy. Recent evidence suggests that this is something which certain ministers find difficult to accept. The 'running battle' between former Home Secretary David Blunkett and Lord Chief Justice Woolf is a warning as to how quickly executive–judiciary relations can deteriorate in the age of twenty-four-hour media coverage.

Guaranteeing security of tenure

The rules governing security of tenure are well-established and remarkably effective. They date from s. 3 of the Act of Settlement 1700 which came into effect with the accession of George I in 1714 (Bailey et al. 2002: 262, n. 23). The Act of Settlement was designed to put a stop to the Stuart practice of removing judges at their pleasure, thereby placing judicial independence on firmer constitutional foundations. No longer would judges have to concern themselves with pleasing the government in order to retain their posts.

The original provision has since been reproduced in s. 11(3) of the Supreme Court Act 1981, while further reinforcement can be found in s. 6 of the Appellate Jurisdiction Act 1876. The recent decision to replace the Lords of Appeal in Ordinary (the Law Lords) with a separate **Supreme Court** also led to minor changes to the law. The security of tenure of a judge of the Supreme Court is now guaranteed by s. 33 of the Constitutional Reform Act 2005.

Their combined effect is that every judge appointed to the High Court, **Court of Appeal** and Supreme Court may only be removed from office on an address (petition) to the monarch from both Houses of Parliament. The exception to this is when the judge is deemed guilty of 'misbehaviour' in connection with his official duties. An example might be a failure to attend court. In such cases, there are a number of alternative procedures available.

However, when misbehaviour is *not* the issue, ministers wishing to remove a senior judge must make their case before Parliament. This is unlikely to prove an easy task. Firstly, given the constitutional implications, they can expect the most severe questioning. Secondly, though the government might be able to 'whip' the Commons vote – though this is by no means certain – it will struggle to do the same in the Lords where the number of cross-benchers ensures that no one party has an overall majority. In addition, the culture of the Upper House has undergone a quiet transformation since the late 1960s. The voting records of today's peers suggest that they increasingly see themselves as a check on both the executive and the Commons. Consequently, it can be assumed that they will demand overwhelming evidence before they agree to an address. The strength of these provisions can be seen in the fact that the only occasion when a senior judge in the United Kingdom has been removed from office via the process of address was in 1830 when Sir Jonah Barrington, a judge of the High Court of Admiralty in Ireland, was removed after it was revealed that he had embezzled funds.

Senior judicial appointments in England and Wales

The relative clarity of the law concerning security of tenure is in marked contrast with the manner in which senior judges are appointed. Indeed, one can go further and say that the ongoing controversy over the appointments process has dominated the debate over judicial independence.

*   The system was based on the convention that the Crown appoints senior judges on the advice of two members of the Cabinet: the Prime Minister and the Lord Chancellor.
*   Fears of political favouritism were compounded by the absence of an open and objective system for identifying and assessing potential candidates for advancement. Traditionally, staff from the Lord Chancellor's Department monitored the performance of leading QCs and judges, and after a variety of interested figures had been 'sounded out' for their views, the fortunate person would simply be invited to take up post.
*   The fact that posts were not advertised so that no one actually knew who had been under consideration, nor why some were preferred for appointment at the expense of others, made this situation even more unsatisfactory.

Political bias

These arrangements gave plenty of ammunition to those who claimed that the integrity of the judiciary was inevitably compromised. Though they did not happen often, accusations of political favouritism did filter into the public domain.[1] However, any notion that political considerations influenced appointments was robustly rebutted by successive Lord Chancellors, none more so than Lord Irvine who held the post from 1997 to 2003. Echoing the views of his immediate predecessor Lord Mackay, he claimed that the secret 'soundings' provided unparalleled insight into individual qualities precisely because the senior judges and legal practitioners whose views were sought could speak freely and in total confidence.

Certainly, it is the case that the days when judicial appointments were regarded as the 'spoils' of office – an unsavoury feature of British history forever associated with Lord Halsbury – steadily disappeared after 1912. There is also a consensus among scholars that all Lord Chancellors since Lord Gardiner (1964–70) have adopted the view that the professional ability of each candidate is the only thing that matters. On this point, it is noteworthy that since 1977 no one appointed to the High Court or above has previously been an MP. Even such a staunch critic as Professor Griffith has concluded that 'being an active member of a political party seems to be neither a qualification nor disqualification for appointment (Griffith 1997: 16–20). If further proof is needed, it should be noted that the men and women promoted by the last three Lord Chancellors have acquired an unprecedented reputation for checking executive power. However, their liberal activism did not disbar them from promotion to the High Court; neither has it blocked their advancement to still more senior positions in the Court of Appeal and House of Lords.

In addition, Parliament has recognised the importance of placing professional ability at the heart of the appointments process. The Courts and Legal Services Act 1990 duly established strict criteria for appointment for high judicial office. Such requirements are, of course, designed to ensure that office holders possess the necessary

Box 3.4 Criteria for appointment to senior judicial positions in England and Wales

Post	Minimum qualifying criteria
Member of the Supreme Court (formerly the Lords of Appeal in Ordinary)	Either (1) two years in high judicial office, or (2) a fifteen-year period as a qualifying practitioner
Lord Justice of Appeal	Either (1) previous appointment as a High Court judge or (2) a ten-year High Court qualification
High Court Judge	Either (1) appointment as a Circuit judge of two years' standing or (2) a ten-year High Court qualification

skills to do the job. However, Lord Mackay (Lord Chancellor 1987–97) also expressed the view that such experience would also encourage a spirit of independence and open-mindedness (Slapper and Kelly 2004: 238).

Social bias

Other critics questioned the independence of the judiciary from a more oblique perspective. This originated in the tradition of allowing senior judges to make unattributed comments about the qualities of potential appointees. In turn, this led to the accusation that judges were highly stereotypical in their outlook and increasingly incapable of coping with the demands for justice emanating from an increasingly diverse society. The main criticism here is that, notwithstanding the objectivity of the Lord Chancellor's staff, too many opportunities were available to senior judges to block the advancement of those to whom they had taken a dislike.

One obvious example is the possible fate of radical barristers who were deemed to have made things 'difficult' in court. In a penetrating critique of judicial attitudes, David Rose (1996) notes the widespread concern among criminal defence lawyers that certain judges disapproved of vigorous cross-examination of police witnesses. It is all too easy to see how, in an unattributed briefing, a judge may warn the Lord Chancellor's Department that to promote to the bench such a person would be risky and ill-advised. This could only have a detrimental impact on an already conservative profession. Given the secrecy and the inability to see or challenge adverse testimony, it made sense for would-be judges to behave with great caution. The key to advancement is to avoid giving offence. While undeniably an excellent stance from a personal perspective, it is not necessarily ideal for entry to a profession which is supposed to uphold Justice in the face of Power.

A second example is more serious still. The judiciary in the UK has long been criticised for being drawn disproportionately from a very narrow social group of well-connected, rather elderly white men. To an extent this is a criticism which one should treat with caution. Historically, judges are drawn from the senior ranks of the legal profession. If that profession is socially unrepresentative, then it follows that this problem will recur among the judiciary. In addition, the nature of the law is such that it will take many years of professional practice before one can be reasonably expected to acquire both the knowledge and the skills necessary to be a credible judge. Of necessity, therefore, the latter is not a profession for the young.

That said, many observers of the legal systems of the UK have insisted that, even when one accounts for such factors, the record of the Lord Chancellor's Department in promoting talented women and members of social minorities is lamentable. According to this critique, judges commenting on the suitability of certain candidates allowed their own social conditioning to influence their observations. The qualities they believed were necessary to make a good judge were precisely those qualities they themselves possessed. It follows that those who most obviously share their *social characteristics* – educational, class, cultural tastes – more easily convinced judges that they possessed the necessary qualifications for the job, even when more objective evidence might lead to a different view.

Change at last: the Constitutional Reform Act 2005

Eventually the government absorbed these objections, though it took some considerable time for it to do so. The main barrier was Lord Irvine. While he acknowledged the need for reform, Irvine was determined to pass on the discretionary powers he inherited to his successors. As a result, the changes he made to the appointments process were minor ones. Unsurprisingly, they failed to stem the flow of criticism (see Box 3.5). However, it took the decision to replace Irvine

Box 3.5 The Irvine reforms

Irvine refused to budge on the central issue of introducing an independent element into the appointments process. He did, however, introduce new procedures designed to make High Court judges more socially representative.

- Those aspiring to appointment to the High Court were allowed to apply for the first time from 1998 onwards.
- Though this did not prevent the Lord Chancellor from making his own nominations in the traditional manner, it opened up an alternative route to advancement. In 2003, for example, of the

175 candidates considered, eighty-three were nominated, while ninety-two applied.

- This was complemented by an advertising campaign to encourage suitably qualified women and members of ethnic minorities to apply. 'Don't be shy! Apply!' went the soundbite.
- Following the recommendations of the Peach Enquiry (1999) a Commission for Judicial Appointments was set up as an independent 'watchdog' of the appointments process. One of its duties was to report on the efficiency and fairness of the process. In addition, the Commission was also empowered to hear complaints from the disgruntled.

Lord Irvine was optimistic that these reforms were beginning to bear fruit. For example, there is at last a female member of the Law Lords, a further two in the Court of Appeal, while the number of women appointed to the High Court stood at eight out of 107 in March 2004 (Slapper and Kelly 2004: 246). More symbolic still was the appointment of Mrs Justice Linda Dobbs as the first non-white member of the High Court in 2005.

Not that this impressed Lord Irvine's critics, foremost among whom was the very Commission he himself created. In their first report on the selection of High Court judges, the Commissioners were so dismayed at what they had seen that they urged the government to halt all new appointments (Dyer 2004). Their particular concerns confirmed what many had been saying for years.

- The Lord Chancellor was far too personally involved in the process. In 2003 the Lord Chancellor made nine new appointments to the High Court, five of whom were nominees. However, of these five, three were personal nominees of the Lord Chancellor himself.
- The so-called 'A' list of preferred candidates was compiled on the thinnest of evidence.
- The consultation process regularly failed to gather information which was either related to the stated criteria or supported by evidence.
- The result was the perpetuation of a senior judiciary dominated by white, well-educated men who enjoyed the reputation as leading barristers (Queen's Counsel).

with Charles Falconer, a moderniser very much in the Blairite tradition, before radical change was considered.

Falconer's chosen vehicle was the Constitutional Reform Act 2005. This particular statute has aroused considerable controversy, largely because of the reform of the office of Lord Chancellor and the removal of the Law Lords from Parliament to a separate Supreme Court. However, those sections which deal with the appointments process have been welcomed more warmly. The details of these changes are summarised in Box 3.6.

At this stage it is, of course, too early to tell whether or not the reforms are likely to silence critics. Much will depend upon the willingness of the Judicial Appointments Commission to assert itself in the face of any resistance from the Lord Chancellor. Who the first chairperson might be will prove vital in shaping the culture and

Box 3.6 The new mechanisms for senior judicial appointments in England and Wales

Appointments to the Supreme Court

As before, these are to be made by the Crown on the recommendation of the Prime Minister. However, the latter can only recommend the name of a person notified to him by the Lord Chancellor. This is a notable departure from previous practice. Even more significant is the fact that the Lord Chancellor in turn is obliged to notify only that person whose name has emerged from the deliberations of a selection commission which he is obliged to convene (s. 29).

This does not mean that the Lord Chancellor is altogether powerless. Firstly, he is able to issue guidelines which the commission must consider. Secondly, along with other leading political and legal figures including the First Minister, he is entitled to be consulted by the commission where no doubt his political stature will make itself felt. More importantly still, the Lord Chancellor is not obliged to accept the first two choices of the commission. This is an important power of veto. Further, any candidate who has been rejected by the Lord Chancellor cannot be nominated by the commission a second time. At the very least this should ensure that the government can keep out of the Supreme Court any person to whom it is violently opposed. Only after the commission has met three times *must* he then notify the Prime Minister of the commissioners' selection.

That said, the loss of formal power is significant. Neither the Prime Minister nor Lord Chancellor can make their own recommendations; nor can the Lord Chancellor reject nominees on a whim. Instead, he must follow statutory procedures if he chooses to exercise this power (s. 30). Finally, any decision by the Lord Chancellor to reject a nomination is bound to provoke adverse comment and will almost certainly result in the government having to answer some awkward questions.

The Judicial Appointments Commission
Appointments to the next three tiers of the judiciary – the Lord Chief Justice and Heads of Division, the Lord Justices of Appeal and the judges of the High Court – will fall under the remit of a long-awaited Judicial Appointments Commission (JAC). This will be a permanent body which will divide itself into committees of four members to identify and assess the merits of suitable candidates. This is also a key departure and one which is clearly influenced by Scottish practice (see below). It is for the JAC alone to produce the name of the person who it feels is best capable of filling the post in question. The fact that only one name can be put forward at any one time is a further blow to ministerial discretion.

This is something which legal reformers must welcome. In addition, they will also be pleased at the prospect of a more open and standardised selection process. Though it is for the Commission itself to decide how to go about its business, it seems unthinkable that the selection process for senior judges will not fall into line with standard practice elsewhere. This is especially so after the damning 2003 report of the Commission for Judicial Appointments set up by Lord Irvine.

Once again, however, the Lord Chancellor retains a significant role. As per recommendations for the Supreme Court, he is entitled to set selection guidelines and can veto initial nominees if he so chooses, though he cannot do this after the first two stages of selection. The one other figure who will play a leading part is the Lord Chief Justice, whose recommendations in respect of appointments to the High Court must be given special consideration.

working practices of the new body. However, it is undeniably the case that the formal power of government to control the appointments of senior judges has been diminished. In addition, those who wish to see a more socially representative judiciary will be heartened by the emergence of an independent element in the identification and assessment of candidates. The fact that the Judicial Appointments Commission is also under a statutory obligation to consider the issue of social representativeness is a further source of satisfaction.

Judicial independence in Scotland

The advent of devolution has had a notable effect on the arrangements for securing the independence of the Scottish judiciary. An important element of this is the manner in which the Scotland Act 1998 clarified the law governing the security of tenure.[2] The key statute – the Supreme Court Act 1981 – only applied in England and Wales. Prior to the passage of the Scotland Act 1998, it was assumed that only an Act of Parliament could remove a senior Scottish judge. However, s. 95 of the Scotland Act created a new procedure which is designed to work as follows (White and Willock 1999: 66). You will see that its essence is similar to the provisions in the Supreme Court Act.

- The process of removal is initiated by the First Minister.
- Whenever he contemplates such a move, he must convene a tribunal consisting of three people under the chairmanship of a member of the Judicial Committee of the Privy Council who will examine the judge's fitness for office.
- If they decide there is merit in removal, their report is laid before Parliament.
- Only if the latter agree can the First Minister make a recommendation to the monarch that the judge be struck from the lists.

A new appointments process

However, it is the impact of devolution on the appointment of senior judges in Scotland which is particularly noteworthy. Prior to 2002 judges were appointed in ways very similar to their counterparts in England and Wales, the main differences concerning the personnel involved. Rules were in place to ensure that appointees had the necessary professional competence. For example, under legislation passed in 1990, promotion to the **Court of Session**[3] depended upon either:

- Holding the position of sheriff or sheriff-principal for five years or more, or;
- Being an advocate (barrister) or solicitor with five years' right of audience before the Court of Session.

However, as in England and Wales, posts were not advertised, interviews were never held and, as a result, these arrangements were subject to precisely the same objections outlined above.

The Scotland Act 1998 changed this to a certain extent. Under s. 95(4), the power to recommend appointments to the Crown passed to the First Minister, who was also placed under an obligation to

Box 3.7 The Judicial Appointments Board for Scotland

Membership
There are ten members of the JAB all appointed by the Scottish executive, to whom they are responsible. Five of the members, including the chair, are lay persons; five are legally qualified.

Remit
* To provide the First Minister with a shortlist of suitable candidates for appointment as: a judge of the Court of Session, Sheriff-Principal, Sheriff and part-time Sheriff.
* To consider ways of making the judiciary in Scotland as socially representative as possible, without compromising the principle of appointment strictly on merit.
* To undertake the business of recruitment and assessment as efficiently as possible.

Guiding principles
These were laid down by the Scottish Ministers. While the JAB is entitled to draw up its own working arrangements, it has to incorporate eight principles, including the necessity of advertising all vacancies and refraining from recommending to the First Minister any candidate who has not been interviewed. The JAB is also obliged to monitor appointments for evidence of racial and other forms of prejudice.

The Board and the First Minister
Like the JAC in England and Wales, the Scottish JAB does not make appointments. Its job is to draw up a shortlist of suitable candidates which it sends to the First Minister. It is the latter, after consulting the Lord President, who makes a final recommendation to the Crown. Having a choice of final candidate is an important advantage to the First Minister and one which the Lord Chancellor lacks. That said, the First Minister does not have an equivalent power of veto.

consult with the Lord President, the head of the Court of Session. However, important exceptions to this were made in respect of the Lord President himself and a second leading judge, the Lord Justice-Clerk. Here, the power to recommend remained with the Prime Minister, an important reminder of the complexities of devolution in Scotland.

The most significant change, however, followed an announcement by the Scottish Ministers in September 1999 that a consultation exercise would soon commence on whether or not to introduce an open and independent appointments process. This began the following summer after the publication of a consultation paper entitled *Judicial Appointments: an Inclusive Approach*. According to Jim Wallace, who announced the results of this exercise in March 2001, there was a clear majority in favour of reform. As a result, Wallace declared the Scottish Ministers' intention to create a Judicial Appointments Board (JAB) as soon as practicable. The JAB duly began its work in June 2002 under the chairmanship of Sir Neil McIntosh.

So far, all the evidence suggests that these arrangements are working well. The only sticking point is a technical one, in that the JAB has not as yet been placed on a statutory footing. The number of appointments made to date (June 2005) is outlined in Table 3.1 below. It remains to seen, however, whether or not a future Scottish executive

Table 3.1 Appointments by the Judicial Appointments Board

Post	Date	Numbers appointed
Senator of the College of Justice[4]	July 2002	2
	September 2004	5
Sheriff-Principal	July 2002	1
Sheriff	September 2003	1
	April 2004	4
	September 2004	1
Part-time Sheriff	December 2002	32
	February 2005	21
Floating Sheriff	December 2002	9
	April 2004	9

will wish to claim the power of appointing the Lord President and the Lord Justice-Clerk. This will, of course, necessitate amending the Scotland Act itself, something which is obviously beyond the power of Scottish politicians to implement.

The spoils system: appointing federal judges in the USA

Before we go on to examine the concept of judicial neutrality, it is worth reminding ourselves that the US Constitution has adopted a rather different approach to protecting judicial independence. The federal nature of the USA is such that judges operate in very different jurisdictions. This section is concerned only with the federal judges themselves, that is, those appointed to sit in a federal court.

The importance of security of tenure is recognised by Article III of the Constitution 'which . . . gives . . . federal judges life tenure

Box 3.8 The principal federal judges in the USA

Title	Judicial functions
Justices of the **Supreme Court**	The nine Justices have three key tasks: to interpret the Constitution, apply it to the most complex and sensitive cases, and establish the rules by which the Constitution may be 'read down'. Their importance is such that they only hear cases on appeal. They are 'appellate' judges.
Circuit Court judges	These are the principal appellate judges in the sense that they will hear far more appeals than the Supreme Court. They are appointed to one of twelve 'circuits'.
District Court judges	These judges, who are also appointed to a particular circuit, are the main trial judges in federal cases.

(subject to removal only if they have committed a serious offence) and a guarantee against salary reduction' (Morrison 1996: 57–8). The exceptions to this are those federal judges who sit on specialised courts or otherwise perform specialised functions. Though they do not enjoy security of tenure, they are appointed for long periods of up to fifteen years. As is the case in the UK, the only way in which a federal judge can be dismissed other than for misconduct is via a motion (of impeachment) passed by the legislature (Congress).

The real distinctiveness of the American system concerns the manner in which federal judges are appointed. Rather than put one's faith in the relationship between a member of the executive and an independent appointments agency (now the dominant model in the UK), the US approach is more obviously rooted in the concept of the separation of powers. Far from trying to bring subtle pressures to bear on government, Article II(II) of the Constitution explicitly empowers the President to appoint federal judges, subject to what is known as the 'advice and consent' of the Senate. In effect, this means that the power to initiate the selection process lies with the President as another 'spoil' of the political battle. At the same time, if a majority of senators are implacably opposed to a Presidential nomination they can block it. However, this assumes at the very least that the President's party is in a minority in the Senate. Even then, however, it is likely that the Senate will exercise caution before vetoing a nominee. An overt display of partisanship may not play well with the electorate and risks a retaliatory response at some point in the future. The fact that no one else can nominate a federal justice also strengthens the President's position.

The reluctance of the Senate to defy the President is supported by statistical evidence. Of the 150 nominations to the Supreme Court, only eleven have been rejected outright,[5] though a number of others have been withdrawn. In recent years, the Senate has shown a marked disinclination to reject. Since a Nixon nominee – G. Harrold Carswell – was rejected in 1970, only one other candidate has failed to be appointed. This was the controversial Judge Robert Bork whose views on key constitutional matters, as well as doubts over his intellectual abilities, placed him 'beyond the pale' in 1987.

In short, the US Constitution does not so much separate power as encourage different political actors to share it, something which is designed to promote, if not goodwill, then at least a degree of co-operation. The fact that the process is so overtly political is its great strength. Those nominated by the President will be subject to interview by the Senate where their views can be tested. This will put both politicians and the public on their guard to ensure that federal judges do not see themselves as creatures of a particular President.

Equally, there can be little doubt that appointments to the federal judiciary, especially the Supreme Court, are highly partisan affairs. Party considerations dominate to a point where the independence of certain Justices seems irrevocably compromised. The label of 'unreconstituted right-winger' certainly seems to have dogged the reputations of Chief Justice William Rehnquist and Justices Antonin Scalia and Clarence Thomas.[6] I shall return to these issues in following chapters.

Judicial impartiality

Judicial impartiality refers to the mental state of judges when hearing and adjudicating upon cases. The ideal is that each judge possesses the following qualities:

*   Disinterest – the judge must not have any personal interest, financial or otherwise, in the case before them.
*   Open-mindedness – they will consider the arguments of both sides dispassionately.
*   Objectivity – judges will concern themselves solely with the facts of the case and the demands of the law itself. All other issues will be 'edited' from their thought processes.

By implication, satisfying ourselves that judges are always impartial is unlikely to prove a straightforward task. The rules concerned with judicial independence will help. If they work as they should, society can be reasonably confident that senior judges are both properly qualified and free from dependence upon ministerial favour. The emergence of a more socially representative judiciary under the new arrangements discussed above should also help conquer institutional prejudices. However, judicial impartiality demands much more than this and, moreover, it is not something that the wider constitution can do much to promote. Instead, this is an area where the courts have come to police themselves.

Self-evaluation, personal interest and automatic disqualification

It is part of the professional obligations of judges to consider their personal suitability to hear the cases allocated to them. The rules give them every opportunity to step down where they feel it appropriate, something which extends to the right of a judge to make a request not to be given an entire category of case. In 1978, for example, Judge Neil McKinnon requested that cases involving an obvious racial element be allocated to others, a request with which his superiors were happy to comply. The courts have also developed strict rules where it is found that a judge has a personal interest in a case. It is assumed that the judge will automatically disqualify himself and, where he has not, his decision will almost certainly be overturned on appeal (*Dimes* v. *Proprietors of the Grand Junction Canal* (1852)).

The precise meaning of the term 'personal interest' is not easy to define. The most obvious example is when the judge has a financial interest in the outcome of a case. However, the notion of 'interest' has much wider implications than this, as can be seen in the famous case of *Re Bow Street Metropolitan Stipendiary Magistrate ex parte Pinochet Ugarte* (1999) where the issue of a political interest was raised for the first time in a higher court. This was in fact a series of cases which drew international attention to the English legal system. The facts of the case were that, upon hearing that the former dictator of Chile, General Pinochet, was in London for medical treatment, a Spanish magistrate applied for his extradition to face charges in respect of Spanish citizens who had 'disappeared' at various points during Pinochet's long reign of terror. While Pinochet's personal involvement is still disputed, it is a matter of record that people acting under his authority committed some truly appalling acts of violence against helpless individuals.[7] However, under international law it was uncertain whether, as a recognised head of state, his extradition was lawful. The Metropolitan Stipendiary Magistrate at Bow Street thought it was. Pincohet's lawyers disagreed and, given the unprecedented importance of the political and legal issues involved, the case was immediately referred to the House of Lords for a definitive ruling.

It is at this point that Lord Hoffman, a hugely distinguished legal practitioner, looms even larger than General Pinochet. Hoffman sat on the initial panel of five judges who decided, three to two, in

November 1998 that it was lawful to proceed with the extradition proceedings. However, before human rights activists could celebrate what most regarded as an unexpected triumph, Pinochet's lawyers petitioned the House of Lords to review its own decision on the grounds that Lord Hoffman had failed to declare a personal interest in the case. The essence of their case was that Hoffman had a clear association with Amnesty International, the respected international human rights pressure group which had been permitted to make a written submission to the court. Hoffman himself was a trustee of an Amnesty charity. In addition, his wife worked for the organisation. Consequently, in January 1999 a new panel of Law Lords took the unprecedented decision of setting aside the decision taken the previous November. Few commentators doubt that the decision was a correct one. Lord Hoffman had a personal interest in the case and should have disqualified himself. In this sense, the decision was a tremendous advertisement for the integrity of the judiciary in the United Kingdom. At the same time, the more so given the evidence presented in the following chapter, it is perhaps unfortunate that the beneficiary of this was one of the most reviled men of the last century. This point is not lost on Slapper and Kelly (2004: 232) who add:

> that it is nonetheless ironic that the first senior judge to have action taken against him for possible political bias was someone whose agenda was nothing more than being against torture and unjudicial killings.

Disinterested bias: the cases of *Gough* and *Locabail*

The problem remains, however, when it cannot be argued that a judge has an interest in a case but is nonetheless felt by one party or another to have behaved in a partial or biased manner. In an earlier case known as *R* v. *Gough* (1983), the House of Lords ruled that the relevant test was not simply whether bias could be clearly demonstrated: the chances are that, unless the judge has behaved in the most foolish of ways, it could not. Rather, the court simply had to satisfy itself that there was 'a real danger or possibility of bias'.

On the surface, this gives the reviewing court far more opportunity to defend the right of aggrieved parties to a fair hearing. It reflects the ongoing influence of Lord Hewart's famous maxim, 'that justice must not only be done, but should manifestly and undoubtedly seen to be done'.[8] Unfortunately, the Law Lords did not list the circumstances which might be covered by such a test. This problem was addressed in two later cases, the most important of which is *Locabail (UK) Limited* v. *Bayfield Properties Limited* (1999) where the court ruled that the test in *Gough* would apply where the presiding judge had personal relations with anyone involved in the case, or where, on a previous occasion, the judge had severely questioned the credibility of such an individual. Finally, in *Director General of Fair Trading* v. *Proprietary Association of Great Britain* (2001), the Court of Appeal ruled that, when assessing whether a danger existed, the court must ask themselves what a fair-minded individual, rather than they themselves, might believe. This is a more objective test which was designed to comply with Article 6 of the European Convention.

With hindsight, though the courts are to be commended for trying to limit the possibility of judicial bias, the various rulings discussed above can each be criticised for what they omit rather than what they include. This point is made with some force by Slapper and Kelly (2004: 233) who remind us that the real purpose of the House of Lords in *R* v. *Gough* was to list the circumstances where the test for bias would *not* apply. In particular, the Lords ruled that the social characteristics of a judge, including his leisure and recreational pursuits and his membership of clubs and societies, would not give rise to the suspicion of bias. The authors go on to acknowledge that this ruling has an obvious public interest justification. If the Lords had ruled differently, it would encourage the mass surveillance of every person appointed to judicial office, together with such a surge in the number of appeals that the UK's legal systems could well be paralysed as a result. At the same time, the Lords decision leaves unanswered what Slapper and Kelly (ibid. 234) call 'a question of profound jurisprudential importance'. Ultimately, despite all efforts to ensure that judges remain impartial, there is no way of knowing when social conditioning influences legal outcomes.

Conclusion

The significance of this last point cannot be underestimated. The focus of this chapter has been a narrow one. I have attempted to explain why the nature of judicial reasoning poses a threat to the credibility of the judiciary and how constitutional and legal systems have responded to this. What I have not done is to examine whether or not these responses have convinced those with an interest in what might be called the politics of the judiciary. It is to this point that I turn in Chapter 4.

•••

✔ What you should have learnt from reading this chapter

* An insight into the difficulties faced by judges when making their rulings consistent with legal principle and the inevitability that judicial decision-making will acquire a strong subjective element.

* The nature of the doctrines of judicial independence and impartiality and why they are central to the integrity of the judiciary.

* The impossibility of ensuring that these doctrines meet the constitutional demands placed upon them.

🔎 Glossary of key terms

Appellate judge A senior judge whose principal task is to hear appeals against decisions taken in a lower court or courts.

Binding precedent An important rule which compels a court to base its rulings on an earlier decision (precedent) taken by a higher court.

Court of Appeal The principal appellate court for cases in England and Wales.

Court of Session Scotland's senior court in civil cases. Members of the Court of Session also serve in the High Court of Justiciary, Scotland's highest criminal court.

Declaratory theory of law The traditional view of judicial decision-making which downgraded the role of individual judges in creating the law.

Judicial impartiality A doctrine which insists that judges only consider relevant facts and disregard irrelevant ones when making their judgements. An alternative name for this doctrine is judicial neutrality.

Judicial independence Another vital doctrine designed to ensure that judges cannot be easily intimidated or otherwise pressurised into coming to a particular decision.

Statute law Law which has been created by a legislative body; in the United Kingdom, statute law is normally associated with law passed by Parliament.

Statutory interpretation The task of applying law passed by Parliament to individual cases.

Supreme Court (UK) Previously known as the Lords of Appeal in Ordinary, or more commonly as the Law Lords, the Supreme Court will be

the highest court of appeal for cases in England, Wales and Northern Ireland, and for civil cases coming from Scotland.
Supreme Court (USA) The highest federal court in the USA with important powers to determine both the meaning of the law and the US Constitution.

? Likely examination questions

Explain the difference between judicial independence and judicial neutrality.

Identify three factors which help to maintain judicial independence.

To what extent are UK judges neutral?

Why do some commentators suggest that judicial impartiality is an impossibility?

Useful websites

www.dca.gov.uk/　Department of Constitutional Affairs

www.scotland.gov.uk/Home　Scottish Executive

www.scotland.gov.uk/Topics/Justice　Scottish Judiciary

www.supremecourtus.gov　US Supreme Court

Suggestions for further reading

Chapter 18 of Oliver, *Constitutional Reform in the United Kingdom* (Oxford: Oxford University Press), 2003 provides a very thorough analysis of the judiciary in England and Wales. An alternative is Rodney Brazier, *Constitutional Practice* (Oxford: Oxford University Press), 1999. Elsewhere, Chapter 3 of Robin M. White and Ian D. Willock, *The Scottish Legal System* (Edinburgh: Butterworths LexisNexis), 1999 is a very sound introduction to the judiciary in Scotland. Developments in the United States can be studied in more detail in Ashbee, *US Politics Today* (Manchester: Manchester University Press), 2004 at Chapter 4. However, those readers who wish to refer to the latest developments in this area ought to consult the websites listed above.

Notes

1.　One of the most prominent of these was the appointment of Sir John (now Lord) Donaldson as Master of the Rolls in 1982. Formerly, Lord Donaldson had played the leading role in Edward Heath's controversial

Industrial Relations Court, a reform which Heath hoped would help reduce industrial militancy in the UK but which provoked genuine fury among the trade unions. That Lord Donaldson was not subsequently promoted during the Labour party's next term in office (1974–9) raised eyebrows. The fact that he was then appointed to head the Civil Division of the Court of Appeal by Margaret Thatcher, a Prime Minister known for her unbending hostility to the trade unions, was widely interpreted as a sign that Lord Donaldson had been brought in to finish the job of curbing trade union power he began in the early 1970s.

Eyebrows were also raised at the behaviour of Lord Irvine. His decision to break with recent precedent and take his place among the Law Lords is perhaps the most famous example of this, though no one suggested that this brought to the government quantifiable advantages. Concern was also expressed over his work in targeting leading barristers, some of whom were seeking advancement, as part of a fundraising exercise for the Labour party.

2. This issue had caused considerable ill-feeling because of the case of Sheriff Peter Thomson. Though not a Senator of the Court of Session, Sheriff Thomson was nonetheless a full-time judge. More importantly, while he was technically removed for misbehaviour, the reasons for his removal were bound up in his participation in the campaign against devolution rather than any obvious personal and professional failings. The fact that Thomson was subsequently denied the opportunity to address Parliament in his own defence when the Order for his removal was being debated in December 1977 only added to the sense of unease (Griffith 1997: 10–11).

3. The Court of Session is Scotland's senior civil court. However, its judges also serve on the High Court of Justiciary, Scotland's senior criminal court.

4. The official title of a member of the Court of Session.

5. For those of you who like these things, this is a rejection rate of 7.33 per cent.

6. Originally nominated by Nixon, Rehnquist was appointed Chief Justice under Reagan in 1986 on the retirement of Chief Justice Burger. Scalia was nominated by Reagan, Thomas by Bush senior.

7. See, for example, the ruling of Lord Brown-Wilkinson in the final House of Lords hearing (*R* v. *Evans*) in February 1999.

8. *R* v. *Sussex Justices ex parte McCarthy* (1924).

CHAPTER 4

Politics and the Judiciary

Contents

Overview

This chapter seeks to explain why the arrangements discussed in Chapter 3 have failed to satisfy the critics of the judiciary. The initial sections focus on the views of the political Left. This variegated group has been foremost among those who have questioned both the independence and impartiality of the judiciary. The fact that civil liberties organisations are closely attached to the Left makes these arguments particularly important. By contrast, the later sections examine the unprecedented criticism aimed at judges by the last two British governments. In addition to explaining why this has occurred, these sections also examine its wider constitutional implications. This takes us on into a discussion of the various techniques ministers have adopted in order to curb the power of the judiciary to challenge their decisions.

Key issues to be covered in this chapter

- The traditional Left-Wing case against the judiciary
- The alleged inability of the judiciary to protect civil liberties in both Britain and the USA
- Ministerial clashes with judges over sentencing policy and judicial review
- The changing nature of executive–judicial relations in the UK
- Attempts to constrain the power of the judiciary

The judiciary in the United Kingdom: a socialist analysis

Throughout the last century, hostility to the judiciary was largely the domain of the Left. The publication of Professor John Griffith's *The Politics of the Judiciary* in 1977 spoke for generations of social reformers who had suffered as a result of what the author believes to be overt judicial prejudice. What made his book especially popular was his attempt to link this bias, in a quasi-Marxist fashion, to the social characteristics of the judges themselves.

Homogeneity, tradition and the judicial mindset

Griffith is openly contemptuous of the way in which senior judges interpret the law to block social reform. A sociological analysis of the judiciary is used to explain why. Table 4.1 suggests that the ranks of the senior judiciary are dominated by people whose education betrays their common upper middle class background. The data contained in Table 4.2 highlights a different problem. In addition to being incorrigibly upper middle class, the senior judiciary is also overwhelmingly middle-aged, male and white.

These data reflect the fact that, despite the expansion of higher education, the law remains a profession in which a disproportionately large number of children from Britain's elites go on to enjoy thriving careers. This is especially so among barristers, where family and other

Table 4.1 The educational background of the senior judiciary (1987–94)				
	Public school		Oxbridge	
	1987 %	1994 %	1987 %	1994 %
House of Lords	90	91	80	82
Court of Appeal	83	77	86	87
High Court	62	80	78	80
All	70	80	80	87

Source: Labour Research (January 1987) taken from Griffith (1997: 20)

Table 4.2 Social characteristics of the senior judiciary

	Average age	Women	Ethnic minorities	Total
House of Lords	66.5	0	0	10
Heads of Division	63.0	0	0	4
Lords Justices	63.0	1	0	29
High Court Justices	57.6	6	0	95
				138

Source: Griffith, 1997: 21

connections can still aid career progression. As we saw in Chapter 3, the composition of the Bar has direct consequences for the judiciary. Poor levels of social representativeness in the former will eventually manifest themselves in the latter.

Why should this matter? Primarily, because Griffith believes that the declaratory theory of law is a myth. Judges, he claims, create the law and:

it is this creative function . . . that makes their job important and makes worthwhile some assessment of the way they behave, especially in political cases. (Griffith 1997: 6)

Secondly, because when they are taken together, judgements such as those in Box 4.1 reveal a pattern whereby judges instinctively side with the forces of conservatism and tradition: private landlords against interventionist local government, employers against trade unions and property owners against those seeking to enforce the Race Relations Acts. In short, when dealing with these cases, the senior judiciary *as a body* tends to decide them in a certain way. Consider the following:

• The British judiciary is socially homogenous to a remarkable degree.
• This leads to a marked conformity in attitudes. Their common background, reinforced by the twenty years most judges spend at the Bar, has resulted in a 'unifying attitude of mind, a political position' (ibid. 7).

- Thirdly, the peculiarities of this common background ensure that this 'unifying attitude of mind' is deeply conservative. The judiciary thus see themselves as 'protectors and conservators of what has been, of the relationships and interests on which, in their view, our society is founded' (ibid. 8).

It will be obvious that this has profound implications for the doctrine of judicial impartiality, which Griffith sees as a mere 'fig-leaf' thinly disguising an unpleasant reality. Nor will this situation improve

---

Box 4.1 Judicial bias: selected cases from Griffith

The Fares Fair Litigation
Wide sections of socialist opinion have long been convinced that the judiciary has a particular loathing for socialist-inspired local authorities. This dates from the 1920s when the courts thwarted the Poplar councillors in their efforts to raise the wages of public sector employees (*Roberts* v. *Hopwood* 1925). However, it was in the 1980s, when a number of large, urban authorities fell under the control of radicalised Labour parties, that the Left was given a reminder of the role senior judges can play in blocking social reform. The most glaring example of this is the decision of the House of Lords in *R* v. *Greater London Council, ex parte Bromley London Borough Council* (1983) which prevented the GLC from carrying out its commitment to lower the costs of public transport. For Griffith, this ruling is notorious for the manner in which the Law Lords appeared to make the law the servant of their political agenda: curtailing the power of a local authority of whose politics they clearly disapproved.

Industrial relations
This is another area in which the judiciary enjoy considerable notoriety, dating from decisions at the turn of the twentieth century in *Taff Vale Railway Co.* v. *Amalgamated Society of Railway Servants* (1901) and *Amalgamated Society of Railway Servants* v. *Osborne* (1910). After a period of relative calm, the judiciary once again became embroiled in controversy from the 1960s. Beginning with *Piddington* v. *Bates* (1960), the courts made a number of rulings which played a key part in the suppression of trade union activity. This was especially so during the 1980s when employers launched a string of successful legal actions against the International Transport Workers Federation, the National Union of Mineworkers and various print unions.

> **Race relations**
> The reluctance of the courts to enforce race relations legislation can be seen in a variety of cases in which *Dockers' Labour Club* v. *Race Relations Board* (1974), *R* v. *Race Relations Board ex parte Selvarajan* (1975) and *CRE* v. *Prestige Group Limited* (1984) are merely some of the most notorious. In these judgements, the courts revealed a deep-seated hostility to legislation designed to interfere with what had been private decision-making. Whether the courts sympathised with racial discrimination is uncertain. What is clear, however, is the extent of judicial sympathy for those who argued that combating racism is not a proper matter for the law.

unless, one, the judiciary becomes much more socially representative and, two, a socialist Parliament chokes off opportunities for adverse judicial interference with the progressive cause.

Civil liberties, law enforcement and national security

Griffith's broad approach – captured in the idea of **corporate bias** – has proved influential among **civil libertarians** who accuse the judiciary of being 'dismally deferential to authority' (Ewing and Gearty 1990: 12). In this respect, the Thatcher years are especially important as it was during this period that a peacetime government deployed its full armoury of repressive powers in pursuit of policy objectives. Even otherwise supportive newspapers expressed concern that Margaret Thatcher's disdain for consensus politics had encouraged her ministers to trample over historic rights (Ewing and Gearty 1990: 3–4). In short, the threat to civil liberties had never been greater. Yet, far from rising to the challenge laid down by government:

> the courts seem to have come to regard themselves as the partners of the executive, tackling problems together, rather than as a separate, autonomous, and sometimes necessarily antagonistic branch of government. (Ewing and Gearty 1990: 12–13)

The combined effect of these cases points to the existence of a powerful doctrine of deference at work within the judiciary. I have touched upon this issue in a previous chapter. It expresses the idea that, if a case involves a core function of government – law enforcement or

Box 4.2 Judges in the dock

The Criminal Trial
A leading legal journalist, David Rose (1996), has argued that, for the bulk of the post-war era, the senior judiciary saw their primary duty as protecting individual police officers from aggressive cross-examination by defence lawyers. Barristers who did this were likely to be severely rebuked, possibly to the detriment of future careers. The most infamous example of this mindset is Lord Denning's rejection of an appeal against conviction by the Birmingham Six in 1988. Denning pointed out that the consequence of granting the men's appeal would be to condemn police witnesses as liars, 'an appalling vista' which his Lordship refused to contemplate. Three years later – with the weight of evidence now overwhelmingly in their favour – the six men were finally freed. However, one can only speculate how many miscarriages of justice occurred throughout this era because police officers were confident of being shielded from the consequences of corrupt practices by the judiciary. The fact that it often took decades before miscarriages were rectified – the Birmingham Six served sixteen years' imprisonment – only amplifies this point.

Curtailing the Power of Local Police Authorities
This is a second area in which the courts were accused of protecting the police from criticism. Part of the problem was the changing nature of local politics which saw the emergence of Left-Wing Labour councillors determined to bring local policing under a greater degree of democratic control. In a landmark ruling – *R* v. *Secretary of State for the Home Department, ex parte Northumbria Police Authority* (1988) – the courts came down firmly on the side of chief police officers and placed severe limitations on the power of the authorities.

The Policing of the Peace Movement
This is in area covered in considerable detail by Ewing and Gearty (1990), who cite a long list of cases dating from the early 1960s. The main areas of contention concern the manner in which the courts:

* Allowed laws designed to combat espionage to be used to punish peace protesters (*Chandler* v. *DPP* (1964))
* Facilitated the use of 'blanket bans' on CND marches (*Kent* v. *Metropolitan Police Commissioner* (1981))
* Assisted local authorities in their use of bylaws to prosecute protesters (*DPP* v. *Hutchinson*; *R* v. *Secretary of State for*

Defence, ex parte Parker; R v. Secretary of State for Defence, ex parte Hayman (1989)).

The Mineworkers' Strike (1984–5)

This remains one of the most controversial episodes in the history of British industrial relations. In order to neuter the strike, the police came up with a variety of tactics, including mass arrests, binding-over orders and the imposition of unjustified bail conditions. Far from challenging the lawfulness of police conduct, the courts were accused of colluding with and even facilitating it, even when this meant the jettisoning of due process standards (*R. v. Mansfield Magistrates, ex parte Sharkey* (1985)). However, the single most important ruling occurred in *Moss* v. *McLachlan* (1985), in which the policy of establishing roadblocks across the country was given the seal of judicial approval. This was a central tactic in the first months of the strike but one of very dubious legality. Court approval confirmed the suspicions of those who believed that there were few powers the courts were prepared to deny the police while the strike persisted.

Covert Surveillance

The 1980s and 1990s witnessed the first attempts by individuals to challenge the validity of covert surveillance operations, the two key cases being: *Malone* v. *Metropolitan Police Commissioner* (1979) and *R.* v. *Secretary of State for the Home Department, ex parte Ruddock* (1987). The latter was especially important since it concerned the use of the Security Service to disrupt the activities of CND by intercepting the communications of its leaders. On each occasion, however, they were rebuffed. To the lawyers involved, the attitude of the courts seemed to be one of deliberate abdication.

Official Secrecy

The principal rulings concern the determination of Margaret Thatcher to preserve what she saw as the integrity of national security in the UK. By far the most famous example of this was the support she received from the judiciary over the *Spycatcher* affair. At the centre of a very complex web of legal arguments was the government's attempt to use injunctions to permanently muzzle the British media. Ewing and Gearty (1990: 157–8) are particularly damning in their assessment of the Court of Appeal and the House of Lords in *Attorney-General* v. *Guardian Newspaper Limited* (1987), which they clearly feel brought the reputation of the senior judiciary to a new low.

national security, for example – the courts will grant ministers very wide discretion to act as they think fit. The civil liberties lobby is now increasingly concerned that this doctrine continues to influence the judiciary in human rights cases.

An early indication of this was the Privy Council's decision to reverse the High Court of Justiciary's ruling in *R* v. *Brown* (2000). This concerned the compatibility of s. 172 of the Road Traffic Act 1988 with Article 6 of the Convention. This provision empowers police officers to request that the owner of a vehicle confirm who was driving it at a particular time. In *Brown*, the defendant faced charges of drink driving. Her lawyers argued that this amounted to compulsion to self-incrimination and was in breach of Article 6. While this convinced the High Court of Justiciary, the Privy Council disagreed. Rather than applying to every single stage of the criminal trial, Article 6 was read down as applying to the trial *as a whole*. Providing a particular stage did not undermine the fairness of the trial per se, there were circumstances in which 'technical' breaches of Article 6 could be permitted. Everything hinged on whether the disputed provision was in the public interest, satisfied the test of proportionality and, above all, was reasonably used. In *Brown*, the justices felt that s. 172 met these criteria and found in favour of the prosecuting authorities.

However, in their commentary Slapper and Kelly (2004: 30) hint that the key factor shaping the Privy Council's ruling was its awareness of the profound impact the High Court of Justiciary's judgement might have had on a range of measures designed to curb road traffic offences, including speeding. There is a clear implication that these public policy considerations competed with legal principle for the attention of the Privy Council judges, and it was this which shaped their reading of Article 6. If true, this might explain the outcome of another Scottish case – *McIntosh* v. *AG for Scotland* (2001) – dating from this time. At stake was another aspect of the right to a fair trial: the presumption of innocence. Thanks to s. 1(1) of the Proceeds of Crime (Scotland) Act 1995, a court was able to impose a confiscation order on property which they believed to have been the result of criminal activity. If the owner of that property wished to challenge the order, he – not the prosecution – would have to show that it had been obtained by honest means. In *McIntosh*, a convicted drug dealer claimed that this provision was in clear breach of the presumption of innocence and thus in contravention of Article 6. Again, the High Court of Justiciary agreed with him and, again, the Privy Council overturned its decision.

In between these two hearings, the Court of Appeal had ruled on an almost identical case – *R* v. *Benjafield and Others* (2001) – which had been brought under companion legislation in England and Wales.[1] In *Benjafield*, the appellate judges used the Privy Council's ruling in *Brown* to justify the reversal of the presumption of innocence. It was felt that whether a reversal constituted a breach depended upon a range of factors, not least of which was the legitimacy of the statute's purpose. On this note, the Court of Appeal would have been only too aware of the bi-partisan view that, without such measures, obtaining the proceeds of serious crimes such as drug dealing and the financing of terrorism would be difficult if not impossible. To the court, such cases are all about striking the appropriate balance. To civil libertarians, too often judges seek a comforting form of words to justify a general unwillingness to offend ministers and provoke a public backlash.

The civil liberties lobby is able to present other evidence to support their claim that a regrettable doctrine of deference is at work. Though they invariably tend to attract the media headlines, cases where the court finds against the government are few and far between. On the contrary, it is cases like *Brown* and those described in Box 4.3 which remain the norm. This point even applies in the highly sensitive area of immigration, where as a result of cases such as *Roth* (2002), ministers have regularly cried foul that the judiciary is unjustly interfering with their discretion. *Roth* was, indeed, a major defeat. However, as the leading analysis in the field demonstrates (Stevens 2004), for the most part the courts have shown considerable restraint in limiting ministerial powers.

- Often an initial defeat is overturned on appeal, as it was in *R* v. *Secretary of State for the Home Department ex parte Saadi* (2001).
- Further, even when judges are agreed that a minister's conduct cannot be reconciled with the Convention, they have gone to some lengths to show how the offending provision may be made compatible with Convention rights. (See the Court of Appeal's ruling

in *R (on the Application of Q)* v. *Secretary of State for the Home Department* (2003).)

• This is also the case with declarations of incompatibility. Ministers made some very angry noises when the House of Lords ruled that Part IV of the Anti-Terrorism, Crime and Security Act 2001 was incompatible with Article 5 of the Convention.

Box 4.3 The doctrine of deference: two case studies

A and Others v. *Secretary of State for the Home Department (No. 2)* (2005)

This remains one of the most notorious rulings made by a senior court in recent years, reversing as it did a legal principle established as early as 1630. At issue was whether, in immigration cases, ministers could present evidence of involvement in terrorism which had been extracted by torture overseas. The case was brought by those originally detained under the now repealed Part IV of the Anti-Terrorism, Crime and Security Act 2001 who argued that the admission of such evidence contravened their right to a fair hearing under Article 6(1) of the Convention. By a majority of two-to-one (Lady Neuberger dissenting), the Court of Appeal ruled that, providing that UK officials had neither connived at nor procured the torture, ministers were entitled to present evidence which had otherwise come into their hands. The view of the court seemed to be one immersed in realpolitick. Torture can never be condoned. However, once it has happened and produced evidence that the minister feels to be reliable, it is not for the courts to rule that such evidence can never be used in an important case where terrorism is involved. The mere use of such evidence will not, of course, prove involvement in terrorism. Ultimately, whether such evidence is convincing is a matter for the relevant court, in this case the Special Immigration Appeals Commission.

In her dissenting ruling Lady Neuberger made the following points:

• The courts have a duty to interpret Article 6(1) with reference to other international treaties, including the Convention Against Torture, which aim at the elimination of such practices in all circumstances.

• Secondly, torture is notoriously unreliable. Yet, it is impossible to see how, given the circumstances in which torture evidence is extracted, the complainants – to be more precise, the special representatives appointed to represent them – can expose this.

- Consequently, where such evidence is central to the government's case, their ability to mount an effective defence is seriously compromised to an extent which Article 6 cannot support.

The journalist Nick Cohen (2004b) makes a rather different point. What encouragement, he wonders, will this ruling give the under-resourced staff of the Foreign Office and MI6 working in very difficult circumstances overseas, to connive at torture in order to provide evidence which gets their political masters in Whitehall off their backs?

R (Roberts) v. the Parole Board and another (2005)

The equivocal nature of judicial attitudes to Article 6 is further revealed in the ongoing saga of Harry Roberts. Mr Roberts is one of the most notorious criminals in English legal history. In 1966 he was convicted of the cold-blooded and seemingly inexplicable murder of three police officers in west London. Though his tariff, which was fixed at thirty years, expired in 1996, the Parole Board refused to review his case to determine whether or not it was safe to release him. Eventually, it ruled that Roberts' case would be heard under a special procedure in which neither Roberts nor his legal advisers would see new evidence against him. Instead, his interests would be represented by a special advocate appointed by the Board to act on his behalf.

Roberts immediately appealed against the Board's decision. However, on 28 July 2004 the Court of Appeal found in favour of the authorities, a decision which was subsequently upheld by the House of Lords (Lords Bingham and Steyn dissenting) the following April. The key to these rulings was whether the Parole Board's duty to protect the public outweighed its duties under the Convention to ensure that Mr Roberts had the chance to see and respond to the evidence against him. The court accepted the Board's arguments that, unless it adopted the special procedure, a fellow prisoner of Roberts who had testified against him would be imperilled. In its view, the Board's statutory duty to the public, together with the appointment of a special advocate to act on Roberts' behalf, ensured that its conduct was compatible with the Convention.

This brought a stinging response from Lord Bingham who questioned whether such a departure from what the other dissenting judge, Lord Steyn, called a 'prisoner's fundamental right to a . . . fair procedure' (Dyer 2005) could be justified when the enabling statute 'contains no hint whatever that Parliament intended such a departure' ((2005), 3rd volume, Weekly Law Reports, at page 172). Roberts' solicitor confirmed that he would appeal to the ECtHR, where both dissenting judges believed he would be successful.

However, this overlooks the striking aversion of the courts to make such declarations, together with the fact that the nature of rulings enables ministers successfully to re-enact the disputed measures in subsequent legislation.

The judiciary and civil liberties in the USA

Despite the popular view of the US Supreme Court as a powerful bulwark against state authority, the arguments of Britain's civil libertarians find a ready audience among their fellow-thinkers in the United States. A number of commentators relate this directly to the recent trend in judicial appointments. According to Tinsley Yarbrough (2002), the composition of the federal courts became a crucial issue to Republican Presidents Reagan and Bush senior (1980–92) as they launched their 'constitutional counter-revolution' against the civil liberties precedents established by the Warren and, to a lesser extent, Burger Courts (1953–86).[2] The strength of this counter-revolution hinged on the ability of these Presidents to:

- Appoint five of the nine Supreme Court justices currently in post, thereby ensuring a conservative majority on this all-important body.[3]
- Secure the appointment of William Rehnquist, a notable conservative jurist originally nominated by Richard Nixon, as Chief Justice in 1986.
- Appoint three-quarters of lower federal court justices in post by the mid-1990s.

Without question, the single most important example of alleged conservative bias was the Supreme Court's dramatic intervention in the 2000 presidential election which effectively decided the contest for George Bush. This is described in Box 4.4. However, this section is more concerned with the allegation from bodies like the American Civil Liberties Union (ACLU) that federal judges have, as Reagan and Bush senior intended, allowed a conservative agenda on law enforcement to compromise their constitutional obligations to protect individual liberty.

The counter-revolution referred to above had many targets, two of the most notable being abortion law reform and the reading of

Box 4.4 Discrediting the Supreme Court? The case of *Bush* v. *Gore*

In the eyes of its critics, the partisan nature of the Supreme Court was brutally exposed during the 2000 presidential election. Prior to this, the Supreme Court had shown 'considerable deference to state authority' (Yarbrough 2002: 120). In other words, the Court had interpreted the Constitution so as to give as much discretion as possible to state authorities. In the case of *Bush* v. *Gore* (2000), however, this trend was reversed. The decision to overrule the Supreme Court of Florida and stop the manual recount of votes it had ordered remains one of the most controversial in America's history.

- In the first place, the action of the Supreme Court was without precedent. Constitutional experts tend towards the view that the final decision should have been left to Congress.
- In the second, no one could provide a satisfactory explanation for a decision so obviously out of kilter with similar judgements made by the same justices.
- Finally, closer examination of three of the justices involved exposed circumstances which, in the UK, would have led to their disqualification. On the eve of the election Sandra Day O'Connor had made a public statement that a Gore victory would be a personal disaster for her. Clarence Thomas' wife was so intimately involved in the Bush campaign that she was helping to draw up a list of Bush appointees more or less at the same time as her husband was adjudicating on whether the same man would become the next President. Finally, Antonin Scalia's son was working for the firm appointed by Bush to argue his case before the Supreme Court, the head of which was subsequently appointed as Solicitor-General.

During his first term as President, Bush junior was denied any opportunity to make his own nominations for the Supreme Court. This did not mean, however, that he failed to make any impact on the process of judicial appointments. An early indication of his determination to put on display his conservative credentials was his decision to exclude the American Bar Association (ABA) from the appointments process. Since the Eisenhower Presidency (1952–60), the ABA has been allowed to comment on the professional qualifications of prospective nominees. A brief hiatus occurred during the 1980s when the ABA clashed with President Reagan over the nomination of Robert Bork. However, the status quo was restored by Bush senior and continued under Clinton. By breaking with the ABA, Bush declared his preference for using the conservative Federalist Society as an alternative source of opinion. Critics suggest that, unless the Democratic party can organise to prevent it, the federal courts will soon be dominated by a new generation of Right-Wing justices, known for their hostility to abortion rights and enthusiasm for the promotion of religious worship.

Shortly into his second term, however, President Bush was given the rare opportunity to make two nominations to the Supreme Court in a relatively short space of time. On 3 October 2005 a new Chief Justice, John Roberts, was sworn in to replace the late William Rehnquist. Known as a pragmatic conservative, Roberts was widely seen in Republican circles as the perfect replacement for Rehnquist. However, on the same day, Bush nominated his personal advisor, Harriet Miers, as replacement for the retiring Sandra Day O'Connor. The close relationship, together with the fact that Ms Miers had never served as a judge, prompted obvious criticism from Bush's domestic opponents. More interesting still, is the fact that America's Right expressed their own disappointment that Bush had not opted for a high-profile conservative with years of experience on the bench. Despite her part in *Bush v. Gore*, Justice Day O'Connor had been heavily criticised by the Right for her liberal stance on the key issue of abortion rights. America's neo-conservatives came to view her appointment as a missed opportunity and one which, in turn, necessitated a rethink on the part of the Bush Presidency.

the Fourteenth Amendment in relation to affirmative action programmes. However, beginning with Richard Nixon's successful campaign for the Presidency in 1968, law enforcement has proved a consistently popular campaigning theme for the Republican party. Nixon was one of the first conservative politicians to question openly the liberalisation of judicial attitudes which emerged throughout the Western world after World War Two. In the USA, this trend is witnessed by the restraints the Warren Court placed on the exercise of police power, a stance which was undoubtedly influenced by the civil rights movement. However, as the latter's potency began to fade, what one might call an 'anti-liberal' backlash followed. It was Nixon's great skill as a politician to anticipate this, much as Margaret

Thatcher was to do in the UK a decade later. His notion of a neglected 'silent majority' of ordinary Americans, whose voices were never heard in government circles, became a standard campaigning theme for conservative politicians on both sides of the Atlantic. By the mid-1970s, liberal voices were largely silenced (Singh 2002: 184). The rulings of the Warren Court were widely condemned as giving both protection and encouragement to the criminal, a somewhat limited analysis but one which nonetheless struck a chord with many American voters.

Bodies such as the ACLU argue that the changing composition of the federal judiciary outlined above has ensured that this critique has come to influence judicial as well as popular attitudes: 'Like the Burger Court before it, a Rehnquist Court majority has been likely to side with the government in the criminal justice arena, expansively construing police powers of search and interrogation' (Yarbrough 2002: 126).

This can be seen at a number of levels. For example, evidence provided in Table 4.3 points to a general predisposition among federal judges appointed since 1980 to decide in favour of the prosecuting authorities at all levels of the federal court system. Today, however, the ACLU is particularly concerned at the failure of the Supreme Court to develop a body of law to protect the individual against the use of covert surveillance. At the heart of the controversy lies the **Fourth Amendment**. According to the ACLU, this was inserted by the Founders to protect the individual from secret or otherwise self-

Table 4.3 The federal courts' record in criminal cases

Nominating President	Probability of deciding against the defendant in criminal cases
Carter (1976–80)	19.15
Bush senior (1988–92)	45.76
Reagan (1980–8)	55.23
Clinton (1992–2000)	42.07

Source: Yarbrough 2002: 129

authorised searches. However, given that the Fourth Amendment was written at a time when techniques such as CCTV could not have been conceived, its ability to protect the individual against the state is dependent upon a high degree of judicial activism. In other words, the Fourth Amendment demands continual reinterpretation in light of technological and other developments.

If one accepts the ACLU's case, this is something that the Supreme Court is disinclined to do. This has been so throughout its history. For example, it was not until 1967 that the Supreme Court finally accepted that the Fourth Amendment protections apply to the interception of communications. However, it has become increasingly marked since 1980.

- The current justices have taken a highly conservative view towards constitutional interpretation. The Rehnquist Court, thanks to the influence of Justice Day O'Connor, has been loath to develop legal doctrine or precedent. Such things are essential if the Constitution, including the Fourth Amendment, is to develop in the way the ACLU and others would like.
- Secondly, there is a marked reluctance to use the guarantee of equal protection to develop additional rights not specifically mentioned in the Constitution.
- Thirdly, in response to the federal government's efforts to combat the epidemic of drug abuse, the Supreme Court has increased the opportunities for warrantless searches in public, especially at borders.
- Finally, and most importantly, the Supreme Court has refused to accept that residents of the USA have a right to privacy in public. Providing they stay at home and do very little when there, ordinary Americans are actually well protected. However, as soon as they venture into the world beyond their porches, their rights to a private life fall away precipitously. Judicial inactivity has exposed the individual to an extraordinary array of privacy abuses, from CCTV to the many techniques which help construct 'data trails' mapping each person's day-to-day activities. In addition, it is this passivity that has encouraged the Bush administration to push ahead with draconian legislation which undermines personal privacy yet further (Stanley and Steinhardt 2003).

I shall expand on these and associated accusations in Chapter 6. For the present, the fact that civil liberties groups on both sides of the Atlantic are deeply sceptical of their respective judiciary's willingness to stand up to an increasingly powerful executive is not without its significance. However, before we return to the British political scene to examine a very different critique of the judiciary, it is important to consider the evidence in Box 4.5. While they are insufficient to counter it in its entirety, it is important to bear such rulings in mind when assessing the validity of the ACLU's rather negative view of the Rehnquist Court.

Box 4.5 An alternative view of the Rehnquist Court

In contrast to the general line of argument above, other evidence supports the alternative view that not all of the Supreme Court appointments made by Reagan and Bush senior fulfilled Republican expectations. This is certainly true of Sandra Day O'Connor, who has played a key part in defending the rights of American women to abortions. There are a number of Supreme Court rulings which have disappointed America's conservatives and religious Right.

- Though weakened a little, the essence of *Roe* v. *Wade* – the pivotal case establishing a federal right to an abortion – has been retained. Undue burdens on a woman's decision to choose were outlawed in *Casey* v. *Planned Parenthood*, While the legality of 'partial birth' abortions was confirmed in *Stenberg* v. *Carhort* (2000).
- A state law forbidding laws aimed to protect homosexuals from discrimination was struck down in *Romer* v. *Evans* (1996).
- The so-called 'Miranda doctrine' which protects suspects in criminal cases was preserved when the Court struck down a federal statute designed to weaken it in *Dickenson* v. *United States* (2000).
- More recently, in *Kyllo* v. *USA* (2001), the Supreme Court ruled that the unauthorised use of a thermal imaging device constituted an unlawful, warrantless search. This ruling opened the possibility of further attempts to bring modern surveillance techniques within the remit of the Fourth Amendment.

The new politics of the judiciary in the United Kingdom

The remainder of this chapter returns to developments within the United Kingdom. Despite the importance of the socialist and civil libertarian critiques, the lack of any opportunity to translate these into constitutional reforms has denuded them of immediate political value. It is this factor which makes the recent, bi-partisan trend in ministerial assaults on the independence and impartiality of the judiciary much more significant. Public criticism of individual judges by ministers has intensified since the late 1980s. Under the Blair government, executive–judicial relations have become so venomous they have threatened the stability of the constitution itself. The underlying cause of these clashes is probably best illustrated via two case studies, the first of which is sentencing policy.

Sentencing policy

As law and order became a more salient issue, control of sentencing policy has acquired unusual political significance. Before the Criminal Justice Act 1991, Parliament had tended to set maximum penalties for each crime, leaving the trial judge to determine what sentence up to the maximum to hand down in each case.[4] In addition, it was the responsibility of the senior judiciary – in England and Wales this meant the Lord Chief Justice – to set guidelines which the lower criminal courts were obliged to follow. The justifications for these arrangements, which accorded the judiciary considerable discretion, were varied.

- Each case differs, often much more than either the public or politicians realise. Only the presiding judge is able to determine a punishment which does justice to all concerned, including the offender.
- This applies especially to the issue of mitigation, obvious examples of which include an early admission of guilt, coupled to genuine remorse. This does not negative guilt. Courts do, however, use it to adjust the final sentence.
- It follows that only another judge, possessing even greater experience and seniority, is in a position to review the original punishment.

• The senior judiciary is also in the best position to monitor the impact of sentencing on other areas of the criminal justice system, notably the Prison Service. It is no accident that leading judges have put themselves in the forefront of the campaign against prison overcrowding. Former Lord Chief Justice Woolf, in particular, has made no secret of his view that custodial sentences should be restricted to crimes of violence or those where no other sentence is likely to have an impact upon the offender.

The problem facing the judiciary is that, by the early 1990s, swathes of opinion had come to associate their discretion with unjustified leniency: in other words, with injustice. A vital point of departure in this respect was the appointment of Michael Howard as Home Secretary on 27 May 1993. During his first party conference in post, Howard made his famous '27 points' speech in which he left judges in no doubt that he expected them to embrace his **neo-conservative** philosophy that 'prison works'. Thereafter, relations between Howard and the judiciary deteriorated swiftly. The strength of ministerial feelings was revealed in an extraordinary speech in October 1995 by the then Conservative party chairman, Brian Mawhinney, who urged party members to participate in a letter-writing campaign designed to expose judicial leniency. By this point, however, Howard had decided to use legislation to force the judiciary into line. The White Paper he published at this time was immediately condemned by senior judges, not least of whom was the late Lord Chief Justice Taylor. In a famous Lords' debate on 23 May 1996, Taylor launched a blistering attack on the government, accusing ministers of pandering to popular prejudice at the expense of justice.

> Never in the history of our criminal law have such far-reaching proposals been put forward on the strength of such flimsy and dubious evidence. (*The Guardian*, 24 May 1996)

It was to be Taylor's last parliamentary debate before ill-health overtook him. Undeterred by the assault, Howard persisted with his plans to restrict judicial discretion over sentencing. Though a rearguard action forced him to introduce important concessions, the Crime (Sentences) Act 1997 duly became law shortly before the dissolution of Parliament.

The details of this statute can be found in Box 4.6. However, with hindsight, the most remarkable political feature of its passage was the support Howard received from his opposite number, Jack Straw. In the course of his reformulation of Labour's law and order policies, Straw had come to see considerable virtue in bringing sentencing policy under greater parliamentary control. The extent of this consensus was finally revealed on 12 January 1999 when Straw announced that s. 4 of the Act would finally come into force later that year. In turn, this led to a new series of clashes between ministers and judges, the more so when Home Office research published the following year suggested that the latter were ignoring statutory pressures to amend their practices. During the period covered by the research, not one burglar and only four drug dealers received mandatory minimum sentences when these could have been handed down. More irritating still for the Government, judges were also reluctant to impose child safety orders

---

Box 4.6 The Crime (Sentences) Act 1997

Automatic Life Sentences for Serious Violent and Sex Offenders
In its White Paper, the government was highly critical of the courts' reluctance to impose discretionary life sentences in cases of serious violent crime. Though the life sentence is mandatory in cases of murder, it can be imposed for a variety of other offences, including rape and manslaughter. Under s. 2 of the Act, the courts in England and Wales are obliged to impose a life sentence on any person convicted of committing a second serious offence from a list of eight (s. 2(5)). The Scottish courts were placed under an identical obligation in respect of a list of ten serious offences (s. 2(6)).

Mandatory Minimum Sentences for Drug Dealers
Under s. 3 of the Act, the courts are obliged to impose a minimum sentence of seven years on anyone convicted of a third offence of trafficking a Class A drug.

Mandatory Minimum Sentences for Burglars
Section 4 of the Act imposed a similar obligation on the courts in respect of a third conviction for burglary. In this case, the mandatory minimum is three years' imprisonment.

Box 4.7 The sentencing provisions of the Criminal Justice Act 2003

The Sentencing Guidelines Council

This body, which replaces the Sentencing Advisory Panel, has the power to issue guidelines to sentencers in England and Wales. Lord Chief Justice Woolf has described the Council 'as a significant incursion into judicial discretion'. While they are unconvinced by this, nonetheless Ward and Davies (2004: 167–8) acknowledge the political symbolism at work. The lay members are there to express the government's view that the Lord Chief Justice cannot be trusted with something as politically sensitive as sentencing.

The New Statutory Definition of Seriousness

A much more serious threat to judicial discretion emerges from s. 143 which redefines the meaning of a 'serious offence'. Generally speaking, the higher courts have tended to view serious crimes as those involving violence or otherwise affecting large numbers of people. Serious fraud is a good example of the latter. One result of this is that persistent petty criminals are not normally considered to be serious offenders, unless they refuse to co-operate with the courts over their punishments. It is this which has caused considerable problems for ministers since it is precisely this type of offender who enrages local communities and fuels fears over crime rates.

David Blunkett's solution was to redefine seriousness in a way which compelled the courts to consider previous convictions, both in the UK and abroad, as an aggravating factor in relation to the offence before them. Convictions which point to a pattern of offending are especially important. Ward and Davies (2004: 175) note that, ministerial protestations to the contrary, the new definition places judges under pressure to consider a custodial sentence in cases where they would not otherwise be minded to do so. Persistent teenage offenders will be particularly affected by this.

The New Indeterminate Sentence for 'Dangerous Offenders'

This is the single most controversial element as far as sentencing is concerned. Like Howard before him, Blunkett's concern was that the courts hardly ever imposed a life sentence where they had the discretion to do so. Under ss. 225–6, a very complex set of rules effectively compel the courts to impose either a life sentence (where the law permits) or, where it does not, the new indeterminate sentence.

- Where a person has been convicted of a serious offence – defined as any offence punishable by either a life sentence or, under normal circumstances, a minimum of ten years – the court must consider whether that person is likely to pose a significant risk of harm to the public through the commission of one of a long list of 153 'specified offences'.
- Moreover, if, prior to his conviction for the initial (serious) offence, the offender has already committed a specified offence, the court must assume that a significant risk of harm exists.
- Only if the court considers it unreasonable to do so, it must then impose either a life or indeterminate sentence.

This final element has enraged senior judges (Dyer 2005). Its effect is that they must find reasons for not doing something they would not be minded to do. Unless the judge is very sure of his ground, he will conclude that he has little choice but to comply with the new law even when every instinct is telling him that injustice will result.

The New Sentencing Regime for Sexual Offences

These are contained under ss. 228–9. While not as threatening to judicial discretion, nonetheless they place a further pressure on judges to impose longer custodial sentences. They do this by creating a new extended sentence in cases of violent and sexual offences. The extended element is designed not to punish but to protect the public. The law now compels the court to consider whether the individual poses a significant risk to the public. Where it believes such a risk exists, it must impose an extension beyond the period in custody which is used for the purposes of punishment. Though it is for the courts to determine the meaning of significant risk, there can be no doubt that ss. 228–9 express a further lack of confidence in their ability to do justice.

Determining the Tariff for Life Sentence Prisoners

Under s. 269, Parliament established statutory rules which the courts must follow when sentencing a person to life imprisonment. This is the culmination of a long running battle which has seen the power of the Home Secretary to set the final tariff progressively removed by the courts. Though the key players in this process were the justices of the ECtHR, Blunkett's reaction suggested that he was the victim of a judicial conspiracy in which British judges were complicit.[5] The result is a provision for three 'starting points' – of fifteen years, thirty years and whole life – which the courts must use when they begin the sentencing process. While the courts can consider mitigating circumstances set out in Schedule 21 of the Act, like ss. 228–9 above, judges are concerned that they create yet another stick with which an aggressive Home Secretary can beat them if they are perceived to be lenient.

established under s. 11 of Labour's own Crime and Disorder Act 1998. Researchers found that judges remained wedded to their pre-existing powers and were heavily influenced by the state of the penal crisis in avoiding custodial sentences (Travis 2000).

This set the scene for the extraordinarily bitter clashes between Straw's successor as Home Secretary, David Blunkett, and the leading judge in England and Wales, Lord Chief Justice Woolf. Whereas Straw had been concerned primarily with the punishment of what he claimed were 100,000 persistent offenders, Blunkett was alarmed at what he felt were inappropriate sentences handed down to dangerous and violent offenders, including murderers. The fears of both men were that the electorate would hold the government to account for these, even when there was little ministers could do – the Crime (Sentences) Act 1997 notwithstanding – to compel the judiciary to respect their wishes. Their response can be found in the sentencing provisions of the Criminal Justice Act 2003.

That these measures, along with those under the Crime (Sentences) Act 1997, cut against the deepest instincts of many leading judges is not in doubt. For example, the idea that the public need additional protection from dangerous offenders (the idea underpinning ss. 225–6 and 228–9) is disputed by one (unnamed) Lord Justice of Appeal who suggests that even the 'most obnoxious' offender will grow out of violent offending, thus obviating the need for these provisions (Dyer 2005). Similarly, Lord Woolf has questioned both the necessity and morality of a whole life tariff which is now the starting point for murder in a number of cases (Hattersley 2004). In light of this it is unsurprising that the judiciary, led by Woolf, fought a rearguard action questioning the integrity of the Act and, where possible, extracting certain concessions. For the record, judicial opposition to the Act is shared by one of Britain's leading academic experts on sentencing, Dr David Thomas. He feels that its principal effect will be the increased use of custody for relatively minor offences which, while it might play well with the public, will not serve the interests of justice (Dyer 2005).

The growing controversy over judicial review
The political significance of this dispute lies in the competing interpretations of the constitutional role of the judiciary. This point emerges even more starkly in the contemporaneous row which

erupted over the courts' ability to review (and quash) the actions of ministers. To remind you, judicial review is a legal device which enables the courts to assess the legality of the manner in which ministers and other officials use the (discretionary) powers granted them by Parliament. Since the passage of the Human Rights Act 1998, such decisions can also be tested for compatibility with Convention rights. The politics of judicial review invert those of sentencing. Here, it is ministers who argue that, in adopting a new and more aggressive stance, senior judges have overstepped constitutional bounds. In so doing, it is alleged, the judiciary has further compromised its reputation for objectivity and impartiality.

The main reason for ministerial pique is that, until the mid-1960s, the judiciary adopted a very passive attitude towards discretionary powers. The courts saw their role as ensuring, one, that the government actually possessed the powers it claimed and, two, had not used them in a way which was either so unfair or irrational that it could never be supported. A particularly famous example of this is *Smith* v. *East Elloe RDC* (1956) which gave the impression – since reversed in the key case of *Anisminic* v. *Foreign Compensation Corporation* (1969) – that the courts would accept so-called '**ouster clauses**' designed to exclude them from reviewing ministerial decisions even when fraud was alleged. However, beginning with *Ridge* v. *Baldwin* (1964), the courts steadily asserted their prerogative to review official decisions. Despite the scepticism of many civil libertarians, there is considerable evidence that this spirit of assertiveness grew apace during the Thatcher-Major years. One minister who was on the receiving end of a series of adverse rulings was Michael Howard, whose propensity to be defeated in the courts drew considerable media comment (Young 1995).

The key cases – those which developed the doctrine itself – are listed in Box 4.8. According to Jowell (2003: 392), the last four cases point to a new stage in the history of judicial review, in which the courts based their rulings on what they regarded as a citizen's legitimate expectations in a democratic polity. This can be seen, to cite but one example, in the case of *Pierson* referred to above, where Lords Steyn and Brown-Wilkinson took the opportunity to remind ministers that their use of discretionary powers could not take place in a legal vacuum. Where a fundamental or higher order right was involved,

Box 4.8 A developing doctrine: judicial activism in the area of judicial review

Re M (1994)
It was established that a minister could be found guilty of contempt for failing to obey a clear instruction issued by a court.

R v. Secretary of State for the Home Department, ex parte Doody (1994)
This created the basis for a subsequent ruling that a reason must always be given to justify the use of a discretionary power.

R v. Secretary of State for the Home Department, ex parte Brind (1991)
An exceptionally important case in which the courts recognised that, even when applying the narrow 'Wednesbury rules' (see Chapter 2), they had to give special attention to any action which infringed fundamental human rights. *Brind* involved the key issue of journalistic freedoms.

R v. Secretary of State for the Home Department, ex parte Leech (No. 2) (1994)
It was established that a prisoner had the right to speak to his lawyer in confidence, unless there was a pressing need to the contrary. Even then, however, any intrusion had to be minimal.

R v. Secretary of State for the Home Department, ex parte Whitham (1997)
In this very famous case, the High Court struck down an order on court fees on the ground that it unlawfully restricted a constitutional right to access a court of law.

R v. Secretary of State for the Home Department, ex parte Pierson (1998)
Following the decision in *Doody*, it was ruled that the decision to raise retrospectively the tariff on a prisoner serving a life sentence without giving good cause was unlawful.

R v. Secretary of State for the Home Department, ex parte Simms (1999)
This ruled that a blanket ban on prisoners giving oral interviews with journalists, that is, regardless of the circumstances, was an unreasonable interference with the freedom of expression.

the courts would only permit it to be undermined when Parliament itself used the clearest, most unambiguous language.

An additional feature of these cases extends to the type of person who brought and benefited from them. It will have struck the reader that many of the leading cases in Box 4.8 concern the rights of convicted prisoners. This has encouraged Slapper and Kelly (2004: 265) to suggest that, in the new judicial culture, there exists a strong desire to extend the protection of the law to those groups whose lack of political influence renders them particularly vulnerable to populist governments. It is unsurprising, therefore, that a second group to benefit were immigrants, especially those seeking asylum. The political importance of asylum cases cannot be understated. Over the last three years they have brought relations between ministers and the judiciary to a new and dangerous low.

Judicial review, human rights and immigration policy
When it entered office in 1997, the Labour government was under no illusions over the sensitivity of this area of policy. Consequently, it ensured the passage of a new statute – the Immigration and Asylum Act 1999 – in order to display its populist credentials. This was subsequently reinforced by certain provisions in the Anti-Terrorism, Crime and Security Act 2001 and, more importantly, the Nationality, Immigration and Asylum Act 2002. The main elements of these statutes are:

• To 'harden' the UK's borders, not least by shifting liability for detecting illegal immigrants to carriers.
• Permitting government to withdraw material support to asylum seekers more easily in the hope of deterring them from entering the UK in the first place.
• Above all, restricting the rights of failed asylum seekers to appeal against decisions to deport them.

That the judiciary would take an interest in these developments was apparent from a series of judgements in the mid- to late 1990s. In this respect the case of *R* v. *Immigration Appeals Tribunal, ex parte Shah* (1999) was hugely important. Its effect was to re-categorise Pakistani women as a distinctive social group in order that they could be granted refugee status. However, it was a second case dating from the same year that provoked the first public burst of ministerial indignation when Jack Straw condemned the ruling in *R* v. *Secretary of State for the Home Department, ex parte Lul Adan and Others* (1999). Straw was rumoured to be so furious that he began to seek ways of standardising asylum policy across the EU in order to prevent a repetition (Travis 1999).

The row over *Lul Adan* set the scene for the much more serious and much more public disagreements listed in Box 4.9. Though the famous case of *A and Others* v. *the Secretary of State for the Home Department* (2005) captured most public attention, it is the cases of *Roth* and *R (on the application of Q)* which are more troubling. By this point, the minister concerned was David Blunkett. His reaction to the second of these rulings in particular was so profound that it led some commentators to accuse Blunkett of wholly unconstitutional behaviour amounting to the deliberate intimidation of the judiciary (Kennedy 2004a). Blunkett's response – that he was doing nothing other than defending the UK's reputation as a constitutional democracy – highlights the gulf in attitudes between the two groups.

A ministerial perspective

For ministers, this 'gulf' has opened up because the judiciary has broken with constitutional tradition by failing to accept their subordinate status. The unelected nature of the judiciary, combined with the fact that they are accountable to no one for the consequences of their decisions, is the decisive element of this critique. It suggests that the courts must be very mindful whenever they overrule ministers carrying out policies which Parliament has approved. If they are not, there is a real danger that they will simply substitute their view for that of Parliament. In a liberal democracy like the UK, this is unsupportable.

This is what Slapper and Kelly (2004: 278–87) refer to as the debate over 'constitutionality'. It is one of three arguments that ministers and their supporters have deployed against judicial resistance to government policies. An alternative approach is to suggest that the courts need to acknowledge that their understanding cannot compare to ministers' when dealing with highly complex matters of public policy, like immigration. Ministers not only have more information; they have access to specialist advisors and consult widely with others working outside Whitehall. In addition, given that it is the minister not the

Box 4.9 Immigration cases and the Human Rights Act

International Transport Roth Gmbh and Others v. *the Secretary of State for the Home Department* (2002)
In April 2000 the government implemented a provision under Part II of the Asylum and Immigration Act 1999 which enabled it to impose a mandatory fine of £2,000 on any carrier who, innocently or otherwise, conveyed an illegal immigrant to the UK. While recognising the hardship this measure caused, ministers defended themselves by pointing out that it was having the desired effect[6] and continued to receive the full support of Parliament. The courts were not satisfied, agreeing with the plaintiffs that the mandatory nature of the fine unjustifiably undermined their rights under Article 6 of the Convention and Article I of the First Protocol. The government was subsequently compelled to amend the law in Schedule 8 of the Nationality, Asylum and Immigration Act 2002.

R (on the application of Q) v. *the Secretary of State for the Home Department* (2003)
This case was brought by asylum seekers who claimed that a variety of Convention Articles had been breached by the government's policy of denying material assistance to any asylum seeker who failed to claim that status immediately upon entering the UK. The government argued that this policy, implemented under s. 55 of the Nationality, Asylum and Immigration Act 2002, was essential to 'flush out' bogus asylum seekers who only entered their claims when facing the threat of deportation. Refugee groups countered by arguing that immigration officials deliberately obstructed the entry of a claim, precisely so that they could deny assistance to otherwise bona fide claimants. In one of the most high-profile judgements of recent times, and citing Lord Ellenborough's famous ruling in *R* v. *Inhabitants of Eastbourne* (1803), Mr Justice Collins ruled that this policy breached three Convention rights, a decision which was subsequently upheld, albeit in a modified form, by the Court of Appeal.

A and Others v. *the Secretary of State for the Home Department* (2005)
This case was settled by the House of Lords. At issue was the legality of the derogation entered into by the government in order to pass Part IV of the Anti-Terrorism, Crime and Security Act 2001. This permitted the Home Secretary to order the indefinite detention of foreign nationals who he believed to be involved in terrorism yet who he

> could not otherwise deport. Unlike the other two cases, there is some evidence to suggest that ministers were not wholly confident of their chances of winning this case, which was just as well since the Law Lords ruled, eight-to-one, that Part IV was both discriminatory and disproportionate. The derogation entered into was overturned as a result.

judge who is responsible for the conduct of government policy, it follows that judges should be especially mindful when gainsaying a minister's interpretation of what his powers entitle him to do. If Parliament is unhappy with the conduct of government policy it has the opportunity to take appropriate, corrective action. However, unless and until it does so, the minister should be allowed to implement their preferred policy. The only exception to this is when they have clearly abused their powers, in which case the courts are right to intervene.

This argument is particularly relevant to the politics of sentencing. Ministers point out that they have an overriding responsibility to ensure that the public and the police retain their faith in the criminal justice system's ability to punish effectively wrongdoers. The policies introduced in the Crime (Sentences) Act 1997 and the Criminal Justice Act 2003 were introduced precisely with this end in view. While they restrict judicial discretion, they do not remove the power of judges to hand down sentences in individual cases. On the contrary, Parliament has approved a framework in which judges are expected to operate, based on the clear premise that such a framework balances judicial discretion with the executive's legitimate interest in promoting public confidence in the courts.

The third and final argument is one which, ironically, returns us to the issue of judicial partiality which was once the monopoly of the political Left. Like Griffith, ministers have also come to disregard any declaratory theory. However, their view of judicial motives is the very opposite of the one which emerges from the pages of Griffith's book. No doubt under the influence of those who received their legal education during the 1960s, an activist trend heavily influenced by political liberalism is now clearly visible. This has been strengthened by numerous other influences, of which the ECtHR is particularly important. However, it is the decision of Lord Chancellor Mackay to promote 'a string of original, creative and non-Establishment High Court judges who have called the government to heel on every front' (Slapper and Kelly 2004: 287) which has brought matters to a head. Unless the judiciary returns to a more conservative assessment of its constitutional role, further debilitating clashes are inevitable.

The judicial perspective

Some judges acknowledge the validity of the third of these arguments. As one of Mackay's more distinguished appointees – Sir Stephen Sedley[7] – has noted:

> What this new generation have absorbed are the new ideas that were developed in the 1970s and 1980s, of a more resilient, more interventionist form of adjudication, being prepared to take a very hard look at the legality of what government does, rather than standing back and saying 'they must know best'. (Quoted in Dyer 2005)

Yet, at the same time, Sedley hints at an ongoing concern many judges have with ministers of a contemporary vintage. This view – which places responsibility for deteriorating relations firmly on government – can be summarised as follows:

- For example, Jeffrey Jowell (Dyer 2005) argues that an 'iron law of governance' immediately operates whenever a party enters office, the key feature of which is that 'whatever the intention of any political party about a rights-based democracy and judicial independence when they're in opposition, whenever they get into power they resent judicial obstruction of their designs'.
- Secondly, it is important to remember the long-term impact of the Thatcher years on the Labour party. Robert Stevens (Dyer 2005) suggests that the effectiveness of her government's unashamed grab for power at the expense of weak and divided opposition is visible in the ruthless way New Labour has swept aside its opponents. The only group of people able to withstand this are the judiciary, which is why Labour ministers have been so unforgiving when crossed.
- An alternative set of explanations focuses on the history and traditions of the Labour party. According to this view, the central part of the Labour tradition has been its faith in parliamentary sovereignty; the notion that Parliament possesses the rightful power to override the objections of a biased and hostile judiciary.

- New Labour has contributed to this tradition through its obsession with 'delivery' in respect of public policy. This results-based culture has become central to Labour's populist programmes in the highly sensitive areas of crime and immigration. For Anthony Scrivener, such a view is wrong in substance and in law, and bound to provoke an adverse reaction from the judiciary.
- On this note, the former Master of the Rolls, Lord Donaldson, questions whether ministers like Blunkett have ever fully understood the subtle way in which the British constitution actually works. Under the constitution, he asserts, the judiciary is actually an independent estate of the realm and one which is not dependent upon the goodwill of either government or Parliament to carry out its fundamental function: to determine the meaning of the law in a way which serves justice and the rule of law.

Political interference with judicial decision-making
Judges support these criticisms of ministerial attitudes with reference to the extraordinary row over Clause 11 of the Asylum and Immigration (Treatment of Claimants, etc.) Bill. This should be seen against a longstanding trend in the use of various legislative techniques to limit the capacity of the courts to review executive decisions.

- One such is the power granted to ministers to make the final adjudication. This is commonplace among land-use issues, where often it is the minister who decides whether and where a new motorway or airport should be built.
- Another is the widespread use of special tribunals to hear complaints over the way in which officials have used their discretionary powers. This practice was originally associated with the emergence of the welfare state. Ministers felt that the common law courts, immersed in their particular traditions, would not be particularly sympathetic to the aims of collectivist governments attempting to provide a standard service to potentially millions of people (Slapper and Kelly 2004: 268). Tribunals staffed by lay persons as well as lawyers offered a way around this problem. Equally, by simplifying their rules, tribunals would also be able to process cases far more quickly than the courts and at minimal cost.

- In more recent years, however, Parliament has been persuaded of the case that tribunals should be extended to highly sensitive areas of public policy. The two obvious examples of this are what is officially known as 'the regulation of investigatory powers'[8] and, secondly, immigration and asylum. By creating new bodies, Parliament is able to establish the rules by which they work. This has proved exceptionally controversial for a variety of reasons. These include: the inability to make personal submissions, denial of the right to choose one's legal representatives, and the refusal to give reasons for decisions.

However, much more important is the association of the movement towards tribunals with the denial of rights to judicial review. In

---

Box 4.10 Judicial reactions to the dismissal of Lord Irvine and the Constitutional Reform Bill

The rawness of judicial feelings was further exposed upon the announcement that Derry Irvine had been replaced as Lord Chancellor by Charles Falconer on 12 June 2003. For many, this was Irvine's 'punishment' for seeking to defend judicial independence against Blunkett. Compounding this, however, was the announcement that, without prior consultation, the office of the Lord Chancellor was to be abolished and the Law Lords removed from the House of Lords into a new Supreme Court.

Despite the fact that it was difficult to reconcile both these offices to the principle of the separation of powers, many lawyers preferred them to the alternatives on offer. In the case of the Lord Chancellor, this stemmed from the tradition (and necessity) of appointing an able legal practitioner. Not only would this lead to a degree of empathy between the Lord Chancellor and the judges with whom he had to deal; it would also deter Cabinet colleagues from clashing with a man whose legal knowledge so obviously outstripped their own. The result, according to the traditionalist account, is far better protection for the judiciary; something which is reinforced by the presence of so many distinguished judges and former judges on the cross-benches of the House of Lords, from where they can subject government policy on a wide range of constitutional and legal matters to the closest scrutiny. According to this account, the loss of these two safeguards leaves the judiciary even further exposed to an aggressive and rapacious executive.

other words, Parliament limits the right to a hearing to the tribunal itself. Even if complainants feel that they have been monstrously ill-treated by the tribunal panel, in theory at least there would be no other legal avenue of redress open to them. A variety of techniques are available to drafters of statutes in their attempts to do this, the main type being 'finality' or 'ouster' clauses. In the past, judges simply reinterpreted the meaning of the word 'final' and ignored them (Slapper and Kelly 2004: 269).[9]

Even then, Blunkett still sought to introduce what has been referred to as 'the mother of all ouster clauses' in his last asylum Bill. Had he not backed down, there is every indication that the judiciary would have simply ignored the statute, thereby provoking a crisis on a scale comparable with that of 1911 when the House of Lords challenged Commons' supremacy over public finance. Yet, the fact that Blunkett was prepared to contemplate such a step indicates the level of hostility simmering under the surface of British constitutional politics in the era of human rights.

Conclusion

This chapter has focused on what one might call the politics of the judiciary. It has emphasised that, despite the efforts to promote a view of judges as both independent and neutral, there are many active within politics who dispute whether this is the case. More significantly, as the final sections demonstrated, there is a real possibility that the resulting tensions may spill over into a constitutional crisis. This prospect also forms an interesting backdrop to the issues discussed in the next three chapters. Despite the Human Rights Act in the UK and the US Bill of Rights, governments on both sides of the Atlantic are intent on qualifying many of the classical civil liberties of liberal democracy. How and why are the questions to which we must now turn.

• •

✓ **What you should have learnt from reading this chapter**

- An awareness of the Left-Wing and civil libertarian critiques of the judiciary in both the UK and USA.

- Better understanding of the reasons why government in the UK has clashed with judges over key areas of public policy.

- An appreciation of the way in which these clashes are rooted in different views of the constitution.

- A sense of why these disputes could lead to a breakdown in relations between the judicial and executive branches.

Glossary of key terms

Civil libertarians A broad group of political activists anxious to ensure that the classical civil liberties described in Chapter 1 continue to receive constitutional protection.
Corporate bias The view that judges in the United Kingdom tend towards an identical approach when deciding certain cases. This common perspective betrays significant bias.
Fourth Amendment The key clause in the US Bill of Rights which lies at the centre of the dispute between civil libertarians and certain Supreme Court justices.
Neo-conservatives A faction of the British Conservative party and their counterparts in the USA known for their enthusiasm for punitive law and order policies and deep suspicion of civil liberties.
Ouster clauses A technique for ensuring that the courts cannot review the decisions of ministers or tribunals set up by them.

Likely examination questions

'The reality is that judges have a political role.' Discuss this view of the judiciary in the UK and USA.

What part has the judiciary played in the development and operation of law and order policy?

Compare and contrast the political significance of the judiciary in the USA and UK.

Helpful Websites

www.guardian.co.uk   Guardian Unlimited

www.homeoffice.gov.uk/   Home Office

 ## Suggestions for further reading

The history of the judicial relations with government in the United Kingdom is covered in some detail in Robert Stevens, 'Government and the Judiciary' and Jeffrey Jowell, 'Administrative Law', in Bogdanor (ed.), *The British Constitution in the Twentieth Century* (Oxford: Oxford University Press), 2003. An obvious starting point for the politics of the judiciary in the United Kingdom is John Griffith, *The Politics of the Judiciary* (Fontana: London), 1997, While the same author also provides an historical overview in *Judicial Politics since 1920* (Oxford: Blackwell), 1993. In this context, a detailed but very rewarding read is Keith Ewing and Conor Gearty, *Freedom under Thatcher* (Oxford: Oxford University Press), 1990. The contemporary American scene is covered in Tinsley E. Yarbrough, 'The Supreme Court and the Constitution' and Robert Singh, 'Law and Order', in Gillian Peele et al. (eds), *Developments in American Politics 4* (Palgrave: Basingstoke), 2002.

Notes

1. At the time, the relevant law could be found in the Criminal Justice Act 1988, as amended by the Proceeds of Crime Act 1995, the Drug Trafficking Act 1994 and the Terrorism Act 2000.
2. There is a tradition in the USA which denotes the Supreme Court by the family name of the Chief Justice presiding over it at any one time. The most recent Court is known as the Rehnquist Court after William Rehnquist who was appointed Chief Justice in 1986.
3. Reagan appointed Sandra Day O'Connor, Antonin Scalia and Anthony Kennedy; Bush senior, David Souter and Clarence Thomas.
4. The most prominent exception to this was the mandatory life sentence for murder.
5. The key cases are *V and T v. the UK* (1999) which removed the Home Secretary's power to set the tariff for juveniles, and *Anderson v. the UK* (2002) and *Taylor v. the UK* (2002) which had an identical effect in respect of adults.
6. Figures for the port of Dover alone found that the number of discovered stowaways had fallen from 12,679 in 2000 to 9,255 in 2001.
7. Mr Justice Sedley joined the High Court in 1992, from where he has gained a reputation as one of the UK's more fearless, liberal judges.
8. This term refers to a variety of covert policing operations. Chapter 6 of this study will examine them in much more detail.
9. This, for example, was the approach of Lord Denning in *R v. Medical Appeal Tribunal, ex parte Gilmore* (1957), where his Lordship concluded that the word 'final' did not mean final when it referred to the ability of the courts to review (and quash) ministerial actions.

Controlling Public Spaces in the United Kingdom

Contents

Overview

This is the first of three chapters which focus on the civil liberties implications of three selected trends in law and order policy. These are:

- Public order law
- Covert policing
- Emergency powers

The aim is to explain what it is about the legislation in these areas which worries civil libertarians; why the latter insist on reforms; and the counter-arguments put forward by ministers. While the primary focus will be the United Kingdom, observations will be made where relevant on comparable developments in the USA. On this note, however, Chapter 5 is concerned exclusively with the United Kingdom. Public order is an area of policy which has grown exponentially in recent years. An overarching concern of civil libertarians is that access to public spaces has been whittled away to a point where the freedoms of expression and assembly are now dependent less on historic rights entrenched in law, than the willingness of the authorities to tolerate them.

Key issues to be covered in this chapter

- The tension between public order law and civil liberties
- The legal and political contexts within which public order law has developed
- The marked increase in preventive powers since 1986
- The fusion of public order policing and crime prevention under New Labour
- The reasons why the civil liberties lobby in the UK remains deeply sceptical over these policy trends
- The justifications offered by governments since 1979 in support of the statutory regulation of access to public spaces

The politics of public order

It is axiomatic (self-evident) that the most important function of government is to maintain order. Firstly, the preservation of order is vital for the preservation of government itself. Accordingly, how ministers deal with those who use political violence is a key measure of their effectiveness and one to which the electorate will look when assessing ministers' fitness to govern. Secondly, without order any hope vulnerable individuals might entertain of leading a remotely tolerable existence – with all this implies for personal liberty – is a forlorn one.

At this point, the voice of Thomas Hobbes booms at us from the England of the seventeenth century.[1] Hobbes' writings are, of course, a product of the times in which he lived: the collapse of the Stuart monarchy and the subsequent attempt by Cromwell to create a Commonwealth in its stead. Yet, despite the passing of the centuries, many people living in contemporary Britain will sympathise with Hobbes' concerns. The modern state's claim to a monopoly of legitimate violence makes the individual highly dependent upon it for protection. Legally restricted in the steps we can take to defend ourselves, we look instead to government to ensure our safety. This is especially so when we choose to leave the relative security of our homes. Without the assurance of state protection when we venture out-of-doors, our civilisation would implode. Every-day commercial activity and social intercourse, the enjoyment of countless leisure pursuits, even the democratic process itself – each depends upon a public confident of conducting its affairs without fear or hindrance.

In addition, according to some criminologists the maintenance of public order is essential in restricting the growth in crime. The '**order maintenance**' model of crime[2] suggests that there is a direct link between effective control of public spaces and the growth of a wide range of crimes, including those like burglary which occur in people's homes. Even **low-level public disorder** can deter the law-abiding majority from spending time in their local communities, thereby encouraging a process of 'colonisation' by criminal elements. Emboldened, the latter begin to expand their criminal ambitions, providing further grist, if any were needed, to the foreboding Hobbesian mill.

Public spaces, the liberal tradition and the European Convention

At the same time, the liberal political tradition urges caution before surrendering control of public spaces to Hobbes' *Leviathan*. Liberals argue that access to public spaces is essential for a variety of fundamental freedoms (thought and conscience; expression; assembly and association) on which both human happiness and democracy itself depend.

- Freedom of expression is important for its own sake. Our ability to express our individuality, whether through our lifestyles or political beliefs, is an essential part of being human. To suffer enforced silence is to suffer a psychological trauma which results in unhappiness.
- Secondly, many people will wish to express their views in association with others. Fellowship is also an essential part of the human condition, especially in politics where many individuals will be anxious to demonstrate their solidarity with others who think as they do.
- In addition, there are the several points raised by J. S. Mill in *On Liberty*. Interestingly, Mill was less concerned with the oppressive powers of government than the strength of social and cultural 'norms'. He argued that any society which develops conventions so strong that they stifle individual expression is doomed to intellectual stagnation and eventual collapse. Mill argued that societies must continually renew themselves via constant exposure to new ideas, no matter how seemingly weird or silly.
- Mill's warnings are particularly important to the intellectual health of a democratic society. To liberals, democracy is an arena, not a process. Public spaces are particularly important in that they enable marginalised groups to connect with the wider electorate. In this way, democratic politics does not become the exclusive preserve of the well-connected. This is especially so when, as the research of bodies like the Glasgow Media Studies Group has established, many groups have real difficulties in attracting media coverage in any other way.

The political importance of public spaces is recognised by the European Convention on Human Rights (see Box 5.1). However,

Box 5.1 Articles 9–11 of the European Convention

Article 9 Freedom of Thought, Conscience and Religion

1. Everyone has the right to freedom of thought, conscience and religion; this right includes freedom to change his religion or belief and freedom, *either alone or in community with others and in public or private, to manifest his religion or belief*, in worship, teaching, practice and observance (emphasis added).

Article 10 Freedom of Expression

1. Everyone has the right to freedom of expression. This right shall include freedom to hold opinions *and to receive and impart information and ideas without interference by public authority and regardless of frontiers* (emphasis added). This Article shall not prevent States from requiring the licensing of broadcasting, television or cinema enterprises.

Article 11 Freedom of Assembly and Association

1. Everyone has the right to freedom of peaceful assembly and to freedom of association with others, including the right to form and to join trade unions for the protection of his interests.

more is at stake than the mere tolerance of those who seek to influence others. The Convention also imposes a positive obligation on government to facilitate the ability of citizens to assemble in public spaces to express both political views and other aspects of their individuality.

Restrictions on Convention rights

The case for relatively unfettered access to public spaces in a liberal democracy is not particularly difficult to make. Yet, even the staunchest civil libertarian must acknowledge that there are circumstances in which it is legitimate to place conditions on the exercise of this freedom. This is acknowledged by the Convention itself, which rejects the notion that the rights listed in Articles 9–11 should be enjoyed unconditionally. Providing they are, one, prescribed by law and, two, necessary in a democratic society,[3] these rights can be limited on a number of grounds, the main ones being:

- The interests of public safety
- The protection of public order, health or morals
- The protection of the rights and freedoms of others
- The interests of national security
- The prevention of crime.[4]

In short, the Convention accepts the need for a balance which falls short of granting unrestricted access to public spaces. Of course, it is unthinkable that any government – Convention or not – is going to allow the streets to be taken over by those preaching treason and sedition, or urging others to commit criminal acts. Rather, the politics of public order concern the restrictions it is permissible to impose on those who do not pose anything remotely proximate to this level of threat. The following list should give some idea of the complexities of this problem.

- Political protest, even when it is peaceful, inevitably causes inconvenience to others. To be effective, protest depends upon high visibility, timing and numbers. Unless they can disrupt the normal pattern of social intercourse, how can the protestors get across their message? Yet, by seeking to disrupt, protestors inevitably compromise the rights of others to go about their own business.
- This problem is aggravated by the issue of cost. Policing public protest is not cheap.[5] Just how far can cash-strapped authorities support the right to protest when it begins to consume resources earmarked for other areas of a law and order budget?
- Thirdly, what should the authorities do when an otherwise peaceful protest is set to provoke violence among others? For example, a so-called 'splinter' group may have attached itself to the main body in the hope of persuading others to commit acts of violence. Alternatively, bystanders witnessing the protest might be so outraged that they begin to abuse the protestors. Under what circumstances are law enforcers entitled to stop the original protest, even when those participating have not behaved provocatively and are not to blame for the violence?
- This problem becomes even more delicate when the authorities are in possession of intelligence that a violent outcome is likely some time before the protest is due to begin. Does it follow that it should be banned simply on the basis that violence *might* ensue?

- Many of these problems also apply to those who choose to express alternative lifestyles which openly challenge conventional morality and notions of good taste. While one might have every sympathy for the residents of a village who suddenly find their peace disturbed by an unlicensed rock music festival, should one extend sympathy to an elderly person who is affronted by the mere presence of young people who occasionally gather outside her home? The levels of distress might be comparable; but should the events preceding them both merit legal intervention?

The growth of statutory regulation of public spaces in the United Kingdom

As implied above, while they would not dispute the validity of these concerns, civil libertarians view the politics of public order from a different perspective. Their primary concern is that governments may seek to use the above as an excuse to criminalise behaviour not because it is violent or threatening to life or property, but simply because it is embarrassing or merely inconvenient. Governments of all countries have used the alleged threat of public disorder as an excuse to repress the activities of their ideological or political opponents. There is no reason to suggest that those of the United Kingdom are beyond such temptation.

In this respect, it is notable just how quickly and extensively the corpus (body) of public order law has grown in recent years. The first statute purposely designed to combat disorder in public spaces was the Public Order Act 1936 (see Box 5.2). For the next fifty years, however, Parliament did not feel the need to pass further legislation in this area. Moreover, the occasions when the Public Order Act was used were few in number. For example, between 1936 and 1980 the controversial s. 3 was used on a mere eleven occasions (Robertson 1993: 74), reflecting the official view that it was an exceptional measure designed to meet a particular threat which had long since passed.[6]

Contrast this with the record of governments elected since 1979. Not only is it the case that the use of existing powers increased dramatically,[7] governments have also asked Parliament to expand public order legislation with an almost ritualistic regularity. Few governments are happy about the prospect of open, mass-based dissent to

Box 5.2 The key provisions of the Public Order Act 1936

Powers to control processions (marches)
Under s. 3, chief officers of police were given the power to impose conditions on processions (that is, marches) if they felt these necessary to prevent 'serious public disorder'. Typically, these involved issues of timing, re-routing and duration. However, and in addition, if they deemed that any conditions they might impose were inadequate for this task, they could apply to the relevant local authority to ban *all or any class* of procession for up to three months. This 'blanket' ban was subject to much parliamentary criticism. Ministers replied that it was the only way in which the police and local government could be protected from accusations of political bias.

The new offence of threatening behaviour
In s. 5 a new criminal offence of 'threatening behaviour likely or intended to cause a breach of the peace' was created. This gave the authorities a new weapon to deal with those who made threats to others without actually carrying them out. The worry for civil libertarians was the subjective element. Firstly, the law did not define what it meant by 'threatening behaviour'. This was to be left to the courts. Secondly, an offence could still occur even when there was no proof that the accused actually intended to cause, or indeed had actually caused, a breach of the peace. This meant that a powerful weapon to control unorthodox but essentially non-violent behaviour in public spaces had been handed to the police.

their policies. However, the pattern of legislation passed since 1986 suggests that the modern executive is peculiarly loath to tolerate it.

The main statutes are listed in Box 5.3. Not that this list should be seen as being comprehensive. It does not include other statutory offences, such as obstructing an officer in the execution of his duty (Police Act 1996 s. 89). The latter is a very effective general provision, not least because it criminalises any attempt to obstruct an officer once he has formed a reasonable view that a breach of the peace is likely to occur.

The primary thrust of these new laws has been to create an ever-wider range of **preventive powers** to enable the authorities to ban or otherwise control most types of gathering. A common target is overtly political protest. However, beginning with s. 39 of the Public

Box 5.3 The main public order statutes: 1979–2005

- The Public Order Act 1986
- The Criminal Justice and Public Order Act 1994 Part V
- The Protection from Harassment Act 1997
- The Crime and Disorder Act 1998 Part I
- The Football Disorder Act 2000
- The Criminal Justice and Police Act 2001 Part I
- The Anti-Social Behaviour Act 2003 Parts III, IV and VII
- The Serious Organised Crime and Police Act 2005

Order Act 1986, what is called 'lifestyle protest' has also become subject to statutory regulation. In addition, the Labour government returned to office in May 1997 has opened another 'front' in the fight for control of public spaces. This is the assault on anti-social behaviour. Led by former Home Secretaries Jack Straw (1997–2001) and David Blunkett (2001–4), the government claims to be the first to systematically tackle a long-neglected problem. Beginning with Part I of the Crime and Disorder Act 1998, Labour has introduced a variety of court orders, most famously the **Anti-Social Behaviour Order** (ASBO), designed to place legal curbs on individual behaviour without first resorting to criminal punishments.

The growth of preventive powers

Generally speaking, preventive powers are designed to give the police and local authorities the ability to regulate access to public spaces by particular groups of people. This can be done by:

- Denying altogether the public or sections of the public the use of particular spaces at particular times.
- Restricting the use of public spaces by imposing certain conditions on the right to assemble.
- Creating a variety of offences to ensure that police officers can compel people to comply with the law.

Some preventive powers apply once people have actually assembled. Others empower the authorities to act *in anticipation* that order may break down and are all the more controversial as a result. The growth in preventive powers dates from 1980 when the new Conservative government embarked upon a review of the Public Order Act 1936. As a result of this, ministers drew attention to what they saw as three deficiencies in the original legislation.

* The police's capacity to control processions was undermined by the absence of a national law compelling organisers to give *advance notice* of their desire to march. This prevented police officers from imposing conditions on processions before they set out.
* Secondly, no statutory power existed which enabled police officers to arrest anyone for refusing to comply with an order subsequently imposing conditions on processions.
* Finally, there was no equivalent power enabling the authorities to control static assemblies. These had become increasingly popular during the 1970s, largely because they enabled protestors to get around the 1936 controls.

All of these matters pointed to major extensions to s. 3 of the Public Order Act 1936. However, it is worth remembering that the immediate cause of the government's decision to order a review was the highly disturbing death of Blair Peach, an anti-racist protestor who died at the hands (and possibly feet) of the Met's notorious and now disbanded Special Patrol Group on 23 April 1979. Mr Peach was protesting at a National Front march through Southall, an area of west London with a high density of people of south Asian origin. The fact that no police officer was ever charged or even disciplined in relation to his death might have encouraged the view that ministers would seek to bring the police rather than demonstrators under greater control. That was not, however, how the government saw it.

Ministerial concerns were dealt with via ss. 11, 12 and 14 of the Public Order Act 1986 (see Box 5.4). During the parliamentary debates it became apparent that these measures would be targeted at the peace movement and, more importantly, pickets on industrial action. In the years preceding the Act, the government had clashed repeatedly with these groups, especially the latter. However, as the Act was passing through its parliamentary stages, a new political problem emerged: the so-called free festival movement. This was a highly variegated movement, the focal point of which was a large 'peace convoy' that travelled throughout the south and west of England each summer. These 'new age travellers', or NATs, were the subject of intense criticism and media

Box 5.4 Preventive powers and the Public Order Act 1986

- Under s. 11, the organiser of *any* procession must give at least six days' notice so that the police can consider what, if any, conditions they wish to impose. This is designed to outlaw spontaneous marches.
- Secondly, s. 12 created three new offices, all of which carry liability to arrest, for failing to comply with any condition imposed by the police. The organisers of processions are particularly vulnerable in this respect, a measure which hints at ministerial intimidation aimed at the leadership of protest groups.
- Further, s. 14 extended preventive powers to static assemblies. The government did concede that, precisely because they are static, assemblies do not impose quite the same threat to public order as processions. Hence, it was not deemed necessary to demand advance notice. However, anyone participating in an assembly ought to know that the police are still empowered to impose various conditions which must be adhered to on pain of arrest.
- Finally, s. 39 broke with centuries of legal tradition by criminalising the law of trespass by giving the police a new power to remove trespassers from land. Further, this power could be activated simply when the trespassers were in a group of twelve or more vehicles. Failure to obey an officer's instruction to move became a new offence, as was the decision to return to the land in question within three months.

comment, much of it wholly distorted. However, that they passed through the Conservative heartland at a time when ministers were highly sensitive to the issue of public disorder made them an inevitable target for the parliamentary drafters.

A very similar pattern emerged in the run-up to the second major public order statute passed by the Conservative government at this time: Part V of the Criminal Justice and Public Order Act 1994 (CJPOA). Once again, the travelling community was a target: in part because it had survived s. 39 of the POA 1986; in part because it had fused with a new generation of political protestors, dubbed appropriately if unimaginatively the '**New Protest**'. The latter tended to focus on animal rights and environmental issues, of which anti-road protest was particularly prominent. Major construction projects at

Twyford Down, Newbury and the East River Crossing of the Thames were each subject to highly effective protest which, in turn, led to complaints flooding in from construction companies that their lawful activities were being thwarted. The other notable group to be targeted in the Act were participants in 'raves', unlicensed music events which became very popular in the early 1990s.

All of these concerns are reflected in the Act, the key provisions of which are outlined in Box 5.5. The overtly discriminatory nature of the legislation prompted huge 'Kill the Bill' protests. Attention also focused on how the police would enforce many of these measures, especially where officers believed that to do so would provoke precisely the disorder the legislation was nominally designed to prevent. However, the one voice most conspicuously missing from these protests was that of the Labour party. Since 1980, Labour had adopted a position very similar to that of the civil rights lobby, the culmination of which was the decision to vote against the Public Order Act 1986. Under the influence of its new leadership, in 1994 Labour reversed this position and abstained on the crucial Third Reading of the CJPOA. Together with similar U-turns over anti-terrorism laws, this signalled the emergence of a new brand of **populist** law and order politics not seen in Labour's ranks up to this point.

Labour's interest in public order law has followed it into office (see Box 5.6). The themes linking together the various provisions are ominous ones, at least for those who believe in an unconditional right to make peaceful protest in the UK. Once again, ministers have focused on the activities of particular groups, of which animal rights

---

Box 5.5 Part V of the Criminal Justice and Public Order Act 1994

Power to remove trespassers from land
This provision can be found in ss. 61–2 of the Act. Basically, it builds on s. 39 of the Public Order Act 1986 by making it much easier for the police to force NATs from private land. It did this in two ways:

- Even when they entered with the consent of the owner, that is, that their entry was not originally an act of trespass, the police can still order them to leave if the landowner changes his mind.

- This applies when there are as few as six as opposed to twelve vehicles.
- In addition, the police are empowered to impound the vehicles (that is, the homes) of those NATs who refuse to follow their instructions.

These sections should be read in conjunction with ss. 77–80 which enable local authorities to move on travellers camping on the roadside or on public land without permission. The fact that s. 80 removed the obligation on local authorities to provide official campsites drew vehement criticism. Taken together, these measures sent out a clear message to the travelling community: there is no room in the UK for people following your lifestyles.

The Act and Political Protest: the New Offence of Aggravated Trespass

Under s. 68, a new offence of aggravated trespass was created. This occurs when a person deemed to be trespassing obstructs or disrupts a lawful activity. Perhaps the most important feature is that the ingredients typical of other public order measures such as serious public disorder or serious disruption to the life of the community are not present in s. 68. Mere obstruction, that is, moral pressure, will suffice. In addition, the police have the power to order anyone they suspect of committing this offence from the area and to arrest them if they fail to comply (s. 69). It is via these measures that the government sought to defend the interests of rural landowners and construction companies from the likes of hunt saboteurs and road protestors.

Power in relation to raves

Unlicensed popular music events remain vulnerable to ss. 63–6 and, depending on the circumstances, ss. 70–1. The first set of provisions gives police officers the power to halt a rave, stop preparations for one and prevent people from attending. They are also empowered to seize vehicles and sound equipment, the latter permanently. Those seeking to circumvent these measures by holding an unlicensed event on private land with the owner's consent would do well to examine ss. 70–1. These enable a chief officer to apply for a ban on any assembly on private land consisting of twenty or more people if that assembly exceeds the limits of the public's right of access. In other words, it is for a purpose not usually associated with the use of private property. It was suggested at the time that this measure was designed to help local authorities to ban Glastonbury-like music festivals.

Box 5.6 Preventive powers under New Labour

Part VII of the Anti-Social Behaviour Act 2003
These measures extended those introduced by the Conservatives in
s. 14 of the Public Order Act 1986 and Part V of the CJPOA. Though
they have a general application, they are largely designed to extend
the provisions aimed at hunt saboteurs and roads protestors to animal
rights activists. This is especially so in the case of ss. 57 and 59.

- Under s. 57, the definition of a public assembly is amended so that
  the police can use their powers under s. 14 of the Public Order Act
  1986 if a mere two people gather together. The previous figure was
  twenty. Ministers had argued that the more vociferous protestors
  succeeded in getting around the 1986 Act by deliberately restricting numbers to a maximum of nineteen and that the extra discretion was needed to avoid the law (and the police) being made
  foolish.
- The following section (s. 58) makes a number of amendments to
  the original law governing raves. The police can: intervene once
  numbers reach twenty (as opposed to 100); deal with gatherings
  in buildings as well as the open air; and, finally, arrest anyone
  making preparations to attend a rave who they have reason to
  believe was aware that it had been banned.
- Finally, s. 59 amended the offence of aggravated trespass so that
  it applied to conduct inside buildings rather than the open air alone.

Combating the Animal Rights Movement
The government's initial response can be found in ss. 42 and 44 of
the Criminal Justice and Police Act (CJPA) 2001. This gave the police
and prosecuting authorities two new powers.

- Under s. 42, a police officer can order a protestor to move away
  from a residential dwelling if he is 'making representations'
  deemed likely to cause harassment to anyone residing there.
- In addition, s. 44 enables the CPS to bring charges against anyone
  who, while not taking part in the protest, it believes to have aided,
  abetted or otherwise encouraged someone else to do so.

The details of s. 42 provoked particular controversy. MPs and
peers pointed out that the wording is so vague that the mere act of
holding up a placard with a graphic image of an animal undergoing
vivisection could suffice to justify police intervention. Undeterred by
such criticism, the government returned to the offensive in Part IV of
the Serious Organised Crime and Police Act 2005. The following

reforms make it easier still both for research companies and the police to suppress protest of this nature.

- Section 125 amends the Protection from Harassment Act 1997 so that either companies or their employees can take out injunctions against protestors on behalf of themselves or others. This rather complex measure is expressly designed to counter the tendency of the courts to interpret the original law in a way which rendered it ineffectual in these circumstances.
- By contrast, s. 126 amended the controversial s. 42 of the CJPA 2001 so that it is now an offence to make representations in a residential area which either cause or *could cause* harassment, alarm or distress. Moreover, the alleged victim does not necessarily have to be living in the dwelling targeted. It is enough that a neighbour suffers, or might suffer, for an offence to be committed. By any standards, this is an extraordinarily wide measure, making it seemingly impossible to protest in the vicinity of residential premises.
- This amendment is complemented by s. 127, which enables an officer to order a protestor from the vicinity of a particular dwelling for up to three months. The original law had not specified a time period.
- In addition, ss. 145–6 create new offences designed to protect any company or person targeted by animal rights protestors simply by virtue of their having either a contractual relationship or a connection with an animal research organisation.

Trespassing on designated sites

These powers were introduced via ss. 128–38 of the Serious Organised Crime and Police Act 2005. The first of these gives a minister the power to designate a site, after which anyone who trespasses upon it (that is, enters without permission where permission is needed) commits a criminal offence punishable by up to a year in prison and a fine. The grounds for designation are very widely drawn. If the site is on Crown land or is owned privately by the monarch or heir to the throne, no other justification is needed. However, where the minister feels that national security is at stake, he can use this power to designate any site, wherever its location.

However, it is the second set of provisions that has really captured media headlines. Under ss. 132–8, any person wishing to demonstrate within one kilometre of Parliament must now seek permission from the Commissioner of the Met and abide by any conditions or directions he or his officers may impose. Again, failure to do so can carry a penalty of up to one year's imprisonment. Despite the government's assurance that the ban on spontaneous demonstrations was the result of the terrorist threat, the general view is that the sole target was anti-war protestor Brian Haw, who has set up camp outside the entrance to Parliament since July 2001. If this is so, it is ironic that a loophole in the law ensured that Mr Haw successfully defended his right to continue to protest in the High Court in July 2005. Two of his supporters, by contrast, were less fortunate; one of whom was arrested under the Act for doing nothing more threatening to parliamentary democracy than bringing Mr Haw a hot meal (Kirkham 2005).

protestors are by far the most prominent. The catalyst for the legislative assault on animal rights activists was the campaign to close down the infamous Huntingdon Life Sciences Centre. The animal rights movement had been complaining about conditions there for a number of years. However, after a television broadcast in 1987, they redoubled their efforts. What was novel about the resulting campaign was the manner in which activists took their protests to the homes of Huntingdon staff and those of companies and banks who supported them. The effects were dramatic and it was not long before leading vivisectionists and the pharmaceutical companies who financed them began to complain about the loss of investment and the possibility of work being transferred abroad.

The government's enthusiasm for tackling the problems raised by these and other activities through repressive legislation is witnessed by the three major public order statutes passed in the last eight years. Nor does this figure include Labour's anti-terror legislation which also has implications for the right to protest (see Chapter 7).

The moral and legal justifications for many, though by no means all, of these measures invariably fail to convince civil libertarians, a point which we will explore in much more detail below. However, no doubt mindful of a former Home Secretary's interdiction that human rights lawyers earn their money too easily, the government was simultaneously engaged in a second legislative programme which also had major implications for a range of civil liberties, including freedom of expression and association. This is the assault on anti-social behaviour.

The campaign against anti-social behaviour
This has its origins in Jack Straw's appointment as Shadow Home Secretary in 1994. Up until this point, if it had a coherent outlook at

Box 5.7 New Labour's measures aimed at curbing anti-social behaviour

The majority of these were created in Part I of the Crime and Disorder Act 1998, Part I of the Criminal Justice and Police Act 2001 and Part IV of the Anti-Social Behaviour Act 2003.

Fixed Penalty Notices (FPNs) for Disorderly Behaviour
The Criminal Justice and Police Act 2001 empowers the police to issue FPNs for eleven of the most common forms of low-level disorder, ranging from knowingly giving a false alarm to the fire brigade to being drunk and disorderly in a public place. These powers should also be read in conjunction with those under Part II giving the police and local authorities additional controls over the consumption of alcohol in public places. In addition, s. 87 of the Anti-Social Behaviour Act 2003 ensures that this provision now applies to 16–17 year-olds, while giving ministers the option of extending it to anyone over the age of ten.

Parenting Orders and Child Safety Orders
Established under ss. 8–9 of the Crime and Disorder Act 1998, a parenting order is a very wide-ranging measure which enables the courts to impose various requirements on parents whose children have either broken the law or are about to do so. One example would be a requirement to ensure that a child attends school. Child safety orders (ss. 11–12 of the Crime and Disorder Act 1998) work in a slightly different way. They apply to children under ten, to whom the court can appoint an adult from outside the family with responsibilities for preventing criminal behaviour.

Anti-Social Behaviour Orders
These orders were originally established in ss. 1 and 19 of the Crime and Disorder Act 1998. They can be handed down to any person aged ten or over whom the court believes has caused harassment, alarm or distress to a member of another household on more than one occasion. Since their introduction in 1999, they have been the subject of considerable controversy. Yet ministers insist that they have improved the lives of some of the most vulnerable people in the country, not least by reassuring the public that anti-social behaviour will not be tolerated.

Dispersal Orders

These powers are available to the police. The first of these, which originated in ss. 14–15 of the Crime and Disorder Act 1998, has been significantly amended by s. 30(6) of the Anti-Social Behaviour Act 2003. It enables a senior police officer to issue an order covering a specific area, as a result of which any officer on patrol who believes that a person is, one, under sixteen and, two, not under effective supervision, can remove that person to their place of residence. The second – which can be found at s. 30(4) of the same Act – applies to any group of two or more assembling in a designated area. To use this power, under which the officer can order the group to disperse, the officer must be satisfied that the presence of the group has or is likely to cause another member of the public harassment, alarm or distress. The officer can also ban members of the group from returning to the area for twenty-four hours.

all, Labour tended to see anti-social behaviour as part of a wider malaise common to all capitalist societies. Thereafter, anti-social behaviour became a central factor not only in Labour's analysis of the causes of crime but also its extensive crime-prevention programme.

By 1997 the government could draw already upon a number of measures designed to combat what is loosely called low-level public disorder. Two examples of these are: the offence of disorderly conduct created by s. 5 of the Public Order Act 1986; and the Protection from Harassment Act 1997 which enabled people to take out injunctions preventing others from intimidating or alarming them. However, for a variety of reasons Labour felt that a more flexible response was needed.[8] This can be seen in the measures included in Box 5.7. As mentioned above, the idea behind this new generation of court orders is to encourage social responsibility without the immediate imposition of a criminal penalty. For example, an anti-social behaviour order (ASBO) places conditions on an individual's future conduct. Only in the event of those conditions being breached will a punishment be handed down.

The ASBO, in particular, has been the subject of fierce controversy. One reason for this is the way in which it uses the civil law test – the balance of probabilities – to secure an order, even when a breach of such an order is likely to result in a prison sentence. In addition, there is a very real danger that these orders are being exploited by ambitious and aggressive local authorities to clear the streets of those whose mere presence is embarrassing. There are numerous examples of this, many of which are associated with Manchester, the self-styled 'ASBO capital' of Britain. Three of the most prominent cases are those of:

- Peter Broadbent, who received an ASBO banning him from sleeping rough
- Leonard Hockey, who died in prison after breaching an ASBO which banned him from begging
- A nameless female prostitute jailed when her drugs clinic issued her with condoms, causing her to breach a condition of her order.

Most significant of all, however, was the local authority's decision in October 2004 to seek an ASBO banning soup kitchens – and hence the homeless – from the city's streets. The council responded by pointing out that it had plenty of 'indoor' facilities to cater for the needs of the homeless, where the latter would receive better care in a safe environment. However, critics suggested that this was a rather transparent ruse to cover the council's determination to protect its 'second city' reputation even when this meant exposing some of the city's most vulnerable people to criminal sanctions (Travis 2004).

Still more disturbing, however, is the evidence that a measure advertised as a means of promoting civility among neighbours is now being used to silence political dissent. The key case is that of Lindis Percy, a sixty-three-year-old midwife, who has emerged, along with Brian Haw, as one of the country's foremost peace campaigners. One of her main targets is the giant American airbase at Menwith Hill in North Yorkshire. On 17 May 2005, Mrs Percy attended court to hear whether or not an ASBO would be imposed on her as a result of her protests. Apparently, actions such as raising a US flag with the words 'No more meddling, please' written on it had persuaded the Ministry of Defence that Mrs Percy had frightened military personnel at the base, including their children. To the relief of many, however, its application for an ASBO banning Mrs Percy from protesting outside the base was thrown out by the judge. Yet peace campaigners and civil rights activists were mindful of the fact that the judge ruled that an ASBO could be imposed if the actions of a protestor (Mrs Percy is a Quaker) were deemed to be intimidating (Wainwright 2005).

Box 5.8 The use of anti-social behaviour measures in England and Wales: 2003–4

In data collected to mark the first anniversary of the enactment of the Anti-Social Behaviour Act 2003, it was revealed that the authorities were responding to ministerial pressure to use the full battery of measures now available to them.

- The police and local authorities took action in over 100,000 cases, an average of 274 each day.
- The courts, meanwhile, issued over 2,600 orders, as many as they had over the previous four years combined.
- A total of 418 'dispersal orders' were included in this figure, the most dramatic of which was the decision of the Metropolitan police to declare sixteen designated 'dispersal areas' across London's West End.
- The number of intensive anti-social behaviour schemes increased from ten to fifty.

Source: Travis (2004)

This case raises, yet again, the possibility that popular crime prevention measures will be exploited by embarrassed authorities for overtly political purposes, even when this possibility was never raised at the time of their enactment. Much the same thing happened with the Protection of Harassment Act 1997, when three of the first five injunctions issued under it were aimed at protestors, and could also prove to be the case with the s. 30(4) provision of the Anti-Social Behaviour Act 2003. Read alongside the government's other provisions against animal rights activists, this will enable the police to intervene even when the designated measures (see ss. 42–4 of the Criminal Justice and Police Act 2001) do not.

Public order law: a civil libertarian critique

The previous section reveals the extent to which government in the UK has sought and acquired new legal powers to control and restrict access to public spaces. That these have the potential to undermine key Convention rights – especially those protected by Articles 5, 6, 9, 10 and 11 – is readily apparent. In defence of these measures, ministers argue that they constitute the optimum balance between these rights and other important aspects of the public interest, notably the maintenance of order. It follows that the 'potential' referred to above is a threat more apparent than real. In response, the civil liberties lobby remains somewhat sceptical about these assertions. In this section, we shall see why.

It is simply not practical to test each of the statutory provisions discussed above against civil liberties criteria. Instead, the aim of this section is to draw out those elements of public order law which capture the essence of the civil libertarian critique. The commentary below is deconstructed into three components:

- The manner in which public order legislation has been drafted
- The changing ingredients of the law
- The net or combined effect of public order law on the relevant Convention rights.

Each of these components questions the notion of balance referred to above, but does so in different ways.

The making of public order law
The first accusation is that public order law has evolved in a rapid, almost frenetic manner, in which ministers have shown little interest in developing any overarching principles to ensure that the law achieves its primary goal without unjustly suppressing individual rights. This is in marked contrast to the recent history of general police powers. The dominant statute – the Police and Criminal Evidence Act 1984 – was both carefully considered and, more importantly, possessed of a single, overriding rationale. The Royal Commission on Criminal Procedure, whose report provided the basis for PACE, was mindful of the need to increase police powers, not least to eliminate the sub-culture among officers that it was permissible to break the law in order to obtain a conviction. Equally, however, the commissioners were adamant that any increase in power had to be matched by new and effective safeguards against abuse.

The contrast with public order law could not be more stark. The latter has a disturbing 'scatter gun' quality to it, with little apparent thought for its civil liberties implications (Manning et al. 2004: 1). This problem is compounded by the obvious influence of private interests. Far from reflecting considered parliamentary and legal opinion, public order law is often driven forward by these powerful lobbies. In the case of Part V of the CJPOA these included rural landowners and the construction industry. Under New Labour, the security needs of vivisectionists and their collaborators in the multi-billion pound pharmaceutical industry have assumed paramount importance.

The result is one where people engaged in controversial activities are being shielded from the consequences of this by their political connections. Laws are being developed which, despite their designation as general public acts, are the servants of particular interests.

These trends ultimately manifest themselves in a dangerous incrementalism. The changes introduced in each new statute are, by themselves, invariably minor. However, when read together, public order laws have exposed the flimsy basis on which the rights of expression, assembly and association are founded in the UK. This can be seen in the way that preventive powers, which once applied to processions, now cover static assemblies, private meetings in part open to public spaces and single-person demonstrations. This is not to say that these measures are wholly without justification. However, when Parliament can happily introduce a major restriction on the right to protest outside its own doors – the very seat of British democracy – in order to silence one individual (Brian Haw), civil libertarians might feel entitled to conclude that a sense of perspective is now wholly lacking. This point is acknowledged in a leading study of the subject (Joyce 2002: 47):

> The response by successive governments to various forms of protest in Great Britain has primarily taken the form of introducing legislation to enable the police to restrict activities associated with it. Under the guise of maintaining public order, successive governments have utilised criminalisation as a mechanism to regulate protest.

Ever-wider discretion

Aside from the incremental erosion referred to above, a second problem is the emergent trend in drafting laws which give exceptionally wide discretion to the authorities. The legal standing of static assemblies is a case in point. The original power to impose conditions on static assemblies was designed to prevent either:

- 'serious public disorder, serious damage to property or serious disruption to the life of the community (s. 14(1)(a) of the Public Order Act 1986);
- or [where] the purpose of the persons gathering is the intimidation of others (s. 14(1)(b)'.
- It was further felt that a person could not be intimidated unless at least twenty people were gathered together.

This is no longer the case, as the following examples illustrate:

- Under ss. 68–9 of the Criminal Justice and Public Order Act 1994, police officers were given the power to intervene and stop certain types of assembly which are, or might prove, in some way intimidating or obstructive or disruptive (s. 68(1)). It can, of course, be argued that any form of protest, unless it is so badly organised that it is has no discernible effect whatsoever, could fall foul of this provision if police officers are so minded.
- This is even more marked in the case of the much-amended s. 42 of the Criminal Justice and Police Act 2001. Under its many provisions, protest within the vicinity of a person's dwelling is now an offence if in the opinion of the police officer it causes, or might cause, harassment, alarm or distress to another. Aside from the power to bring charges, the officer can also issue an instruction not to return for three months. Whether officers will do this will depend upon their understanding of the terms 'harassment, alarm or distress' (the statute does not define them) and, whether in the absence of complaints, they believe that someone could have suffered such a reaction. For civil libertarians, this places far too much discretion in the hands of an individual, who becomes the arbiter of what is or is not acceptable.

The full implications of this last point will be considered below. More generally, civil libertarians argue that this type of measure raises the key human rights principle of proportionality. Is it really correct that a person could face criminal charges merely for displaying a poster which is neither abusive nor insulting, but which merely expresses his distaste for vivisection? Those who engage in such practices are entitled to the protection of the law. Yet, should this extend to silencing *any* public criticism when that takes place near their dwellings? The government clearly felt that it should. However, in the words of Brian Haw, is it right that such fundamental freedoms in a liberal democracy should contain laws which result in 'making serious criminals out of peaceful protestors'? (Kirkham 2005).

A very similar problem exists in respect of s. 30(6) of the Anti-Social Behaviour Act 2003. Young people aged under sixteen have every reason to feel aggrieved that they are being penalised for no other reason than their membership of a perennially unpopular social group. To activate powers under this section, all the officer concerned needs is authorisation from a senior colleague. Other than that, providing his suspicions are reasonable – that is, that a person is under sixteen and not under effective supervision (s. 30(6)) – he can act upon them without further evidence. The unfairness of this has been recognised by the High Court which accepted the argument of an unnamed teenager ('W') that this provision exposed him to a very real loss of liberty when he had not transgressed the law in any way.[9] This ruling will no doubt come as a relief to civil libertarians (Liberty helped 'W' to bring the action) and exposes the government to similar rulings in respect of s. 30(4) which empowers the police to disperse any gathering of two or more people in a designated area. If this proves to be the case, ministers will only have themselves to blame.

Goodwill, not rights

In their famous dissection of the parlous state of civil liberties in the UK, Ewing and Gearty (1990: 94) argue that the right to express one's views in public has been progressively removed from the realm of law and placed at the mercy of personal caprice.

> [B]y 1979, the freedom to engage in peaceful protest in this country [the UK] was . . . dependent not on the law but rather on the benev-olent exercise of discretion by those in power.

Civil libertarians add that this situation has ossified in the quarter century since. The key point, however, is that the goodwill on which we are all dependent can be withdrawn so easily: personal or corporate prejudice thus become the real arbiters of the rights of expression and assembly. In this respect, a number of possibilities present themselves. Firstly, police officers might act on their own prejudices, a well-documented trend two centuries old. The most infamous example of this was the extraordinary police operation against NATs at Stonehenge on 31 May 1986. The so-called 'Battle of the Beanfield' offers the starkest reminder of what the police will do when sufficiently motivated (Ewing and Gearty 1990: 125–8).

Secondly, that the corporate interests of the police will influence their responses. It should be remembered that policing protest can be expensive and massively inconvenient to senior police officers who find themselves short of manpower for other duties. In such circumstances, the simplest solution is to ban protest altogether. If evidence of this effect is needed, it can be found in the decision of the Met to ban anti-arms protestors from Europe's largest armaments fair at Docklands in September 2005, a decision justified on the grounds that the Met's resources are overstretched by the terrorist threat to the capital (Muir 2005).

More worrying still is a third possibility: that senior police officers will come under intense political pressure to suppress forms of protest which challenge or otherwise embarrass the government of the day. This could occur for any number of reasons:

- Governments are often opposed to protest on ideological grounds, that is, that it challenges the sovereignty of Parliament and the democratic process.
- Ministers see certain protestors as their political enemies who they need to silence for electoral purposes. This is especially so when opinion poll evidence suggests that the government is failing to win the political argument.
- In rarer cases still, ministers may perceive the purpose of the protest to be the removal of the government itself. This accusation was made during the prolonged mineworkers' strike of 1984/5 when many commentators suggested that the NUM could only succeed in its attempt to save pits from closure when the Conservatives had been removed from office.
- Alternatively, ministers may object to the principle of extra-parliamentary protest where it proves disruptive to important commercial interests. Pharmaceuticals have been mentioned already. A more prominent example, however, was the policing of the visit of Chinese President Jiang Zemin in October 1999. The determination of the Met and the Cambridge constabulary

to keep protestors away from a man notoriously sensitive to criticism encouraged suggestions (strenuously denied) that the Foreign Office had applied unconstitutional pressure on senior officers.

• Finally, protest inconveniences members of the public. As a result, it might reflect poorly on the government's ability to perform the key task of maintaining order.

A conservative perspective on law and order

After skimming through the substantive content of public order law, it is all too easy to assume that government has laid claim to the UK's streets in a way that threatens a variety of fundamental freedoms. Perhaps this is an inevitable consequence of a study such as this. Why would government grant itself such powers if it was not prepared to use them? However, any assertion from civil libertarians that vital freedoms have been forfeited in an unjustified drive towards a 'law and order society' have to be considered against the counter-claims of their conservative opponents, a group which now includes the collective leadership of the Labour party. As a result, many of the points made in this section constitute something of a bi-partisan consensus between the leaders of the UK's two principal parties.

Individual rights, the democratic will and the rule of law
The politics of what I have loosely called protest are wrapped up in competing analyses both of democracy and the rights and duties of the individual in a pluralist society. In response to the accusation that the evolution of public order law has been devoid of principle, a conservative might argue that this body of law actually reflects one of the oldest and most fundamental features of civilised society: the necessity of self-restraint. Any action which disrupts or threatens to disrupt the lives of others is, by definition, questionable, even when it is peaceful. This does not mean that such behaviour will be automatically outlawed. Indeed, public order law does not do this. Merely that the authorities have a duty to regulate public spaces so that the rights of some (including the right to live undisturbed) are not overlooked.

Some Conservative (as opposed to conservative) thinkers go further and argue that forms of behaviour which challenge the status quo are especially questionable (Scruton 2001: 60). The reason for this stems from the Conservative view that society is held together by shared values which are themselves the product of a uniform culture, chief of which is the idea that responsibility to others has primacy over self-interested decisions (Ingle 2000: 30). It follows that behaviour which openly challenges this culture poses a threat, no matter how minor, to the coherence of British society as a whole. One of the most famous expressions of this view is the then Home Secretary Douglas Hurd's description of the New Age Travellers as 'mediaeval brigands' whose selfishness and fecklessness contrasted so clearly with the hard-working and thrifty people whose lives they had so adversely affected (Ewing and Gearty, 1990: 126).

In addition, both Conservative and Labour leaders argue that strong public order laws are not so much antagonistic to liberal democracy as essential in its defence. Accordingly, political protest is inherently problematic. Viewed from this perspective, an organised minority is seeking to use its collective power to persuade others to do something they are not otherwise minded to do, or cease to do something which is perfectly legal. This has obvious implications for the rule of law, a point which featured prominently in the Conservatives' election campaign for 1979 and has re-emerged under the Blair government over the debate on animal rights protest.

Further, whenever protest challenges government policy, albeit unwittingly, it challenges some of the key principles underpinning parliamentary democracy itself. A conservative interpretation of the UK constitution tends to see democracy largely as a process by which the actions of a strong government are legitimised. In the United Kingdom there is a clear understanding that *any* party with a working majority in the House of Commons has the right to form a government and implement its political programme. Many people – perhaps even a majority – may disagree with key elements of this programme. However, for as long as the government retains the support of Parliament, its opponents must accept its claims to obedience, though obviously not approval.

Supply and demand

This 'rights versus responsibilities' argument has acquired a particular prominence in the last forty years or so, largely, it is alleged, because too many people resident in the UK are unwilling to accept that their rights to enjoy public spaces are dependent upon a clear and overwhelming acceptance of their civic responsibilities. This reflects a long-standing complaint by neo-conservatives such as Lord Tebbit that moral standards have been steadily undermined since the emergence of the 'permissive society' in the 1960s. It is certainly the case that, ever since the disturbances between the 'mods' and 'rockers' on England's south coast in the early 1960s, British society has become increasingly prone to bouts of public disorder. In the 1970s and 1980s, the dominant trends were urban rioting (there were major outbreaks in 1976, 1980, 1981, 1985, 1991 and 1995) and industrial violence. Since then, however, though outbreaks have been on a smaller scale, their capacity to cause misery and fear cannot be underestimated.

More worrying still, some forms of protest have become indistinguishable from acts of extreme violence. This is most obviously true of sections of the animal rights movement. To return to the example of s. 42 of the Criminal Justice and Police Act 2001, ministers will argue that they simply cannot permit protests to take place outside people's homes when there is a chance that they could result in attacks on the property and the people living in it.

This argument counters the point that the growth of public order law results from a separate agenda pushed forward by a combination of ministers, law enforcers and private interests in defiance of the public good. For the current government, it applies with additional force to those measures aimed at tackling anti-social behaviour. The Labour party's position on this issue has hardened to a point where provisions such as ASBOs and **dispersal orders** are absolutely essential in promoting liberty and security in some of Britain's most deprived communities. This point was made by David Blunkett in response to various criticisms of s. 30 of the Criminal Justice and Police Act 2001. He pointed out that the presence of certain individuals is now the single most pressing issue in many inner urban areas, especially the few remaining local authority housing estates. The same point was made rather more forcefully by Inspector Darr of the Cumbria police, who described the opponents of the curfew on children he introduced in the town of Wigton as 'liberal hand-wringers' out of touch with the needs of 'real people' (Cohen 2004a).

Exaggeration and distortion

The final point made in defence of public order law accuses the civil liberties lobby of dabbling in the excesses of inductive logic. In other words, they select particular examples – the Battle of the Beanfield being a case in point – and draw general conclusions from them. This ignores the fact that these episodes are invariably the product of a highly specific set of circumstances which do not often materialise (Waddington 1992). The result is to ignore the fact that, for the most part, access to public spaces remains largely unfettered in the United Kingdom.

The current government would no doubt wish to point to the various policies that have actually enhanced access to public spaces. A very obvious and direct example of this is the dramatic expansion of the 'right to roam' brought about by the Countryside and Rights of Way Act 2000. In addition, ministers can also claim to have brought about improvements via a more indirect route: the elimination of fear. One example of this is the concerted attempt to destigmatise homosexuality, most recently by allowing gay partners to enjoy the legal protections offered to married couples. More prominently, Labour has sought to improve the ability of ethnic minorities to go about their lawful business via a series of changes to race relations legislation, the police complaints procedure and the criminal law. In the latter case, the government's determination to extend the law on incitement to religious (as opposed to racial) groups other than Christians[10] is particularly noteworthy. So, too, is its willingness to develop and extend the concept of an 'aggravated' element to certain crimes. This is designed to send a message to those whose criminal behaviour is motivated in part by racism or religious bigotry.[11] As a result, such criminals can expect noticeably longer sentences once their guilt has been established.

In the final analysis, however, the Prime Minister and successive Home Secretaries have insisted that the ability to move and associate in public depends on the willingness of others to behave responsibly and respectfully. Where this self-limiting ethos is lacking, a liberal democratic government has a duty to intervene, precisely so that the weak and vulnerable can enjoy the same rights as those who are stronger and more confident. The new preventive powers, ASBOs, dispersal orders – all are designed to redistribute power in favour of those whose freedoms would be otherwise severely limited.

Conclusion: a cause for concern?

This chapter began – and concluded – with a discussion of how competing analyses of the purpose of government in a democratic **polity** shape our appreciation of the politics of public order law in the UK. In between, we were able to see how the latter has evolved and what it is about this process which so concerns civil libertarians. The fact that the law has grown so quickly – with each new increment going on to form the justification for the next – without any obvious consideration of how this will effect liberty over the long term is a key feature of this. So, too, is the sub-text; that seemingly reasonable laws can all too easily be abused, especially when those in authority are desperate for political cover. This is not to say that all senior politicians are **Machiavellian** schemers. However, there is a certain mindset among ministers, in particular, that winning and staying in office is a hard business. Where one can gain an advantage, one should not be too squeamish about doing so. This hints at the 'iron law of governance' described by Professor Jowell in Chapter 4. It suggests that strong tendencies to appease the powerful and silence one's critics continue to shape the values of government, regardless of political persuasion. If true, the subject matter discussed in the next chapter poses an even greater threat to the liberties of the individual.

....

✔ What you should have learnt from reading this chapter

- An appreciation of why the freedoms of expression and association are so important in a liberal democracy.

- A more detailed understanding of how the European Convention seeks to protect these freedoms.

- A comprehensive survey of the way in which public order law has evolved in the United Kingdom.

- An awareness of why the civil liberties lobby and mainstream politicians clash over the extent to which these laws threaten the quality of democratic life in the UK.

🔍 Glossary of key terms

Anti-Social Behaviour Orders These are the central plank in the government's campaign to combat incivility and low-level disorder which has become such an important electoral issue in recent years.
Dispersal orders These are included in s. 30 of the Anti-Social Behaviour Act 2003. They give the police wide-ranging powers to clear certain groups of people from the streets.
Leviathan The title of Thomas Hobbes' classic work of political philosophy which aimed to provide a justification for state power.
Low-level public disorder A term describing a category of behaviour which causes immense irritation to many people. The current government is very sensitive to this problem, largely because it believes that low-level disorder is the decisive factor in explaining the fear of crime.
Machiavellian A term used to describe cynical or cunning behaviour among politicians. It derives from the family name of Niccolò Machiavelli, a Renaissance political philosopher whose work *The Prince* is still studied today.
New Protest This emerged in the mid-1990s and incorporated a range of direct action techniques designed in the main to halt large construction projects.
Order maintenance A criminological theory which states that the suppression of low-level disorder (vandalism, nuisance neighbours, and so on) will have a trigger effect on reducing the number of crimes committed in other categories.
Polity A particular form of government or constitution.
Populist politics A style of political campaigning designed to appeal to a majority of voters regardless of any other factor. Populist politicians are often derided for their opportunism and lack of integrity.
Preventive powers These are statutory powers enabling the authorities to ban or place conditions on various forms of gathering in public places.
Trespass Historically, this was a civil offence which could not be punished with a criminal sentence. One commits the offence of trespass by entering private property without permission and refusing to leave. The exception to this is when the law recognises a public right of way or some other licence to enter.

? Likely examination questions

Outline the ways in which police powers have increased in recent years.

In what ways has the Labour government since 1997 been 'tough on crime'?

Helpful websites

www.liberty-human-rights-org.uk/   Liberty
www.opsi.gov.uk/acts.htm   UK legislation

Suggestions for further reading

The history of public order law is explained in Chapter 4 of Ewing and Gearty, *Freedom under Thatcher* (Oxford: Oxford University Press), 1990. Peter Joyce, *The Politics of Protest* (Basingstoke: Palgrave), 2002 covers the impact of political protest on the development of this area of law. Ewing and Dale-Risk, *Human Rights in Scotland* (Edinburgh: Thomson–W. Green), 2004 at Chapters 8 and 9 discuss this area of law from a Scottish perspective. Those readers wishing to discover more about New Labour's attitude to order-maintenance are encouraged to read Patrick Slaughter, 'Of crowds, crimes and carnivals', in Roger Matthews and Jock Young (eds), *The New Politics of Crime and Punishment* (Cullompton: Willan), 2003. Meanwhile, Robert Reiner, *The Politics of the Police* (Oxford: Oxford University Press), 2000 at Chapter 6 provides an ever-polished assessment of police power and accountability.

Notes

1. Hobbes' *Leviathan* remains one of the most important works of political philosophy ever written.
2. More popularly known as 'zero tolerance', this model has proved both influential and controversial in equal measure both in the UK and USA. In the northern city of Middlesbrough, former police Inspector Ray Mallon routed his many critics in policing and political circles to become mayor on the basis of popular approval for his zero-tolerance policing tactics.
3. An important qualification which means that government must behave in a way compatible with the common-sense understanding of democratic standards.
4. The precise nature of these qualifications varies from Article to Article.
5. Two useful case studies capture some of these issues. The extent to which the policing of protest can become prohibitively expensive was revealed after media enquiries into the Met's decision to allow controversial cleric Abu Hamza to preach outside the Finsbury Park mosque in north London for the twenty-two-month period between his expulsion from the mosque and his arrest on terrorism charges. The total cost

of the operation was £874,387. The fact that Hamza was breaking the law by preaching on the highway only adds to the remarkable nature of this story (O'Neill 2005).

6. This provision was aimed at the British Union of Fascists (BUF) whose heyday soon came and went. During World War Two, the BUF leadership soon found itself on the receiving end of the full force of state power when it was interned under emergency legislation. The legality of this detention was and remains highly controversial and was the subject of one of the most important legal opinions ever expressed on the subject of the liberty of the person: Lord Atkin's minority opinion in *Liversridge* v. *Anderson*.

7. For example, s. 3 of the 1936 Act was deployed on no fewer than seventy-five occasions between 1981 and 1984 (Ewing and Gearty 1990: 113).

8. An infamous example of the government's imagination running ahead of common sense was Tony Blair's vision of police officers 'frog-marching' drunken youths to cash machines whereupon, in an extraordinary example of state-sponsored larceny, bank accounts would be emptied to recompense the public for the inconvenience it had just suffered.

9. On 20 July 2005 Lord Justice Brooke ruled that the police did not have the power to use force to remove a child from an area subject to a dispersal order.

10. The interests of Christians are, in any case, protected by the laws on blasphemy.

11. This reform was first introduced in Part II of the Crime and Disorder Act 1998 and amended in Part V of the Anti-Terrorism, Crime and Security Act 2001 which added religious hostility as a qualifying ingredient.

Is Big Brother Really Watching You? The Politics of Covert and Mass Surveillance

Contents

Overview

In the previous chapter we gained some insight into the ability of government in the United Kingdom to control the use of public spaces. By contrast, the subject of Chapter 6 is a broad category of powers that enables the political authorities to undertake a different set of policing functions. These powers are categorised as covert and mass surveillance. Whereas Chapter 5 considered the implications for civil liberties when a body of law expands without a clear rationale, the principal theme of Chapter 6 is how the enjoyment of basic freedoms is threatened by the absence of openness and accountability at the heart of the state.

Key issues to be covered in this chapter

- The implications of covert and mass surveillance for civil liberties
- The statutory regulation of covert surveillance in the UK
- Civil libertarians and the politics of surveillance
- A case study of Part I of the Regulation of Investigatory Powers Act 2000
- Covert surveillance: the executive response
- Covert surveillance in America: the USA/Patriot Act
- The emergence of mass surveillance

The politics of covert and mass surveillance

When carrying out order-maintenance operations, the authorities always labour under a certain handicap. Public order policing is a highly visible activity. Eyewitnesses often challenge the official version of events, while journalists are on hand to follow up accusations of abuse of power. This normally suffices to encourage a degree of self-restraint, especially when those subject to police attentions are capable of mounting an articulate public defence of their actions. By definition, covert (hidden) policing or, as I have called it here, covert surveillance,[1] removes many if not all of these pressures. Covert surveillance can be distinguished from public order policing in a number of ways.

- Though its eventual aim might be the conviction of individual criminals, this is not necessarily its *primary* purpose.
- Covert surveillance is mainly concerned with the accumulation of intelligence; the data which uncovers those behavioural patterns that may help establish the target's role in a complex criminal network or, better still, anticipate a course of action.
- In consequence, covert operations may continue for a considerable period of time, during which an intimate portrait of an individual's life will have been acquired.
- Further, covert policing is often carried out by organisations falling within the 'ring of secrecy' lying at the heart of the state.
- This poses great difficulties for anyone anxious to ensure that such operations are compatible with the liberal democratic tradition. The two standard mechanisms of accountability – parliamentary scrutiny and actions brought in the ordinary courts – immediately run up against the outer surface of this ring of secrecy. In which case one is left to wonder how the individual can be reassured that this tremendous capacity to invade his privacy is never abused.

The methods of covert surveillance are discussed in much more detail below. However, the last decade has also witnessed the rise of *mass surveillance* in the UK; a set of techniques which involve the acquisition of vast quantities of personal data on an indiscriminate basis. Whereas the traditional techniques target particular individuals, mass surveillance mines personal information on almost everyone. Little wonder that some critics have seen in this the emergence of an Orwellian 'Big Brother' state (Kennedy 2004b: 259–80).

Privacy and the European Convention

The combined effect of covert and mass surveillance calls into question our ability to enjoy a private life. This right is recognised in Article 8 of the European Convention and contains a number of elements. These include the sanctity of family life, together with the inviolability of one's home and private correspondence.

- Article 8 is predicated on a simple idea: in a 'free' society, it is the individual, not the state, who is the sole and undisputed owner of his or her person, identity and history.
- It suggests, further, that when we pass on information about ourselves, we do so on the assumption of confidentiality. It is not for the other party to do with this information what they please.
- A further justification for protecting privacy is that, without it, the intimacy necessary for family life is wholly absent, something which also has major implications for professional and business activities.
- In addition, there is a strong relationship between privacy rights and the rule of law. If personal information has been accumulated on us without our knowledge, we are denied the right to challenge its accuracy.
- The right to privacy also protects democracy itself. A cowed population, frightened that any expressed opinion will find its way back to government, is hardly the stuff of which robust, democratic practice is made.
- In addition, the ability of political parties, pressure groups and the media to conduct their affairs without interference also depends upon the maintenance of privacy. Should the government be able

---

Box 6.1 The European Convention of Human Rights on privacy

Article 8 Right to respect for private and family life
1 Everyone has the right to respect for his private and family life, his home and his correspondence.

Box 6.2 Justifying interference with privacy under the European Convention on Human Rights

- Firstly, the capacity of the state to interfere must be in accordance with the law. Officials can act only when the law permits them to.
- Secondly, interference must be necessary in a *democratic society*. This reminds the authorities that democracy can only function when individuals are free to think thoughts and exchange ideas, no matter how controversial, without these being relayed to government. Any interference with the right to privacy must be consistent with democratic values.
- Thirdly, Article 8(2) also aims to introduce an element of proportionality into the use of this power. In particular, it insists that interference can only be justified if it takes place: (1) in the interests of national security, public safety or the country's economic well-being; or (2) for the prevention of disorder or crime; or, finally (3) for the protection of health or morals, or the rights and freedoms of others.

to gain intelligence on those it regards as a political threat, it could all too easily disrupt their activities.

While the Convention does not regard it as unconditional, human rights lawyers insist that the right to privacy is so profound that interference should be subject to strict conditions. Paragraph 2 of Article 8 acknowledges this (see Box 6.2). As a result, the legality of covert surveillance is dependent upon a *statutory scheme* which limits the circumstances in which these techniques can be used. In addition, such a scheme must include mechanisms which guard against abuse and which allow those who fear their privacy has been unlawfully compromised to raise their grievances. The next section will examine how government in the United Kingdom has responded to these demands.

Covert surveillance in the United Kingdom: the movement towards statutory regulation

Covert surveillance in the UK has a long history. During the Interregnum (1649–60), officials urged that the postal system be made a state monopoly in order to ease the interception of private correspondence. Shortly after the Restoration, a Royal Proclamation affirmed the power of officials to carry out interceptions under the authority of the Crown.[2] These instances point to a powerful tradition that covert surveillance was a matter for government alone. Consequently, those who undertook surveillance operations drew their authority from ministers acting under the Royal Prerogative and it was to these ministers, rather than the Parliament and the courts, that they were accountable.

That this tradition survived the onset of democracy tells us much about the culture of Britain's political **Establishment**. Periodically, ministers would reassure MPs that covert surveillance did not result in abuse, principally by publishing the criteria used to issue warrants authorising an operation.[3] Yet, even when the legality of certain operations was called into question, it was never suggested that the existing arrangements were anything other than fundamentally sound.[4] Similarly, the judiciary were very reluctant to undermine the status quo. This did not stop aggrieved individuals from taking their cases to court. However, the most the judiciary were prepared to concede was that anyone subject to covert surveillance could reasonably expect government to abide by the published criteria (*R* v. *Secretary of State for the Home Department, ex parte Ruddock* (1987)).

In the footsteps of Mr Malone

It is at this point that the Convention makes a decisive impact. The key case is *Malone* v. *the UK* (1984) when the complainant challenged the legality of a tap on his telephone, mainly on the grounds that the invasion of his privacy was authorised by executive order rather than by law passed by Parliament. Whereas the House of Lords had previously rejected this argument, the ECtHR ruled in his favour, insisting that any interference with privacy had to be firmly grounded in *and hence limited by* law passed by the legislature.

Nor was this a mere technical argument. As implied above, the Court insisted that, in passing such a law, Parliament would have the opportunity to consider how other key aspects of the Convention, notably the creation of an effective means of hearing complaints, might be put in place.

Box 6.3 The regulation of covert surveillance in the UK

The Interception of Communications Act 1985
This statute was the first of its type. It created a new regime for issuing warrants to intercept communications, while also creating a Commissioner and Tribunal to offer some form of oversight and a means of redressing grievances. The Interception of Communications Act went on to become a 'template' for many of the statutes which followed.

The Security Service Act 1989
This placed the work of the Security Service (MI5) on a statutory footing. In addition, it created a system by which property warrants could be issued, as well as a Security Service Commissioner and Tribunal.

The Intelligence Services Act 1994
This updated the law on the issue of property warrants to MI5. It also created a limited form of parliamentary oversight of the agencies which comprise the 'secret state' in the UK: the Security Service, the Secret Intelligence Service (MI6) and Government Communications Headquarters (GCHQ).

The Security Service Act 1996
This expanded MI5's remit (lawful sphere of operations) to include assisting the police in the fight against serious crime.

The Police Act 1997
Part III of this wide-ranging Act created a statutory system for issuing property warrants to police officers. It was accompanied by the creation of a new Chief Commissioner of Surveillance to oversee this process.

The Regulation of Investigatory Powers Act 2000 (RIPA)
This is the dominant statute for most covert surveillance operations in the UK. It repealed the Interception of Communications Act 1985, extended statutory regulation to a range of other areas and overhauled the system of oversight and redress. In Scotland, however, Part II of RIPA does not apply. This is instead covered by a separate piece of legislation passed by the Scottish Parliament: the Regulation of Investigatory Powers (Scotland) Act 2000.

The Anti-Terrorism, Crime and Security Act 2001
This introduced certain amendments to RIPA, notably with regard to the retention of communications data.

The Malone ruling compelled ministers to reconsider the legal status not just of intercepting communications but of covert surveillance per se. This did not happen overnight. The Thatcher government (1979–90) was at first prepared to place only the law governing interception on a statutory footing. However, given the risk of further adverse rulings, it was only a matter of time before statutory regulation spread to other areas. In this respect, it is notable that elements within both MI5 and the Home Office[5] had begun to press for reform on the grounds that greater openness would help counter the view that the Security Service was run by paranoid, Right-Wing extremists. Thanks to the decision of the Blair government to codify many of these provisions, much of the law can now be found in a single statute: the Regulation of Investigatory Powers Act 2000 (RIPA).

Investigatory powers

This section offers a brief analysis of RIPA and associated statutes. Its purpose is simply stated: to identify precisely what steps government in the UK can take in order to uncover highly personal information by covert methods.

Intercepting communications

The law on interception can be found in Part I of RIPA. Traditionally, interception of communications meant opening and reading private correspondence such as letters and telegrams. However, technological change resulted in a new generation of techniques which enable the authorities to listen in to a much wider range of private communications, including telephone conversations, and pager and mobile telephone signals (s. 2). Interceptions are authorised by warrants issued by ministers, not the courts. There are, however, restrictions on the number of people who can apply for them and the grounds on which they can be sought. (The details of these can be found in Box 6.7.)

In addition, thanks to powers in Part I, Chapter II of RIPA, the law on interception now extends to communications data. Under s. 21(4), this term refers to traffic data and billing data incidental to the communication but attached to it. As a result, it does not reveal the contents of the communication, only the use of the service. This places considerable obligations on communications services providers

(CSPs) to retain their data should they receive an order demanding that they pass it to the authorities.

When RIPA was being debated, ministers argued that because communications data does not involve 'listening in' on communications, the authorisation regime need not be so demanding. This manifests itself in three ways.

- The number of institutions who can apply for communications data is marginally greater and includes bodies such as the Inland Revenue.
- Authorisation is given by a member of staff within each organisation who has been designated for this purpose by ministers. This effectively means that the acquisition of communications data is a self-authorised process.
- Communications data can be sought on eight rather than four grounds, including items such as protecting public health and assessing and collecting monies owed to the government.

Interference with property

Interfering with property denotes a number of different activities which involve entry on or interference with property without consent. It covers anything tangible which may be then photographed, copied or removed for analysis elsewhere. The power to interfere with private property has two sources.

- The Security Service can seek property warrants from ministers under s. 5 of the Intelligence Services Act 1994. The grounds for doing so are broad; that the information sought is likely to be of substantial value in assisting MI5 in the execution of its duties.
- The police and other bodies like Customs and Excise must refer to Part III of the Police Act 1997. Police officers can seek property warrants where interference is necessary for the prevention and detection of serious crime. To an extent this gives the police a little more flexibility since there are circumstances when a chief officer can authorise such actions on his own authority. However, the more sensitive operations, such as those that take place in a dwelling, must be approved by an independent Commissioner.

Intrusive surveillance

This is defined by s. 26(3) of RIPA as a form of covert surveillance which:

- Is carried out in relation to anything taking place on residential premises or in a private vehicle;
- And which involves either the presence of an individual or a surveillance device.

The purpose of intrusive surveillance differs from interference with property in that it is designed to build up a comprehensive intelligence picture of the target. This is especially so when a surveillance device – a 'bug' – is used. This enables the authorities to acquire continuous, 'round-the-clock' intelligence for the duration of any operation. Intrusive surveillance thus represents potentially the most profound threat to privacy of all the techniques available.

In ss. 32 and 41 of RIPA the power to authorise intrusive surveillance is granted to ministers (who authorise the operations of MI5) and a variety of other authorising officers, including the heads of every police force in the UK. However, whereas a minister can authorise intrusive surveillance on his own authority, senior police officers must first seek the permission of a Surveillance Commissioner (s. 36). This is virtually identical to the procedure for authorising property warrants in Part III of the Police Act 1997. Exceptions occur in cases of urgency. Even then, under s. 37, the Commissioner can quash any authorisation which fails to satisfy the tests of necessity and proportionality. The decision to quash a warrant, or refuse to authorise one in the first place, can be appealed against to the Chief Surveillance Commissioner. Though his decision is final, he must report such occurrences to the Prime Minister.

Directed surveillance, including the work of Covert Human Intelligence Sources (CHIS)

These categories of surveillance were brought under a statutory regime for the first time in Part II of RIPA. They are considered by the Office of Surveillance Commissioners to be non-intrusive in the sense that they do not involve either the interception of private communications or the presence of a person or recording device on private property. 'Directed surveillance' is a broad term defined in s. 26(2) of the Act. It refers to covert surveillance undertaken to acquire private information about an individual carried out by non-intrusive means. A typical example of directed surveillance is the use of agents to record the movements of people in and out of a particular set of premises. CHIS (defined in s. 26(8) of RIPA) are different again. They are either recruited from among the family or known associates of the target, or placed there by the authorities. In both cases, the CHIS will exploit their relationship with the target by acting as an 'informer'.

Once again, because they are not deemed to be intrusive, the rules governing directed surveillance and CHIS are rather more permissive.

- Under s. 30, ministers are entitled to designate various bodies that have the power to authorise their own directed surveillance operations.
- So far the Home Secretary has granted this privilege to twenty-eight bodies in respect of directed surveillance, twenty-three of whom can also use CHIS. The range of bodies included on this list far exceeds law enforcement agencies and extends right across the public sector, including various NHS Trusts and the Pharmaceutical Society of Great Britain.
- The grounds for authorising these types of surveillance are also widely drawn, being almost identical to those which permit the acquisition of communications data.

Simply because these methods are non-intrusive does not mean, however, that they are non-controversial. Directed intelligence could be easily abused in order to acquire embarrassing evidence of personal indiscretions to silence a forthright critic of the government. Similarly, the widespread use of CHIS will render ordinary family and social life impossible. The fact that this technique is forever associated with totalitarian regimes lends further weight to this concern.

Oversight and redress
As part of the government's plan to make investigatory powers largely immune from legal action, the Act also overhauled the existing systems of oversight and redress. The details of this can be found in Box 6.4. The important point to note is that, despite the changes, the distinctive 'model' which first emerged in the Interception of

Box 6.4 The system of oversight and redress established under RIPA

The Interception of Communications Commissioner

Appointed by the Prime Minister under s. 57(1), the Commissioner's principal task is to review the system for issuing interception warrants and the acquisition of communications data. His key power is the statutory duty (s. 58) on anyone involved in the business of interception to assist him, something which includes the provision, on request, of documents and information.

Other Commissioners

In addition, an Intelligence Services Commissioner is appointed by the Prime Minister under s. 59. He has virtually identical functions to the Interceptions Commissioner, though his work is confined to the Security and Intelligence Services *other than the interception of communications*. In other words, the Intelligence Commissioner focuses on the issue of property warrants and intrusive surveillance.

The political sensitivities of the situation in Northern Ireland are reflected in the fact that a separate Investigatory Powers Commissioner for Northern Ireland must be appointed under s. 61. His work focuses on intrusive and directed surveillance (Part II of RIPA) as it applies to Northern Ireland. If and when devolution is restored, the First and Deputy Minister will be involved in the appointments process and will receive reports.

RIPA also extended the work of the Chief Commissioner for Surveillance (CSC) established by Part III of the Police Act 1997. The latter was appointed to review the use of property warrants issued by chief police officers. Thanks to RIPA, the CSC's remit has been extended to include the warrants issued to police officers and other public authorities to undertake intrusive and directed surveillance. To help him, his staff have been expanded into a team of Assistant Commissioners and inspectors under a new Office of Surveillance Commissioners (OSC). It is worth stating, however, that the work of the OSC does not overlap with that of the Commissioners mentioned above.

The Intelligence Services Committee (ISC)

In 1994, under s. 10 of the Intelligence Services Act, a parliamentary committee was finally added to the mechanisms of oversight. Its membership, including the chairperson, is determined by the Prime Minister who also receives and can edit any reports. It is not unfair to say that the ISC has been subject to considerable criticism for its alleged reluctance to tackle politically sensitive issues.

The Investigatory Powers Tribunal (IPT)

Created under s. 65 of RIPA, the IPT absorbed the roles of three separate bodies – the Interception of Communications Tribunal, the Security Service Tribunal and the Intelligence Services Tribunal – which had been created under previous statutes. It also took on part of the work of the Chief Commissioner for Surveillance established under the Police Act 1997. Its brief, in short, is to hear complaints on any one of the following grounds:

- Breaches of the protected Convention rights by any of the Security and the Intelligence services
- The use of the various investigatory powers established under RIPA
- The use of the powers to interfere with property granted to the Security and Intelligence Services under s. 5 of the Intelligence Services Act 1994
- The use of near-identical powers to interfere with property granted the police and Customs and Excise under Part III of the Police Act 1997.

Currently, it has eight members. The President and Vice-President – respectively Lord Justice Mummery and Mr Justice Barton – both hold high judicial office. The other six members are all legally qualified. Apart from taking over the work of all three pre-existing tribunals, the IPT has modified its procedures somewhat. In the past it was not common practice for any of the tribunals to correspond with complainants after a complaint had been lodged. However, the IPT reserves the right to ask the complainant for additional information, possibly in the form of a personal interview. The fact that the Tribunal also has its own website from which forms for registering a complaint can be downloaded is further recognition of the need for a greater degree of openness.

Communications Act has survived. The task of reviewing authorisation is allotted to various Commissioners whose reports, subject to government-imposed restrictions, are published. In addition, a separate Tribunal exists to hear complaints. However, like the system for issuing authorisations, the courts proper are excluded from this process.

Covert surveillance and civil liberties: a case study

The politics of covert surveillance no longer, if they ever did, centre on the question: are these techniques compatible with liberal democratic principle? Whether they are or not, governments with access to the relevant technology will continue to use them. Instead, debate has focused on whether the regulatory regimes established to control the use of these techniques are capable of providing the necessary levels of protection. Box 6.5 identifies the principles civil libertarians would like to see reflected in the enabling legislation.

Given the breadth and depth of the statutory regulations above, it is impossible in a study of this nature to test each and every provision against the principles outlined in Box 6.5. Instead, a secondary case

---

Box 6.5 Regulating covert and mass surveillance: a civil libertarian perspective

- Covert and mass surveillance should be used only when vital national interests are at stake. On this note, a clear distinction must be drawn between the latter and the political interests of the governing party. This is problematic in the UK where ministers have claimed the exclusive right to determine the meaning of the national interest at any one time.
- As a result, these techniques should not be used to combat day-to-day criminality, including public order situations (popular though this might be). If this were not so, surveillance would become so pervasive that the entire population would be caught in its embrace. Civil libertarians see this as a wholly disproportionate response, one which cannot be justified by the benefits it seeks to gain.
- The third point is one of the most important. This insists that surveillance is authorised by warrants issued by people of independent judgement. This immediately calls into question the British tradition of allowing ministers to issue warrants in certain circumstances.
- Further, very strict rules should be put in place to ensure that disclosure of any information gained is strictly limited.
- Finally, and most importantly of all, a rigorous system of oversight and redress must be established, both to uncover and deter abuse.

study will be used, one which focuses exclusively on Part I, Chapter 1 of RIPA dealing with the perennially sensitive area of intercepting communications. Those readers who wish to do so are invited to refer to Box 6.7 as they read through the following commentaries.

The historical context

The main reason why civil libertarians insist on such strict rules is that the record of security and intelligence sources in particular reveals a clear tendency to abuse their powers. In the United Kingdom there is overwhelming evidence that the Security Service went through a phase during the 1970s and 1980s when, using the most tortuous definition of national security, it systematically directed its resources at trade unionists and Left-Wingers (Dorrill 1993; Ewing and Gearty 1990) engaged in lawful and democratic activities.

Two issues emerge from this era. Firstly, the ability of Cabinet Ministers to keep the activities of the Security Service under control is extremely suspect. Secondly, there is the possibility that ministers collude with officials in these unconstitutional practices, especially when they share a similar perspective on security matters. In this respect, the relationship between Sir John Jones (Director-General of MI5 1981–5) and Prime Minister Margaret Thatcher provides something of a benchmark for unconstitutional practice. This came to light in a number of revelations, the most famous of which were those of Cathy Massiter.

On 24 August 1997 another Security Service operative, David Shayler, drew attention to this disturbing period once again with his revelations that MI5 still retained records on leading members of the government – Jack Straw and Peter Mandelson being the most prominent. In a subsequent interview, Shayler raised the political temperature still further when he claimed that MI5 also kept files on leading journalists who were seen to be 'disruptive'. The notion that elements within MI5 were still prepared to conduct campaigns against their political critics received confirmation from an unnamed insider who added that leading figures were often targeted simply in order to find out who their associates were (Norton-Taylor 1997).

The Shayler affair continued to rumble on for a number of years after his initial allegations. By the time he was finally put on trial, however, attention had shifted to still more disturbing developments

Box 6.6 The Massiter revelations

During a Channel 4 television programme broadcast in 1985 Cathy Massiter revealed what many had long since suspected: that MI5 routinely tapped the telephones of high-profile trade union officials, leaders of the Campaign for Nuclear Disarmament and the then National Council for Civil Liberties. More embarrassing still, Massiter went on to claim that the inspiration for these operations came from ministers themselves. Particularly controversial was the decision to routinely tap the phone of Dr John Cox, then the Vice-President of CND, an organisation with which the government was engaged in a bitter political battle. Official justification for this was Cox's membership of the Communist Party of Great Britain. However, Massiter suggested, and many others agreed, that this was a mere excuse, designed to mask the real purpose of the operation: to provide information which might assist ministers in their propaganda war.

Constitutional experts have pointed out that these actions were in defiance both of the Maxwell-Fyfe Directive, which then determined the permissible extent of MI5 operations, and internal guidelines on intercepts (Ewing and Gearty 1990: 52–3). However, the fact that senior MI5 officers shared the government's security agenda, coupled with the likelihood that these actions would never be detected, meant that they were only too happy to do the ministers' bidding. Subsequently, additional anecdotal evidence confirmed that the authorities had placed permanent 'taps' on the phones of numerous other individuals simply to discover what it was they were up to.

- Greenpeace protestors planning to unfurl a large banner on Big Ben found the police waiting for them, even though they had changed their plans at the very last moment.
- Bus companies which had agreed to take striking miners to picket lines were called by police officers demanding details minutes after bookings had been taken.
- TGWU officials discovered that Ford managers were already informed of their 'bottom line' on pay awards prior to the commencement of negotiations.

in Northern Ireland. On 8 December 1999 Sinn Fein President Gerry Adams called a press conference to display a bugging device found in a vehicle used belonging to his party. Given the implications for the peace process, it is highly unlikely that a warrant authorising this operation would have been signed by a Secretary of State. However, the most damning case of all concerned the involvement of a variety of security and intelligence agencies in the murder of Belfast solicitor Patrick Finucane in February 1989. The subsequent inquiries by Lord Stevens, who was since appointed to and retired as Commissioner of the Metropolitan Police, revealed a catalogue of collusion between the police and security services on the one hand, and Loyalist paramilitary organisations on the other. Mr Finucane was very probably murdered in order to protect the life of a double-agent named 'Steak knife' whom the same forces had recruited from the leadership of the Provisional IRA and who was about to be assassinated by a Loyalist death-squad. This sordid episode became more complex still when it was revealed that an ultra-secret intelligence unit within the British Army had successfully sabotaged Stevens' first inquiry in order to prevent him getting at the truth.

Box 6.7 Part I of the Regulation of Investigatory Powers Act 2000 in detail

Part 1, Chapter 1: the Interception of Communications
The interception of communications is lawful only when it is authorised by a warrant issued by a designated member of the government, or, in the case of Scotland, the Scottish executive. In order to ensure compliance with the Convention, a warrant can be issued only when it is necessary:

- In the interests of national security
- For the purpose of safeguarding the UK's economic well-being
- For the purpose of preventing or detecting serious crime
- For the purpose of giving effect to any international mutual assistance agreement.

The Secretary of State must also consider the following:

- Whether or not the conduct authorised is proportionate to what it seeks to achieve (a key ECtHR influence)
- Whether or not the information sought can be reasonably obtained by other means
- That satisfactory arrangements are in place both to ensure that the disclosure of information is limited to the minimum necessary

and that additional material obtained inadvertently is not examined at all

- Most importantly, the secretary of state is under a statutory duty to make sure that each warrant contains a variety of details. This is to ensure that a paper trail is created which will assist all of those charged with ensuring that abuses do not occur.

Finally, the Act also aims to guarantee that those involved in the process of applying for or authorising warrants are denoted by their professional experience and political status.

- Typically, this includes the heads of the intelligence and security services, the Director-General of the National Criminal Intelligence Service (who acts on behalf of the chief constables of England and Wales), the Metropolitan Police Commissioner, and chief constables of Scotland and the Police Service of Northern Ireland.
- Similarly, the fact that warrants must be signed either by a senior minister or a senior official authorised by a senior minister, adds to the sense that only people inoculated against 'the ways of the world' are involved.

In theory at least, they are people of proven judgement, not easily frightened and fully aware of their constitutional responsibilities. Most importantly, they are in a position to keep one another under mutual surveillance.

The permissiveness of language

The points made in the previous section place the arguments in Box 6.5 into sharper relief. The issue we must now address is whether or not the statutory regulations currently in place satisfy the criteria for effective protection. Suffice to say that, despite the not unimpressive detail in which the Act is written, civil libertarians remain deeply sceptical on this point. Instead, they suggest that the Act's depth is designed to create a 'smokescreen' which reassures the public while allowing government to carry on much as they it did in the days before Malone.

This criticism – that there exists a considerable gulf between image and reality – can be seen in the criteria *authorising the use of intercepts*. To remind you, interception is lawful when it is deemed necessary on four grounds, all of them seemingly grave. Unfortunately, on closer inspection, the gravity of at least some of these criteria is not quite as imposing as it might first appear.

Two examples should suffice to make this point. The first of these refers us to the meaning of the term 'national security'. Historically, Parliament has not defined this term with any degree of strictness. The nearest it has come to a definition is in s. 1(2) of the Security Service Act 1989 where the term is linked to a number of criteria. Many of these are unobjectionable: espionage, terrorism[6] and sabotage, for example. By contrast, the phrase which links national security to 'actions intended to overthrow or undermine parliamentary democracy by political, industrial or violent means' is much more problematic. If one interprets this expansively, any form of effective extra-parliamentary protest which challenges laws and policies endorsed by Parliament falls under this definition. It means that MI5 can legitimately target political protestors and trade unionists. More importantly from our immediate perspective, it also means that ministers can grant MI5 warrants to intercept their communications.

The second example concerns the meaning of the term 'serious crime'. This term is defined in RIPA at s. 81(2)–(3). Once again, some of the ingredients of serious crime seem inherently reasonable.

- Under s. 81(2)(a), a serious crime is linked to the severity of punishment, namely criminal conduct which carries the reasonable expectation of at least a three-year prison sentence for a first-time offender aged twenty-one or over.
- Under the next sub-section, s. 81(3)(b), a crime is also classified as serious whenever it involves the use of violence.

However, later on in s. 81(3)(b) a crime also becomes serious simply when it involves 'conduct by a large number of persons in pursuit of a common purpose'. Its effect is that covert surveillance can be aimed at a wide variety of people who engage in some form of collective action. Like the definition of national security, civil libertarians fear that this is an invitation to disrupt peaceful political protest. As a result, the only restraining factors are practical ones: limits on resources and confidence that abuses will not be uncovered.

A blurred lens
The importance of these criticisms becomes more pressing when one considers the effectiveness of the system of oversight and redress. To

help you make better sense of civil libertarian concerns in this regard, I have grouped these into three points.

Authorisation and Whitehall officialdom: the Law and Order Society
The first of these questions the democratic accountability of the authorisation process. Governments have traditionally argued that, because the Home Secretary is accountable to Parliament for the use he makes of his power to issue warrants, he will abide strictly by the law for fear of being exposed at a later date. Aside from the obvious fact that MPs can only begin to enquire into such matters when they are aware of them, this defence assumes that the Home Secretary is in a position to genuinely study each application,[7] including the background intelligence. It has, however, long since been recognised that the problem of ministerial overload is so great that the number of hours Cabinet Ministers have to devote to their departmental duties is alarmingly low. One analysis suggests that a typical minister spends only two-thirds of his working time on departmental matters (Coxall, Robins and Leach 2003: 223). In turn, this makes them highly dependent upon the advice of their leading civil servants, on whose judgement many of them come to rely. Civil servants are not only in the perfect position to influence ministerial decisions; the extent of the latter's workload is such that they will be called upon to 'take' the decision in the sense that it is highly unlikely that a Home Secretary is in a position to challenge their view.

> [H]ow much serious consideration can be given by a Minister absent from his office, engaged in pressing matters of state? In view of the sheer volume of interception warrants, and in view of the sheer volume of the Home Secretary's other duties, it seems unlikely that his personal involvement can seriously be seen as an effective means of control. (Ewing and Gearty 1990: 69–70)

There is impressive statistical evidence to support this view. In 1990 the number of interception warrants issued across the UK stood at 539. Five years later that figure had risen to 1,047, an increase of 94.2 per cent (*The Guardian*, 7 June 1996). Moreover, the use of interception warrants has grown considerably since then. In 1996, in his last full year in charge of the Home Office, Michael Howard signed 1,073 interception warrants. In 1999 Jack Straw signed 1,645,

Table 6.1 Authorised interception warrants in 2003

	Warrants issued during 2003	Warrants still in force at the end of 2003	Modifications made to warrants
Home Secretary	1,878	705	2,525
Scottish Executive	105	41	319
Total	1,983	746	2,844

Source: Annex to the report of the Interceptions Commissioner for 2003

averaging four-and-a-half per day. If, as is claimed, it takes twenty minutes to review carefully each request, Straw spent up to one hour, forty minutes each day on this task alone (Clark 2000). As Table 6.1 indicates, by 2003 that number was just shy of 2,000, or an average of five-and-a-half each day. A minority of these are signed by Scottish ministers. Yet, even taking this into account, the question is still begged whether Douglas Hurd's successors are in a position to consistently and conscientiously follow his sterling example.

This is not simply a matter of constitutional niceties. One of the most influential analyses of the senior civil service in the UK is the 'Whitehall village' model. This suggests that relations between ministers and civil servants are rather fluid, just like they are between neighbours in a small, close-knit village. In addition, it points out that, in their dealings with ministers, civil servants also 'have their own networks of informal contacts and official committees which operate across departments' (Coxall, Robins and Leach 2003: 223). It is to these that civil servants will refer during decision-making and who, as a result, will be able to exert considerable indirect influence.

Nowhere is this village atmosphere as marked as it is in respect of national security (Lustgarten and Leigh 1994: 426–7). These authors – and they are not alone – go on to note the extraordinary levels of empathy which exist between Home Office officials and the law enforcers with whom they come into regular contact. In particular, they refer to a 'presumption of regularity'; in effect that all is well inside bodies such as MI5 and that a key part of the Home Office's political role is to ensure that would-be critics are deterred from finding evidence to challenge this. Martin Kettle (1983: 221) puts matters even more bluntly:

> the Home Office (in the person of its civil servants) has *its own line*, quite independent of any party line . . . This line is largely dictated by its need and desire to sustain the agencies which it, nominally, controls. But, of course, it is heavily dictated to by the agencies themselves. And if *they* put their foot down, then so will the civil servants and so too (as their records show) will the Home Secretaries who, again nominally, run the department.

From a democratic perspective this is, indeed, a bleak and grim vista. It suggests that, even in the rare event of wrongdoing being brought to the attention of the Home Secretary, there is little likelihood of anything being done about it. Disturbing the fragile balance of relations in the village is one reason for this. Any Home Secretary determined to assert himself over his department is in for a long and bloody battle. In addition, as brilliantly demonstrated in the political satire *Yes, Minister*,[8] most senior ministers simply do not want to be made aware of such matters. If they are informed, they are under enormous pressure to act. If they do not, and a public scandal subsequently breaks out, their careers could be over. It is, in short, a situation which cries out for the rectification offered by independent scrutiny and oversight. The question is: though such mechanisms are in place, are they necessarily any more effective?

A compromised Commissioner
Like his predecessors and counterparts elsewhere, the Interceptions Commissioner has faced considerable scepticism over his ability to provide meaningful oversight (Ewing and Gearty 1990: 75; Lustgarten and Leigh 1994: 63). There are many reasons for this, so many that the following is a mere selection.

- The Commissioner is appointed by the Prime Minister to whom he is responsible. The only restriction on the latter's choice is that the person appointed must hold or have held high judicial office. This immediately lends itself to the views expressed by the likes of Griffith (see Chapter 4) that the Commissioner will be a pro-Establishment figure only too ready to sympathise with those involved in interceptions.

- This is possibly reflected in the nature of his reports which have been full of expressed satisfaction with the legality of operations but without accompanying explanations.
- More importantly, perhaps, his relationship with the Prime Minister restricts his ability to publicise and act upon his concerns. His annual report is primarily a matter for the Prime Minister, who can censor those findings he regards as threatening to national security. The tradition is now for the Commissioner to include certain matters – no doubt those which are truly controversial – in a confidential annex, the contents of which remain secret.
- This leaves completely unanswered the question of what the latter can do if he suspects that the Prime Minister or his senior ministerial colleagues are deliberately obstructing the course of justice.

A second set of problems concern his resources. There is no evidence from his latest report (for 2003) that the current Commissioner – Sir Swinton Thomas – has any staff at his disposal. Twice each year he visits the three security and intelligence agencies, four police forces including Special Branch and the Strathclyde constabulary, Customs and Excise, and three government departments including the Home Office and the Scottish executive. In addition, he has voluntarily agreed to take on responsibilities for monitoring intercepts in the Prison Service. As part of his statutory duties he also visits a limited number of communication service providers (CSPs). After

Box 6.8 Members of the Intelligence Services Committee

- Rt Hon. Paul Murphy MP (Chairperson)
- Ben Chapman MP
- George Howarth MP
- Dari Taylor MP
- Baroness Meta Ramsay of Cartvale
- Rt Hon. Michael Mates MP
- Rt Hon. James Arbuthnot MP
- Richard Ottaway MP
- Rt Hon. Alan Beith MP

Source: Cabinet Office Briefing

requesting the details of all warrants, he then selects a number at random in order to more fully assess their legality. While no one should question Sir Swinton's enthusiasm, it is questionable whether he has the time or the resources to uncover abuses.

In particular, there remains the possibility that certain intercepts take place without warrants. Just how far can the Commissioner go in order to find out whether these exist?

The watchdog which neutered itself

The Intelligence Services Committee (ISC) currently consists of the nine parliamentarians listed in Box 6.8. The Chairperson is a former Secretary of State for Northern Ireland while the other eight members have years of parliamentary and in some cases ministerial experience behind them. That the ISC has enjoyed something of a chequered history is something of an understatement. No sooner had it been formed than rumours began to circulate that its first Chair – another former Northern Ireland Secretary, Tom King – had immediately blocked, at the request of senior Cabinet members, demands that the allegations of people like Cathy Massiter be fully investigated. Nor was its cause helped when John Morrison, a former Deputy Chief of Defence Intelligence, was effectively removed from his post as the committee's first investigator after he participated in a television programme which was highly critical of the disputed intelligence claims made by Tony Blair to support the invasion of Iraq.[9] However, it was not until summer 2005 that the several criticisms of the ISC received the endorsement (for what it is worth) of academic research. Somewhat to their surprise, a team of scholars based at Brunel University found their unpublished findings the subject of a major feature on BBC Radio Four's *Today* programme. The ensuing debate focused on their central accusation; that the committee continues to fight shy of fully and openly investigating issues of real political sensitivity. This failing is apparently particularly noticeable during the 2001 Parliament when the chair fell to an ultra-loyalist Labour MP, Ann Taylor.

At the root of the ISC's difficulties is a single, unpalatable feature:

The chairmanship of the committee has tended to go to MPs as a consolation prize for not being awarded a top ministerial post. So the chairperson owes their [sic] ongoing career to the Prime Minister, which does not encourage rigorous scrutiny of government actions.

Compounding this problem is the apparent emergence of a mentality among committee members which has resulted in an unhealthy attachment to the 'ring of secrecy'. One unnamed MP expressed his frustrations on this point at the time of the ISC's report into the Anglo-American invasion of Iraq, with the strong implication that committee members tended to forget the loyalties they owed to Parliament, the implication being that the committee is chock-full of former ministers content to enjoy the enhanced status that comes from being inside the ring of secrecy (White and Wintour 2003).

This has led to a further criticism. Though they acknowledge the important work done by the ISC in this respect, the Brunel team feel that it has concentrated on the rather narrow area of expenditure and value-for-money. A more expansive approach is called for if the ISC is to regain some of the credibility it has lost, the more so in light of the recommendations of the Butler Report

A Tribunal without teeth

A rather different set of criticisms concern the Tribunal. The history of this body which dates from 1985 is marred by the secrecy in which it has carried out its work. This relates to a criticism of tribunals in general: their rules can all too easily be manipulated to deny complainants the legal privileges they might find in an ordinary court. Aside from the problem of actually finding out whether one's communications have been intercepted, in the event of a complaint being registered it is not easy to see how the complainant can be satisfied that justice has been done. There are a number of reasons for this:

- In the event that the Tribunal decides to investigate a complaint, it will request that the relevant body send all the relevant information it possesses. Though it is obliged under law to do this, it is not clear how the Tribunal can satisfy itself that its request has been fully complied with.
- Secondly, while the Tribunal may offer the complainant the opportunity of making further representations, which may include an oral hearing, it is under no obligation to do so.

Table 6.2 The work of the Investigatory Powers Tribunal in 2003	
Number of complaints received in 2003	109
Number of complaints carried over from 2001–2	67
Number of investigations completed in 2003	100
Number of investigations still to be completed	76
Number of investigations from 2001–2 still to be completed	10

Source: Annual Report from the Interception of Communications Commissioner for 2003, para. 30.

- At no point, however, will it be possible for the complainant to challenge the evidence provided by the agency or department concerned. On the contrary, complainants are wholly reliant on the ability of the Tribunal to act on their behalf. In this respect, that Tribunal members are appointed by the Prime Minister, who can also remove a member after five years, gives further pause for thought. That in the course of its history, which dates from 2000, the Tribunal has never upheld a single complaint,[10] either in respect of intercepts or any other matter, simply encourages further speculation that its role is more symbolic than real.
- Finally, from a constitutional perspective, the decisive factor is that the decisions of the Tribunal cannot be appealed against. As Hilaire Barnett (2004: 685–6) notes: 'The weakness of the Tribunal . . . is reinforced by the absence of any appeal therefrom and the prohibition against questioning of the Tribunal . . . before any court of law . . . This arrangement is far different from that pertaining in the United States, where security matters are regarded as being within the competence of the courts (*United States* v. *United States District Court* (1972)'.

The problem of location
Ultimately, however, the most debilitating defect of these arrangements may prove to be their location at the heart of a nation state. This is the likely consequence of the fast-accelerating trend towards international co-operation in intercepting communications. Since 1947, the Anglo-Saxon powers (the US, UK, Canada, Australia and

New Zealand) have been developing an increasingly sophisticated 'eavesdropping' system, codenamed '**Echelon**'. It was this system which lay at the centre of the Katharine Gun scandal, when Mrs Gun, a translator at GCHQ, revealed that US agents had used a combination of bugs and powerful recording equipment to uncover the negotiating positions of various UN delegations in advance of key votes on the most recent Iraqi war. Prior to this, the Echelon network had been the subject of a highly critical European Parliament report in which MEPs warned all citizens to be aware that any electronic communication could be swept up and analysed (*The Guardian*, 30 May 2001).

Of far greater significance, however, is the scandal which broke a year earlier. During a television interview, Mike Frost, a former Canadian intelligence agent, claimed that he was ordered by his superiors to arrange for the interception of the personal communications of two British Cabinet Ministers whose loyalty had been questioned by the Prime Minister of the day, Margaret Thatcher (Blackstone 2000). In this way, Echelon offered the perfect mechanism for sidestepping any domestic laws designed to guard against abuse. By asking a fellow Echelon member to carry out covert surveillance it is nigh-on impossible for bodies like the Commissioner and Tribunal to uncover who made the request and why. The all-important paper trail will simply not exist.

Nor is it the case that concerns are confined to the UK's relations with the USA and the other Anglo-Saxon powers. The steady growth of police co-operation among the member states of the European Union has raised similar fears that operations are taking place at a level beyond the reach of national mechanisms of accountability. This is especially so after the signing of the EU Convention on Mutual Assistance in Criminal Matters on 29 May 2000. The significance of this is noted by Fignant (2004: 251–3), who adds that:

> the regulation under Title III of the Convention for international interception of telecommunications . . . [is] detailed and far-reaching . . . [and] will not be encountered in any other mutual assistance treaty.

Though safeguards have been put in place, the tone of Fignant's analysis questions whether they will prove sufficiently robust to deter abuse. Indeed, one of the main features of policy developments within the EU's Third Pillar[11] has been the reluctance of the member states to allow judicial or other bodies operating at the pan-European level to monitor mutual police operations. It follows that, unless and until this is rectified, speculation over the real as opposed to the stated purpose of mutual assistance will continue.

The Establishment response

Ministers respond to these objections in a variety of ways. The first and by far the most important concerns the proportionality of covert surveillance in relation to the goals it tries to achieve. Accordingly, it is too easy to focus on the shortcomings of bodies like MI5 and hence lose sight of the far more serious threat posed by international criminal organisations. Moreover, this threat has grown considerably in recent years; in part because of the new organisational arrangements made possible by modern technology, and also because of the ability of criminals to cross borders and blend into communities which offer them both anonymity and protection.

The principal consequence of this is that breaking into such organisations is far harder then it was in the past. This is certainly the case with the al-Qaeda network. Infiltrating PIRA, with its famed cellular structure, proved difficult enough. This is why PIRA were able to plant so many 'lilywhites' – operatives working in isolation with no previous record of PIRA membership – in mainland Britain. However, the semi-independent nature of al-Qaeda operatives makes them more or less impervious to penetration by security agencies. This means that, despite the views of civil libertarians, law enforcers must have available a wide range of techniques, including interception, and the legal discretion to determine when to use them whenever their professional consciences dictate.

With some justice, the government can also point to the irony that the integrity of the law enforcement agencies is further compromised by the very thing they need to protect their operations. The 'ring of secrecy' will always encourage endless speculation and conspiracy theories. However, it must not be forgotten that much has changed in the way the relevant law enforcement agencies operate since the mid-1980s. For example, successive leaders of MI5 beginning with Sir Anthony Duff have pursued a policy of greater

Box 6.9 Openness and constitutionality in the Security Service

The first official insight into MI5 came in July 1993 when a booklet – *MI5, the Security Service* – was published. This document, which has been since updated, was part of Stella Rimington's[12] commitment to greater openness. It was at pains to point out that some 70 per cent of MI5's resources were devoted to the fight against terrorism, with counter-subversion counting for less than 5 per cent of expenditure. By 1998, the year in which the third edition of the booklet was published, that figure had fallen to 0.3 per cent, monies which predominantly went to pay the pensions of retired agents. In the same passage, it was also pointed out that 'The Security Service currently has no investigations in this area'. In March that year, as if to emphasise the changed nature of MI5, Sir John Jones died at the age of seventy-five.
Source: *MI5, the Security Service* (London: HMSO), 1993, 1998

openness, one which has demonstrated that the obsessions of the Jones era are very much a thing of the past. This point has been acknowledged by even the most forthright critics (Lustgarten and Leigh 1994: 58–9).

Not that everything that went on during the Jones era was wholly without justification. For example, in the aftermath of the mass expulsion of 105 Soviet embassy personnel in 1971, the USSR and its allies developed new techniques designed to destabilise British democracy. Evidence leaked to *The Sunday Times* (11 January 1998) strongly suggests that the KGB had indeed infiltrated a number of trade unions and protest organisations; at the very least, they were able to divert not insignificant funds to them. This did not mean that the UK citizens involved were guilty of serious crimes such as treason or sedition. However, it is possible that not all of them – including Dr Cox – were properly aware of the manner in which they were being exploited.

A robust regulatory regime
Whatever its shortcomings, ministers insist that the system of regulation put in place since 1985 is a huge improvement on what had gone

before. This defence places great emphasis on the way in which the various duties created under the law reinforce each other. Do note the following:

- Part I of the Act places multi-layered obligations on those to whom it grants powers. This does not guarantee that the law will be always obeyed. It does, however, raise considerably the consequences of abusing the law and being found out.
- The fact that these people have the benefits of years of experience and a proven record to defend gives extra credence to this point.
- The Act also insists on a clear 'paper trail' which will help both Commissioner and Tribunal uncover the decision-making process. The absence of key documents will provide the clearest indication that something has gone seriously wrong.
- Further, the fact that so many people within Whitehall have access to this paper trail means that it is very difficult for 'rogue' operations to take place. These might still happen. However, the professional consequences for anyone discovered to have abused their powers could be severe. One can only assume that a rogue element would have to be very well motivated to take such a risk.

For all their alleged failings, the various Commissioners are all highly experienced individuals, fully versed in the unique nature of covert policing. This 'insider' status is by no means the disadvantage critics make out. The drafting of high-profile outsiders with reputations for a fearless search for the truth might make the civil liberties lobby feel better. However, it is likely that the agencies themselves will simply use their unmatched knowledge and experience to make the task of an overseer virtually impossible. By contrast, if the person concerned is someone they perceive to be sensitive to their peculiar difficulties, the chances are that they will be more inclined to reciprocate. Intellectually, this may not be a very satisfactory argument. It is, however, rooted in unavoidable political realities (Reiner 2000: 171).

Similarly, it should be noted that the much-maligned Tribunal has overhauled its procedures considerably since 2000. The fact that its website offers clear advice on how to register a complaint is obviously important. However, the real change has emerged in the enhanced flexibility and openness which can only be to the benefit of those who see themselves as victims of abuse. In addition, critics of the fact that the Tribunal (in its present or previous incarnations) has never upheld a complaint have to recognise that this may be more a reflection of the type of person who complains than any failings on the Tribunal's behalf. Though the following passage ostensibly concerns the work of MI5 in general (as opposed to the particular business of interceptions), it also holds good for the latter.

> Some of the complainants are repeaters who, as the Commissioner expressed it informally, are 'plain barmy'; the existence of this problem was confirmed from the other side by Mr John Wadham, [then] Legal Officer of Liberty. It is apparently a difficulty common to complaint systems in this field, for the same opinion was expressed by the Australian Inspector-General. (Lustgarten and Leigh 1994: 439)

Covert surveillance in America: the USA/Patriot Act

Very similar concerns over covert surveillance have emerged in the USA. The people of the United States are not strangers to terrorism. In 1996, part of Oklahoma City was devastated by Timothy McVeigh in a bizarre act of revenge against the federal authorities for their role in the destruction of a religious cult in Waco, Texas. However, despite the loss of life such attacks failed to provoke the dramatic reappraisal of national security which followed the destruction of the World Trade Center and parts of the Pentagon on 11 September 2001. The key to this was the realisation that the perpetrators had been absorbed into mainstream American society, undetected and undisturbed, before carrying out their grisly deeds. That some of the hijackers even received training as pilots while resident in the USA only added to the sense of outrage.

To date the principal legislative response to 9/11 is the USA/ Patriot Act. The controversy it generated needs to be seen in the light of the Fourth Amendment to the American Constitution. Under its terms, the Founders placed various legal hurdles in the way of any government wishing to gather information on Americans *by interfering with their property*. This is a hugely sensitive issue for Americans since it touches on one of the original motivations behind the rebellion against British rule (Singh 2002: 200). This has never been taken to mean that private property cannot be searched under any circumstances. However, if the authorities wish to enter private property they need a warrant which, in addition, can only be obtained when a certain evidential test has been passed. The effect of this is that:

- Warrants can be issued only by courts which are then responsible for ensuring that the warrants are used for the proper purposes.
- Courts can only issue warrants when law enforcers have shown 'probable cause', that is, that the request is linked to reasonable suspicion of involvement in a particular crime.
- At some point, the owner of the property must be informed of the warrant. The thinking behind this is that it will force the authorities to declare their intentions, while enabling the property owner to make their own representations to the courts especially in respect of any items which may have been seized in the process.

In theory, these restrictions offer individuals in the USA far greater protection than their counterparts in Britain. However, the American Civil Liberties Union (ACLU) points out that, as in the British case, the history of covert policing in the USA reveals a clear propensity to bypass Fourth Amendment restraints, often via secret agreements with private individuals and companies (Stanley 2004: 9). For civil libertarians, these and other incidents remind ordinary Americans that any attempt to weaken the Fourth Amendment must be resisted. This is why the USA/Patriot Act is viewed with such suspicion. In their eyes, each of the items in Box 6.10 constitutes a clear breach of the Fourth Amendment. Compounding these fears is the context in which the Act became law.

- Congress passed this law in such a hurry, without giving itself time to consider its full implications.
- The man whose handiwork it is – former Bush Attorney-General John Ashcroft – was in desperate need of political cover once al-Qaeda struck. During Bill Clinton's Presidency (1992–2000) the then Senator Ashcroft confirmed his reputation as the standard bearer of the Republican party's far right by blocking the efforts of Clinton's Attorney General, Janet Reno, in her efforts to combat domestic terrorism. His view was that the federal government was pursuing a vindictive agenda against ordinary Americans doing nothing other than exercising their constitutional rights to bear

Box 6.10 The surveillance provisions of the USA/Patriot Act

Delays in informing property owners of secret searches
Under s. 213 of the Act, the Federal Rules of Criminal Procedure were modified so that the authorities can wait for a much longer period before informing the property owner that a search has taken place. Nor is this provision confined to terrorism and foreign intelligence cases.

'Pen register' searches
The subject of s. 214 is what is known as 'pen register' searches. In the UK, the term is 'communications data'. The FBI has been able to carry out pen register searches lawfully for some years. However, because the information sought was of a technical nature – the actual conversation or email would not be disclosed – it was agreed that the FBI need not show probable cause when applying for warrants. The Act builds on this provision by enabling the FBI to obtain pen register warrants on people, not property. This will give the FBI considerable operational flexibility, while making it far harder for the issuing court to track the use of those warrants they issue.

New search powers
The controversy over s. 218 concerns the ability of the FBI to conduct either physical searches or intercept communications. Under rules agreed in 1978, the courts accepted that, where it could show that the 'primary purpose' of such a search was to gather intelligence on suspected foreign agents, the FBI did not need to show probable cause. Thanks to s. 218, instead of foreign intelligence being the primary purpose of a physical search or interception, it now merely has to be a 'significant purpose'. This is a much less demanding test and opens the way for the mass use of secret searches including the property and communications of political protestors.

Expanded Powers to Access Personal Records
By far the most controversial measures within the Act can be found in s. 215. In light of the scandals referred to above, Congress was anxious to prevent the executive using the Cold War as an excuse to pry into the personal affairs of US citizens. Under the Foreign Intelligence Surveillance Act 1978, Congress duly imposed important restraints on the FBI's ability to obtain personal records.

> Thanks to s. 215, however, this situation has changed in a number of important respects:
>
> - The FBI can now seek warrants from the relevant court to obtain personal information concerning US citizens as well as foreign nationals. However, the only restriction is that a warrant issued by the FISA would be unlawful if it focused *exclusively* on records detailing activities protected by the First Amendment.
> - Secondly, a warrant issued under s. 215 can authorise the FBI to obtain anything tangible. Previously, under the FISA (1978) only personal records could be obtained.
> - Thirdly, and of great interest to civil libertarians, the ability of the FISA court to refuse a request from the FBI is severely compromised. Critically, the FBI does not have to satisfy the 'reasonable cause' test demanded by the Fourth Amendment. Instead, it merely has to show that the information requested is being sought for a terrorism investigation, in which case the court must issue a warrant.

arms. His willingness to downgrade the terrorist threat to US interests was to haunt him once the full horror of the September 11th attacks became apparent. According to his critics, the USA/Patriot Act was inspired by Ashcroft's sense of vulnerability over terrorism and far exceeds what is actually necessary to deal with this threat.

The dangers posed by these measures can be illustrated via the ability of the FBI under s. 215 to obtain the records of books borrowed from public libraries. For the ACLU, the issues listed below constitute a grave threat to Fourth Amendment principles quite out of proportion to the current menace to national security.

- In the event that the FBI's target is found to have withdrawn a particular title which interests investigators, the latter can request that librarians release the names and addresses of anyone else who has withdrawn the volume in question even though they cannot demonstrate probable cause.
- Another example would be the discovery that a target had been assisted by a charitable organisation. This is quite commonplace in the USA where recently arrived immigrants often receive material and legal support from such bodies. The result might well be that

the charity in question is forced to divulge the details of all other recipients of its services.

- In addition, the FBI is able to place a comprehensive and indefinite 'gag' on anyone served with a warrant under s. 215. This has profound legal implications under both the Fourth and First Amendments. Those whose personal records are sought will be denied the opportunity to challenge the legality of the decision to invade their privacy. In addition, though the First Amendment guarantees freedom of expression, s. 215 denies it to anyone who is forced to hand over information and who would otherwise prefer to inform the targeted person. The fact that the First Amendment rights are being suspended indefinitely only adds to the unease this provision has generated.
- Finally, the FBI is protected from having to make itself fully accountable for the use it makes of these powers. In particular, it is under no obligation to reveal how often it makes requests nor the social and personal profiles of those it targets.

Conclusion: towards the mass surveillance state

Despite its undoubted importance, it is increasingly likely that covert surveillance will form the preamble to a far wider debate. This is the result of the inexorable rise of mass surveillance, something which has become possible thanks to the extraordinary revolution in digital technology. As mentioned above, mass surveillance differs from covert surveillance in two important senses: it is neither covert, nor is it targeted at a particular person or group. This has dramatically increased government's ability to accumulate, store and retrieve data. It is already much in evidence in the UK. The most visible example of this is the dramatic growth in CCTV cameras in public places. However, potentially far more threatening is the emergence of a database which will contain the DNA profile of any person who has been arrested by the police. A sense of what this might mean for privacy can be gleaned from Box 6.11.

The Identity Card Bill
The remainder of this section will focus on the government's current proposals to introduce a national identity card. Initial justifications for

Box 6.11 The law on gathering and retaining DNA samples

DNA samples can be taken from various forms of body tissue. The law recognises two basic categories: intimate and non-intimate, the essential difference being that, whereas an intimate sample cannot be taken from the body without consent (PACE s. 62), a non-intimate sample can.

Acquiring Samples
Labour's promised expansion to the DNA database was introduced in s. 80 of the Criminal Justice and Police Act 2001 and, later, s. 10 of the Criminal Justice Act 2003.

- The net effect is that anyone arrested for a recordable offence who has not yet done so can be forced to give a sample for recording and retention on the DNA database.
- Nor does the order have to come from a senior officer which has been the case previously. Middle-ranking inspectors are empowered to do this, a change in policy which highlights the routinised nature of this activity. In effect, an inspector can order the taking of biological data from virtually anyone whom they arrest.

Retaining Samples
The importance of these reforms must be seen in conjunction with those brought about by s. 82 of the Criminal Justice and Police Act 2001. This empowers staff who manage the database to retain DNA samples of:

- Anyone charged with an offence but subsequently acquitted
- Anyone who gave a sample for the purposes of elimination in a case where another was subsequently convicted.

This is a far cry from the law as it originally emerged. Under the original provision (s. 64 of PACE), DNA samples could only be retained in the event of a conviction for the offence investigated. However, as is clear from the above, the strict rules put in place to ensure that DNA samples taken in all other circumstances were destroyed have been now considerably relaxed.

such a card centred on a number of propositions (Home Office press notice 5775, dated 25 May 2005):

- That the theft of personal identity is too easy. The ID scheme will enhance the liberty and security of the subject by protecting against this.
- That the use of false identities is a key factor in the commission of a variety of crimes.
- The card will enable vital public resources such as social security benefits to be protected against fraud.
- The card will also help the authorities tackle a number of illegal activities, most notably people trafficking.

A draft Bill was published on 26 April 2004 but, despite quickly passing through the Commons, it met insurmountable political obstacles in the House of Lords and was duly dropped prior to the 2005 general election. However, this decision was merely a temporary setback. Upon its re-election, Labour reintroduced the measure in substantially the same form on 25 May 2005.

The National Identity Register is designed to be a huge database which will contain a variety of details on each person's life and movements. As things stand, most of these details are fairly innocuous. However, Schedule 1 gives ministers the opportunity to add new categories of information providing these are in keeping with the purposes of the Bill. Given that these are so broad, one example being the efficient provision of public services, the terms of Schedule 1 would appear to give ministers considerable discretion when using this power. In addition, as the accompanying Explanatory Notes point out, there is nothing in the Bill to prevent Parliament passing amendments in future that create new statutory purposes which permit the authorities to allow entirely new categories of information onto the Register.

These issues are for the future. In spring and summer 2005 the Bill was subject to considerable debate. Most public attention focused on the issue of cost, an understandable reaction when non-government sources, including researchers at the London School of Economics, put the cost of each card as high as £300. Similarly, questions were again raised over the security of the scheme. However, the overriding concern among civil libertarians is the way in which the Register and the Identity Card combine to create a data trail of each person's

Box 6.12 The Identity Card Bill

The National Identity Register
It is this, rather than the ID card itself, which is the key to understanding the Bill. The National Identity Register (NIR) is both 'a record of registrable facts' and any other information which is permitted by Schedule 1 of the Bill. This will include, in addition to a person's name, previous names and date of birth, a host of other data including a list of residences and residential status. Most importantly of all, however, it will include details of each occasion when information contained on the NIR is passed to another. The full significance of this and the threat it poses to civil liberties will become apparent below.

The other main points to note are that the government has devised two ways of forcing people to enter. The first of these is that it will in future be impossible to obtain an ID card without doing so, something which, as you will see shortly, could soon make life very awkward indeed. Secondly, the Secretary of State can, at a time of his choosing, issue an order to individuals to register on pain of a fine of up to £2,500 on each occasion such an order is ignored.

The Compulsory ID Card
It is not clear how ID cards will be introduced. The easiest will be to make applying for a card a condition of receiving a 'designated document' such as a passport. In any case, it will be impossible to obtain a card unless an entry has been made on the National Identity Register. What is clear, however, is how they will work, regardless of their exact specifications.

- The card will record registrable facts available on the Register
- It will also enable people to receive information recorded in a 'prescribed part' of the Register to which the individual will not have access.

The second of these provisions relates to a power which will enable ministers and the companies who issue the cards to obtain a variety of information from public and other bodies in order to verify the application. What this information might consist of will not be known to the individual applicant.

In the event that members of the public become a little uneasy about these provisions, the government can fall back on a power which effectively means that an ID card will become necessary to access certain public services. Ominously, the Explanatory Notes (at para. 18) point out that, for the purposes of the Bill, this term has a wider meaning than is commonly understood.

movements and behaviour. This is so because on each occasion that a card is used to validate identity it will also be recorded on the Register. Precisely because the card will be necessary to access a wide variety of public services, which will almost certainly include things such as banking, property and accommodation services in addition to the staples of health care and social security, the pattern of a person's daily life will soon be recorded. The only exceptions to this are people who spend the bulk of their lives at home and pay for everything in cash.

This raises a number of legal and philosophical issues which combine to question the justice of the scheme.

* The liabilities of criminals are being passed on to the law-abiding majority.
* This will entail a considerable, possibly large financial cost which will place many families in real difficulties.
* It will also entail a second 'cost' in the form of vulnerablility to technological failure and criminal predations.

In addition, civil libertarians point out that ID cards undermine critical features of the British legal and cultural traditions, in particular that this type of interference was justifiable only when the state could show good cause, that is, that the loss of privacy was the result of reasonable suspicions of criminal activity. Mass surveillance of this type cuts away at this. Even more so than DNA retention, it is indiscriminate and leaves a nagging doubt that the British state is busy recording and collating information on every aspect of our lives. While this is unlikely to be the case, at least for the moment, it is the stuff of which a cowed, uncritical and humourless society is made. To illustrate this point, Nick Cohen (2004c) quotes at length from the late A. J. P. Taylor.

> Until August 1914 a sensible, law-abiding Englishman [sic] could pass through life and hardly notice the existence of the State, beyond the post office and the policeman. He could live where he liked and as he liked. He had no official number or identity card. He could travel abroad or leave his country for ever without a passport or any sort of official permission.

For much of the twentieth century this situation steadily unravelled because of the growth of the welfare state. However, at least the loss of privacy could be linked to the tangible benefits. This is the final objection of civil libertarians, who dispute whether the scheme can do even the modest things claimed for it. To cite one of many examples, benefit fraud is not for the most part the result of bogus identities. Most offences relate to unlawful entitlement claims,[13] something that an ID card can do nothing to stop.

Nor do the government's plans for compulsory ID cards necessarily mark the limits of ministerial ambitions. On 29 June 2005 medical leaders warned their colleagues at a BMA conference in Manchester that the possible threat to civil liberties posed by ID cards pales by comparison with the implications of the *Connecting for Health* programme (Carvel 2005). This is the official name for a very ambitious IT programme which will see the personal medical records of 50 million people in England and Wales placed on a central database. In turn, these records would then be accessible to as many as one million health-care workers. While acknowledging its advantages, doctors have expressed their concern that they and their patients are 'sleepwalking' into a nightmarish situation. Part of the problem, once again, is security. To work properly, the database will necessitate multiple points of access. Viewed together with the notorious lack of security in hospitals, this is a recipe for unlawful access, identity theft and deliberate falsification of records; employers, insurance companies and tabloid journalists merely being at the top of a long list of those who would pay handsomely for such information.

In addition, the logic underpinning the government's desire for a 'data trail' implies that law enforcement agencies, the immigration authorities, the Inland Revenue, the Benefits Agency and countless others be given access to medical information; possibly the single most fertile source of information yet to be tapped in the fight against crime. Certainly, it is no defence to say that the sharing of medical information outside the ranks of health-care professionals would fall foul of the Data Protection Act 1998. Parliament could amend this whenever a sufficiently determined government is minded to do so.

There is not, as yet, any suggestion that ministers are planning a raid on patients' records. Yet it is a measure of the rising anxiety about their real intentions that their plans for something as seemingly well-intentioned as a national database for medical information should produce such scepticism. On the same theme, one can also criticise the government's latest plans for curbing traffic congestion, the essence of which lies in charging the owner of a vehicle each time it is used on the public roads. Such a scheme can only work if each vehicle is fitted with a tracking device linked to some sort of positioning system. Though it might not necessarily ease overcrowding on the UK's roads, its value to the authorities as they seek to map and chart our lives in ever-greater detail should by now be obvious.

....

✔ What you should have learnt from reading this chapter

- The nature of the threat posed to privacy and other fundamental freedoms from covert and mass surveillance.

- The specific features of covert surveillance, along with the justifications for their use.

- The reasons why civil libertarians on both sides of the Atlantic are so sceptical about the real purposes of covert surveillance and what it might mean for the quality of democratic life in Anglo-Saxon democracies.

- The still more greater threat emanating from mass surveillance.

𝒫 Glossary of key terms

Central Intelligence Agency (CIA) Created in 1947, the CIA is responsible for directing intelligence gathering outside the USA and collecting, correlating and interpreting reports received in return. In this respect it combines the role of the UK's SIS (see below) with intelligence officials in the Cabinet Office. Its current Director is Porter J. Goss, who was appointed on 21 April 2005.
Echelon spy network An integrated system of eavesdropping bases run by America's National Security Agency with support from the UK, Canada, Australia and New Zealand. Echelon uses a combination of spy satellites and ground stations which detects electronic signals and stores them on powerful computers whenever key words are registered. Echelon has generated considerable controversy in recent years, with some analysts seeing it as a grave threat to the privacy of anyone using a modern communications device anywhere in the world.
Establishment In British politics, this term refers to an interconnected and mutually reinforcing group of politicians, officials, business leaders

and journalists who seek to control the political destiny of the nation. They are also seen as highly resistant to change.

Federal Bureau of Investigation (FBI) Established on 26 July 1908, the FBI is America's principal law enforcement agency. In addition to investigating violations of federal law, it also has responsibility for internal security, including terrorism. It is likely that the Bureau will be forever associated with J. Edgar Hoover, its controversial Director from 10 May 1924 to 2 May 1972. Aged seventy-seven when he died in his sleep, Hoover was widely regarded as America's most consistently powerful official during the post-war years. His virulent anti-communism and feud with Bobby Kennedy have since become the stuff of legend. The current and sixth Director is Robert S. Mueller III, who has held office since 4 September 2004.

Government Communications Headquarters GCHQ is based in Cheltenham, Gloucestershire and first came to national prominence in 1984 when Margaret Thatcher successfully banned any staff member from joining or retaining their membership of a trade union. The purpose of GCHQ is to intercept and interpret a vast number of electronic communications. As well as having electronic and other technical experts on its payroll, GCHQ also employs a number of linguists. One of these – Mrs Katharine Gun – exposed the involvement of the American and British governments in secretly recording the conversations of various UN delegations via the Echelon system. Sacked from her job and at one time threatened with a criminal prosecution, Mrs Gun is regarded as a heroine by many civil libertarians (see the Liberty website). The Director of GCHQ is currently Sir David Pepper.

Secret Intelligence Service (SIS) Otherwise known as MI6, the SIS is technically under the control of the Foreign Office. It works overseas to gather intelligence on the UK's enemies, invariably by recruiting a network of paid informers. The SIS are the 'spies' to the Security Service's 'spy-catchers'. However, despite the glamour attached to its work, the SIS has been severely criticised in recent years, not least because of its failure to penetrate the secrets of Saddam Hussein's regime. Its current head is Sir John Scarlett, a controversial appointment given the widespread view that Sir John's independence had been compromised over the construction of the infamous dossier on the case for the 2003 invasion of Iraq.

Security Service Better known as MI5, the Security Service exists to protect national security from people living in the UK. After being embroiled in a series of scandals which came to light in the 1980s and 1990s, the Service has gone some way to improve its image, not least through an impressive website. It currently employs 2,200 people and is led by Dame Elizabeth Manningham-Buller, the second woman to hold this position. According to its website, MI5 devotes 67 per cent of its resources to countering terrorism.

? Likely examination questions

In what ways have law and order policies since 1979 eroded civil liberties?

In what ways does the practice of intercepting communications undermine fundamental freedoms in the UK?

Why are bodies like the ACLU so concerned about the USA/Patriot Act?

Helpful websites

www.aclu.org   ACLU

www.cabinetoffice.gov.uk/intelligence/   Intelligence Services Committee

www.pmo.gov.uk/   Interceptions Commissioner

Iwww.ipt-uk.com   nvestigatory Powers Tribunal

www.usdoj.gov/   US Department of Justice

Suggestions for further reading

This is a very difficult chapter to resource, largely because so much of the material is drawn from statutes and a variety of public law textbooks. One of the most accessible accounts of covert surveillance from a civil libertarian perspective remains Ewing and Gearty's *Freedom under Thatcher*, where the relevant chapters are 3, 5 and 6. Helena Kennedy, *Just Law* (London: Chatto and Windus), 2004 has many interesting observations to make about mass surveillance at Chapter 13. Similarly, Charles Tiefer, *Veering Right* (Berkeley: University of California Press), 2004 offers fascinating insight into the Bush administration's use of such techniques at Chapter 3. However, by far and away the best store of articles on these issues can be found on the websites of Liberty and the ACLU respectively.

Notes

1. The term 'surveillance' is defined by s. 48(2) of the Regulation of Investigatory Powers Act 2000 as the monitoring and observing of and listening to persons, and the recording of information gained as a result. 'Covert surveillance' is defined by s. 26(9)(a) of the same Act as surveillance calculated to ensure that those subjected to it are unaware of it.
2. It was later established in 1711 that authorisation had to take the form of a warrant signed by one of the principal Secretaries of State.
3. This happened on six occasions between 1951 and 1982.

4. This was the Report of the Birkett Committee into the Marriman case.

5. Principally, these were the new Director-General of MI5, Sir Patrick Walker, and the Permanent Secretary at the Home Office, Sir Clive Whitmore. It is worth noting that the main barrier in the way of reform was Lady Thatcher herself. When Walker's predecessor, Sir Anthony Duff, who served as Director-General 1985–7, suggested that a limited form of parliamentary oversight might be to the Service's advantage, his offer met with overwhelming Prime Ministerial resistance.

6. Though we shall see in Chapter 7 that the legal meaning of the term 'terrorism' is loaded with dangers, at least from a civil libertarian perspective.

7. Lord Hurd – Home Secretary 1985–9 – insisted that he personally read and authorised each application.

8. Most notably in *The Whisky Priest*, an episode from the third series.

9. Mr Morrison had been appointed on 21 June 1999.

10. See para. 30 of the Annual Report of the Interception of Communications Commissioner for 2003.

11. This term – which dates from the Treaty on European Union (the 'Maastricht Treaty') – refers to co-operation in policing and criminal justice matters.

12. Mrs Rimington was appointed Director-General of MI5 in 1992.

13. The most obvious example is when a person claims Job Seeker's Allowance (unemployment benefit) while working.

CHAPTER 7

Emergency Powers

Contents

Overview

This is the third and final case study. Its subject is the body of legislation developed by British governments to deal with emergency situations. An obvious example of this is wartime. Since 1974, by contrast, the term 'emergency' is almost exclusively associated by ministers with the very different threat posed by terrorism. It is a stance mired in controversy. Emergency powers enable ministers to suspend normal constitutional arrangements, including traditional guarantees of individual freedom. This can, of course, be justified but only if the threat to the national interest is so great that no other action is viable. However, as has been pointed out on many occasions in recent months, whereas the menace posed by Nazi Germany was unquestionable, that of militant Islam is not. The Blair government disagrees and has proceeded with a legislative programme which elicits the fiercest disputes over civil liberties in an already troubled era.

Key issues to be covered in this chapter

- Emergency powers and civil liberties
- The history of anti-terrorism legislation in the UK
- The main points of controversy concerning the Terrorism Act 2000 and subsequent legislation
- Civil libertarian objections to anti-terror laws
- The counter-arguments offered by ministers of both main parties

A short history of anti-terrorism law in the United Kingdom

Anti-terror laws have a long pedigree (Walker 2002: 1), though the frequency with which they are passed has increased dramatically since the mid-1970s. The first Prevention of Terrorism (Temporary Provisions) Act 1974 (PTA) became law in the immediate aftermath of what remains one of the most notorious terrorist outrages in mainland Britain: the **Birmingham pub bombings** of 21 November 1974.[1] That government advertised this measure as a short-term response is evident in its title. Yet, in the years which followed, this body of law not only survived but, in the process, was significantly extended. Today, the principal statute is the Terrorism Act 2000, though crucial additions have been made via the Anti-Terrorism, Crime and Security Act 2001 and the Prevention of Terrorism Act 2005.[2] In light of the terror attacks on London in July 2005, we can expect this body of law to be modified still further in future.

The Terrorism Act 2000

Anti-terrorism law was not mentioned in Labour's 1997 election manifesto. However, shortly after coming into office[3] the Blair government announced its intention to replace the Prevention of Terrorism Act 1989 (PTA)[4] with a new statute, one which would not need annual parliamentary renewal. Ministers claimed that they were simply responding to long-standing requests for such a measure, most notably the October 1996 review of the PTA by Lord Lloyd. Other commentators were less convinced. In their eyes, such scepticism stems from the volte-face (an act of turning round to face the opposite direction) ordered by Blair and Straw as part of their electoral strategy. After years of opposing the annual renewal of the PTA, the Labour leadership suddenly ordered its backbenchers to abstain. This led to considerable ill-feeling within Labour's ranks, compounded by the support Straw gave to the Conservatives as they tried to pass a controversial amendment to the PTA in April 1996. Under these circumstances, it is unlikely that the new government wished to give its backbench rebels periodic opportunity to accuse it of bad faith. Placing this body of law on a permanent footing would go some way to achieve this.

Box 7.1 The Terrorism Act 2000 at a glance

Part I	ss.1–2	Redefines – and considerably broadens – the legal definition of terrorism.
Part II	ss. 3–13	Empowers ministers to 'proscribe' various organisations. It also creates various offences connected with membership of and support and assistance for such organisations.
Part III	ss. 14–31	Focuses on 'terrorist property', in particular how law enforcement agencies might lawfully seize it. In addition, it imposes legal duties on various people to disclose information concerning terrorist property to the police.
Part IV	ss. 32–9	Codifies police powers to conduct terrorist investigations, notably to 'cordon off' areas and obtain information.
Part V	ss. 40–53	Lists the range of powers available to counter-terrorist agencies when they suspect a person of terrorist activity. These mainly concern stop and search; entry, search and seizure; arrest; and port and border controls.
Part VI	ss. 54–64	Contains various miscellaneous provisions, mainly offences not covered elsewhere.
Part VII	ss. 65–113	This details the 'non-permanent' provisions which apply to Northern Ireland only and which were due to lapse the month after the Terrorism Act became law.
Part VIII	ss. 114–31	Contains a miscellany of general and technical provisions.

On 17 December 1998 the Home and Northern Ireland Offices duly published a joint document announcing a review. After an official consultation period which lasted until 16 March 1999, the government included a Terrorism Bill in the Queen's Speech later that year. Despite opposition to a variety of clauses, most notably the definition of terrorism itself, the Bill duly became law as the Terrorism Act 2000[5] on 20 July that year.

At the time of its enactment, the government's principal concern was to 'normalise' law enforcement in Northern Ireland, where ministers hoped that the measures contained in Part VII of the Act could be phased out as security improved. As events transpired, they were to be disappointed in this wish. However, fourteen months after the Terrorism Act became law, **al-Qaeda** struck in New York and Washington and changed the politics of terrorism forever.

The Anti-Terrorism, Crime and Security Act 2001 and the Prevention of Terrorism Act 2005

The dramatic events of 11 September 2001 are so well known that the slightest repetition is unlikely to improve understanding. The response of the government was to rush through Parliament a new

---

Box 7.2 The Anti-Terrorism, Crime and Security Act 2001 at a glance

Part I	ss. 1–3	This contains numerous provisions which add to the state's existing powers[6] to uncover terrorist property. Primarily, they enable law enforcers to 'freeze and seize' assets, while compelling financial institutions to breach client confidentiality and pass information to the authorities. In keeping with the Terrorism Act 2000 (Part III), they create a new offence of failing to report suspicions of terrorist financing.
Part II	ss. 4–16	This largely complements the measures contained in Part I above, mainly by making it so much easier for the Treasury to freeze the assets of foreign governments and nationals resident in the UK.
Part III	ss. 17–20	Part III gives the authorities additional powers to obtain otherwise confidential information, especially from public authorities.
Part IV	ss. 21–36	The most controversial element of a controversial Act, Part IV put in place new arrangements for immigration hearings involving suspected foreign terrorists.

Part V	ss. 37–42	This extends the law on racially aggravated offences to offences aggravated by religious hostility. This is an early indication of the government's awareness that the effect of its own legislation could be the increase of 'Islamophobia', both among police and immigration officers and the general public.
Part VI	ss. 43–57	This strengthened controls in respect of weapons of mass destruction.
Part VII	ss. 58–75	Part VII has a similar effect to Part VI but this time in respect of pathogens and toxins.
Part VIII	ss. 76–81	This contains measures to promote nuclear security.
Part IX	ss. 82–8	An identical aim to Part VIII but in relation to aviation security.
Part X	ss. 89–101	This contains a series of controversial measures which enable the police to search for a person's identity by making suspects remove facial coverings and allowing them to record identifying body marks. It also enabled a variety of specialised forces, including the Ministry of Defence police, to assist in general policing operations, a development which raised important issues of accountability.
Part XI	ss. 102–7	This is also a highly contested part of the Act and one which enables the authorities to insist that communications service providers retain communications data long after it is required for billing purposes. Rather than place these arrangements on a statutory footing, Part XI makes provision for a Code of Practice to ensure standards are maintained.
Part XII	ss. 108–10	This strengthens the law on international corruption.
Part XIII	ss. 111–21	A miscellany of provisions with one 'stand-out' issue: the reintroduction of a general offence of failing to disclose information about terrorism.
Part XIV	ss. 122–9	A set of supplemental provisions including those for the review of the Act.

statute: the Anti-Terrorism, Crime and Security Act 2001 (ATCSA). This fact alone was provocative enough. Critics of anti-terror laws in the UK have always objected to the manner in which they pass their parliamentary stages, leaving parliamentarians little time for detailed scrutiny. The credit that the Blair government had built up over the more stately passage of the Terrorism Act 2000 largely evaporated after the ATCSA became law, an issue which recurred over the passage of the Prevention of Terrorism Act 2005.

By far the most controversial provisions were those created in Part IV. They allowed the Home Secretary to order the indefinite detention of suspected foreign terrorists who could not be deported because such an action would breach their rights under the European Convention. As we saw in Chapter 4, this was eventually ruled unlawful by the House of Lords in December 2004, a decision which gave ministers little alternative but to draw up new legislation.

The result is the short Prevention of Terrorism Act 2005. However, one of the great ironies of this episode was that the new law is, in key respects, far more draconian than the one it replaced. Most importantly, its provisions now extend to anyone resident in the UK. Surprising though it might seem, it is once again possible for extensive restrictions to be placed on a person's freedom of movement and association by ministerial fiat (decree) alone.

Box 7.3 The Prevention of Terrorism Act 2005

ss. 1–9   These are the most important sections of the Act in that they enable ministers to impose various control orders over those they perceive to be a terrorist threat. These come in two types. Non-derogation orders enable ministers to impose a variety of restrictions, including house arrest. By contrast, derogation orders enable ministers to order indefinite detention, though only after a court has given its authorisation.

ss. 10–12   These establish a set of mechanisms by which people upon whom control orders have been imposed may appeal against such decisions.

ss. 13–16   The final sections of the Act create further mechanisms for oversight and review.

The implications of anti-terrorism legislation for civil liberties

The previous section explains why and how anti-terror laws have developed. In keeping with the approach adopted in the previous chapters, a more comprehensive analysis now follows, one which considers in detail anti-terror laws' implications for individual freedom.

The definition of terrorism

No other aspect of the Terrorism Act has attracted so much adverse comment as the new definition in s. 1. Ministers argue that it simply reflects the diverse and changing nature of the terrorist threat to the UK.

- Firstly, a variety of new groups prepared to use terror have emerged since the 1970s.
- Some of these threaten vital British interests by targeting governments abroad.
- Others fall under the category of domestic terrorism and include certain nationalist groups in Wales and Scotland and, as we now know, British Muslims engaged in a **jihad** against everyone and no one.
- Further, it is by no means certain whether completely new categories of terror groups will emerge in future.

Box 7.4 The definition of terrorism in British law

In s. 1 of the Terrorism Act 2000, the term 'terrorism' refers to the use or threat of action where the following conditions are present:

- The action (or threat) involves: (a) serious violence against a person, or, (b) serious damage to property, or, (c) endangering the life of another, or, (d) the creation of a serious risk to the health or safety of a section of the public, or, (e) plans to interfere with or disrupt an electronic system (such as air traffic control).
- The action (or threat) is designed to either (a) influence the government or (b) intimidate the public or a section of it.
- The action (or threat) is made for the advancement of a political, religious or ideological cause.

• Finally, the history of contemporary terrorism shows that a variety of tactics, not all of which are aimed at people or governments, are now in use. On all counts, it is essential that the definition of terrorism is sufficiently flexible to permit the authorities to take immediate action against these, rather than having to refer constantly to Parliament for new powers.

Civil libertarians argue that, this aside, the definition of terrorism is still too wide. As we saw in the previous chapter, it is the ambiguity of the language which lies at the heart of the issue. A common-sense understanding of the term 'terrorise' might follow that of the *Oxford New Dictionary* (at page 1915): '[to] create and maintain a state of extreme fear and distress'. By contrast, s. 1 of the Terrorism Act opts for a much broader definition. In one scenario, an environmentalist who, aiming to promote his 'ideological cause', threatens serious damage to earth-moving equipment which has the effect of intimidating the driver and some of his colleagues, falls foul of the Act. This protestor can become, *if the police and prosecuting authorities wish it*, a terrorist.

Such a scenario might seem far-fetched. For civil libertarians, however, it is quite inappropriate that peaceful protestors should face such legal intimidation. Understanding these concerns – whether or not you agree with them is a different matter – is absolutely essential for a full appreciation of the politics of terrorism.

Proscribed organisations and the freedom of expression
The power to proscribe enables ministers to outlaw certain groups or movements. This means that it is unlawful to belong to or to support a proscribed organisation in any other specified manner. Ministers argue that, regardless of the implications for freedom of expression and association, the openness of British society cannot be exploited by terrorists whose methods, to say nothing of their aims, are antithetical to democratic values. There is, of course, a paradoxical element to this. However, in their defence, ministers can point to the fact that the freedoms involved are not unconditional ones under the European Convention and can be legitimately restricted in certain circumstances. In addition, a number of safeguards have been put in place to ensure that these powers are justly used.

- The Proscribed Organisations Appeals Commission (POAC) hears appeals against ministerial orders and has the power to quash them.
- No evidence presented to the POAC can be used by the prosecution in any criminal proceedings.
- Anyone convicted of an offence in connection with a proscribed organisation can appeal against conviction upon an order for deproscription.

Civil libertarians may not be convinced by these concessions. For example, under s. 3 of the Terrorism Act, one of the criteria for proscribing an organisation is that it is 'otherwise concerned with terrorism'. It is suggested that this has a 'catch-all' quality to it, which, when read in connection with the definition of terrorism itself, gives ministers far too much latitude to impose bans. Similar problems emerge in respect of some of the offences created to enforce this law (see Box 7.5). You will note the generalised nature of these provisions which, as the government acknowledged, is to deny those who sympathise with proscribed bodies the chance to discuss their views – no matter how absurd, *or how just*, they might be.

Box 7.5 Offences relating to proscription under ss. 12–13 of the Terrorism Act 2000

- For example, under s. 12 it is an offence to offer support to a proscribed organisation. However, the apparent reasonableness of this provision is undermined somewhat when one discovers that, thanks to s. 12(2), offering support may consist of doing nothing more than assisting in the arranging of a meeting, knowing that this might be addressed by someone who professes to be a supporter of that organisation. A mere three people assembled in private is sufficient to expose a person to prosecution and a ten-year prison sentence.
- Under s. 12(3), a person who addresses a meeting and *furthers the activities* (whatever this might mean) of a proscribed body faces a similar punishment.
- Finally, under s. 13, any form of public display – including choice of clothing – which shows any kind of allegiance to a banned group is also an offence.

Terrorist property and the totalitarian state

Part III of the TA 2000 creates a variety of powers and duties in respect of 'terrorist property', a broad term which includes more than financial assets. That government would wish to target such property is obvious. In addition to disrupting terrorist acts, it is also a means of gathering vital intelligence. Further, in recent years, many terror organisations have globalised their operations, thereby increasing their dependency on the international financial system. This might make them more potent; it also makes them more vulnerable.

The question remains: how far can government legitimately go in demanding access to financial information before it undermines the principle of confidentiality on which banking and financial services depends? In this respect, s. 19 of the Act is peculiarly important since it imposes a duty on bankers and other professionals to disclose information to the authorities wherever it is suspected that an offence in connection with terrorist property has occurred. Failure to do so is punishable by up to five years imprisonment. The ATCSA further extended the powers of police officers to demand account details, in some cases for a period of up to ninety days.

A number of civil liberties issues are raised by such measures.

- The United Kingdom's reputation as a liberal democracy is compromised by the practice of compelling people to spy and inform on others.
- Secondly, evidence from the United States suggests that enlisting banks in particular has very unfortunate consequences for those who fall under suspicion. Cases have been reported where, even after the FBI has ended its investigations without bringing charges, the individual concerned has had his banking services withdrawn with little prospect of opening an alternative account elsewhere.
- The third issue, once again, concerns the freedom of expression. While legal advisers are given partial exemption from a duty to disclose (s. 19(5)), this does not apply to other professionals such as journalists. Indeed, when this issue was debated in Parliament, the government made it clear that a journalist investigating the financing of terrorism could face charges for failing to pass on notes (including contacts) to the authorities. This is anathema to journalists and could result in them turning to other stories

instead. Whether this can be reconciled with the jurisprudence of the ECtHR in respect of the flow of political information is an interesting conundrum.

Terrorist investigations, family life and the exposure of abuse

These issues – confidentiality and freedom of expression – also dominate the debate over terrorist investigations. This can be best illustrated via a discussion of ss. 38–9, 58 and 103 of the TA 2000.

Obligations under s. 38B

The new s. 38B, which was inserted into the Act by the ATCSA, re-established a highly controversial law which had been originally dropped on the advice of Lord Lloyd in 1996[7]. The official reasoning behind this U-turn is that, post-9/11, the threat to national security is now such that government has the right to demand the co-operation of all in the fight against terrorism, even when this involves unpalatable choices.

- The new s. 38B once more makes it a criminal offence for anyone to fail to disclose information relating to terrorism.
- Clearly, this provision goes much further than s. 19 discussed above, which applied only to professionals and business people and only then in respect of terrorist property.
- As a result, an intolerable pressure may be placed upon family members and other intimates to inform on each other, or face a serious criminal penalty. Walker (2002: 108) adds that, as a result, s. 38B may well be challenged under Articles 8 and 10 of the European Convention.

Silencing the critics

The latter three sections all create a variety of offences designed to help the authorities protect the integrity of terrorist investigations. Two new offences are created by s. 39 which criminalise the disclosure by a civilian of any information relating to ongoing terrorist investigations. Ministers point out that, in the course of their professional and business activities, a number of people will become aware of such investigations and hence be in a position to warn those under suspicion. The offences under this section are designed to deter this.

The offences listed under ss. 58 and 103 have the same goal, but seek to effect it in a different way. They criminalise the retention, or making, of any record relating to an investigation. The impact of these provisions is potentially so much greater because it is the mere act of making a record, rather than its communication, which creates criminal liability. The government's view is that such a law is necessary to deter '**whistle-blowers**' who, for a variety of reasons, ranging from financial gain to a misguided sense of public duty, are minded to pass on the secrets to which they are privy.

These offences pose a troubling but interesting question: under what circumstances does the individual owe primary loyalty to a state on which they depend for protection? While accepting that all these measures – even s. 38B – can be justified, civil libertarians insist that they make it far too easy for ministers to silence those who seek to uncover official incompetence and wrongdoing. All of them can be used to prosecute academic researchers, journalists and high-minded officials desperate to bring a scandal to the public's attention. The weaknesses of Parliament as an instrument of scrutiny are legion. Hence, it can be argued that, without such people, unconstitutional and criminal conduct at the highest levels would never come to light. Anyone vaguely familiar with the history of the Troubles in Northern Ireland can attest to this. Yet the government was adamant that it would not create any exemptions, even to journalists. Sceptical civil libertarians are apt to conclude that ministers wish to retain maximum discretion to prosecute where their personal, political interests are at stake.

Counter-terrorist powers, pre-trial investigations and the right to a fair hearing

Counter-terrorist powers are contained in Part V of the Act, with special provisions for Northern Ireland in Part VII. They raise a rather different set of civil liberties issues. As Box 7.6 makes clear, some of the most sensitive aspects of the criminal law are undermined by the various counter-terrorist powers listed in the Act. The government's position is simple: that the experience of terrorism is such that police officers must be able to act *instinctively*, especially when intelligence is less than comprehensive. On occasion, and this

Box 7.6 The criminal law and the Terrorism Act 2000

Principle	Corresponding provision in the Terrorism Act
The need for reasonable suspicion before the powers of stop, search and seizure can be used.	This is contravened by ss. 44–5 which enable officers to stop and search people in designated areas for items connected to terrorism, even when they cannot justify this. Though it has to be affirmed by the Home Office, designations are authorised by senior police officers (s. 44). The official reviewer of the Terrorism Act, Lord Carlile, has expressed considerable misgivings about the use of s. 44 authorisations, along with the so-called 'short stops' at borders which can also happen without reasonable suspicion.
That the power of arrest relates to reasonable suspicion (in US law 'probable cause') that a specific crime has been committed.	Under s. 41, a person can be arrested without warrant if a police officer reasonably suspects them of involvement in terrorism. This is a far less stringent test and one which allows officers to act on a 'hunch' rather than a properly formed opinion.
That, once arrested, a person should be either charged or released as soon as possible.	Thanks to s. 308 of the Criminal Justice Act 2003, a person arrested under the Terrorism Act can be detained without charge for up to fourteen days. This is ten days longer than is the case for other serious criminals.
When defending oneself against criminal charges, the onus of proof falls on the prosecution.	This is reversed at various points in the Act, most notably in cases of money-laundering connected with terrorist property (s. 18) and the possession of articles which gives grounds for suspecting that they are connected with terrorism (s. 57).
That oral testimony by prosecution witnesses during a criminal trial must be	In the Criminal Justice (Terrorism and Conspiracy) Act 1998, Parliament accepted that, where the accused was charged with membership of a proscribed

| corroborated (supported) by evidence. They cannot be based on suspicion alone | organisation in Northern Ireland, senior police officers could make uncorroborated evidence before a court. Despite innumerable criticisms of this provision, it was included as s. 108 of the Terrorism Act. |

applies particularly when foreign terrorists are being investigated, the unique problem of uncovering decisive evidence has to be reflected in the rules governing the trial process itself.

The implications of some of these measures for civil liberties are summarised in Box 7.6. The legality of the provision now included in s. 57 has been brought before the courts (*R v. Secretary of State for the Home Department, ex parte Kebilene* (2000)), though the Law Lords accepted government arguments that reversing the onus of proof does not necessarily undermine the right to a fair hearing.

Border controls, immigration and detention without trial

This is the one area of anti-terrorism legislation which has gained an extraordinarily high public profile. Following its defeat in the Lords, the government steered through Parliament the Prevention of Terrorism Act 2005. This repealed Part IV of the ATCSA and replaced its provisions with a new regime of control orders. The aim of the Act had not changed. The control orders enable ministers to impose obligations on those suspected of terrorism which, in turn, will 'prevent or restrict the further involvement by individuals in such activity' (Explanatory Notes to the Act at para. 3).

As mentioned in Box 7.3, the orders are divided into two categories: non-derogating and derogating. Given the fact that Parliament has given ministers the discretion to impose any obligation providing they believe it to be necessary for public protection (s. 9(2)), the distinction between the two may be more apparent than real. In essence, however, a derogation order will involve the imposition of obligations which amount to indefinite detention without trial. For this reason, they will breach a person's rights under Article 5 of the European Convention and will thus necessitate entering a derogation under the Human Rights Act.

The determination of the government to reintroduce the principle of detention without trial meant that two, key concessions were inevitable. Detention will, initially at least, take the form of house arrest rather than imprisonment; while anyone resident in the UK is liable to receive an order, regardless of nationality. The implications of these provisions is the subject of a coruscating analysis by Gareth Pierce, one of the most revered criminal defence lawyers of her generation (Pierce 2005). Her objections to these laws – which are summarised below – are based in part on legal principle but much more on her experiences in representing those who were imprisoned as a result of the original detention orders under Part IV of the ATCSA.

• The non-derogation orders are anything other than a humane alternative to detention orders. Pierce suggests that those in receipt of orders are forced to live in a surreal world where they know that the slightest infringement of the order can result in their immediate imprisonment. Non-derogation orders will work only to the extent that the authorities make their terms as clear as possible and provide considerable support thereafter, something which was not immediately in evidence.

• Worse, however, they offend against the very essence of justice. As the experiences of those who endured similar measures in apartheid South Africa attest, such orders permanently brand those to whom they are given, especially any children they might have. This is akin to transferring liability from people whose guilt has not been established to those whose innocence has never been questioned. The fact that the restrictions they will undoubtedly impose (telephone usage, access to the internet, visits from family and friends) will affect equally any and all members of a household only adds to the iniquity of this failing.

• The way in which these measures offend against conceptions of natural justice reappear in her third criticism: that those in receipt of an order have little opportunity to amend their behaviour so as to convince the authorities of their innocence.

• This is aggravated by the often dubious quality of the evidence against the detainees. In her article, Ms Pierce is particularly bitter about the willingness of the British government to rely on information extracted under torture. However, it was the tenuous nature of some of the intelligence gained through more orthodox methods which caught the eye as a result of the exchange between another leading human rights lawyer, Ben Emmerson, and an MI5 officer in May 2004 (Bright 2004). The case involved an appeal by one of the original detainees against the order imprisoning him without trial. During the exchanges it was revealed that the order was based on an intelligence report that the man concerned had supplied a pair of boots, a sleeping bag and some telecommunications equipment to one of three Islamist groups operating in Chechnya. Had he supplied either of the other two, he would not have come under suspicion. The point Mr Emmerson was trying to make is not simply that such evidence is often flimsy, but that its legal significance relies upon the interpretation placed upon it by the security and intelligence services. Should this ever be enough to justify the measures which can be imposed under the PTA 2005? Civil libertarians think not; ministers disagree.

Anti-terrorism law and the civil liberties lobby

You will have gained by now a clear sense that the *potentially* malign impact of anti-terror laws on civil liberties is at once extensive and profound. This point has been recognised by no less a figure than Lord Carlile of Berriew, the current reviewer of the legislation. In his report for 2004, he draws attention to the following:

- The absence of suitable training for special advocates appearing for organisations under threat of proscription.
- The vagueness of the offences created under ss. 11–13 which criminalise membership of and support for a proscribed (banned) organisation.
- The obligations imposed on the public by ss.14–19 in respect of reporting suspicions of business transactions involving terrorist property.
- The power of police officers to make arrests under s. 41 without an evidential base for their decisions.
- The stop, search and seizure powers under ss. 44–5 which his Lordship believes to be significantly overused.

However, like the government, Lord Carlile also believes that these laws are justified by the pressure of events and the integrity of those who implement them. One of his Lordship's predecessors, Lord Colville, expressed this view in the following way:

> The exercise of powers given by the PTA 1989[8] will affect civil rights. There may well be a restriction of personal liberty, or a suspension of one or more of the usual aspects of a fair trial, or an invasion of privacy and family life, or a restriction on the freedom of expression, or freedom of assembly and association. But that is the price a community is obliged to pay, for the prevention of terrorist outrages, which cause death, injury or damage. (Report of the Operation of the Prevention of Terrorism Act 1989 for 1999 at para. 15).

Whereas human rights organisations concur with the first of these sentences, they continue to express grave reservations over the second. This section seeks to explain why.

Ineffective parliamentary scrutiny
The first point is that, too often, ministers rush anti-terror laws through Parliament, thus denying MPs the chance to subject them to meaningful scrutiny. The original Prevention of Terrorism Act passed through its parliamentary stages in seven days during the last week of November 1974, something which set an unfortunate precedent repeated in 1996, 1998, 2001 and 2005. Because the government can always rely on its loyalists to support it, the net effect is to pass the power to legislate to the Home Secretary.

This is not always wise. In 1998, senior police officers in Northern Ireland were given the power to make uncorroborated statements in court as evidence of offences connected with proscribed organisations. This was much criticised as being a gross infringement of the rule of law. However, detailed debate was impossible and the measure was passed. Since when, as critics noted, the police in Northern Ireland never used it, largely because they sensed it would not be acceptable to judges. Precisely because they were not under the same compulsion to listen, ministers persisted with a measure which brought them much opprobrium but no convictions.

Ministerial duplicity
For critics of the British government, such behaviour is explained by the fact that, far too often, ministers exploit emergency situations in

order to pass laws of a highly dubious nature. One of the most famous of these instances also dates from the passage of the Criminal Justice (Prevention of Terrorism) Act 1998 but reappeared during the debates on the Terrorism Act two years later. When Parliament was recalled to pass this piece of legislation, the Home Secretary insisted that it was part of a joint response, agreed with the Dublin government, to the **Omagh outrage** (Straw 1998). His critics, however, remained perplexed as to why a domestic emergency was used to pass highly controversial measures aimed at conspiracies to overthrow foreign governments. In their eyes, the real purpose of the Act was the appeasement of what Gearty (1998) refers to as 'Britain's favourite despots', who had been pressurising London to bring criminal charges against their own political exiles. Accordingly, Omagh offered the perfect opportunity to introduce a measure in an emergency situation where government whips allied to a **guillotine motion** would see it through without too much adverse questioning.

This is, self-evidently, a strong accusation. It is repeated, however, by Faisal Bodi (2000a; 2000b). Picking up on Gearty's central theme, Bodi argues that the manner in which the West has propped up Middle Eastern regimes has generated political ferment and oppression in equal measure. Denied legitimate opportunities to protest at home, many critics have been reduced to advocating violence from abroad. For Bodi, the definition of terrorism in s. 1 of the Terrorism Act is designed exclusively to silence such people. This is so because it refuses to accept that political violence can ever be acceptable. Neither does it consider the possibility that certain regimes are so oppressive that the violence they show to their own people provides these so-called 'terrorists' with a lawful excuse[9]. His conclusion is equally blunt: key aspects of Britain's policy on terrorism are based less on necessity than the demands of '[the late] King Fahd, Hosni Mubarak and the **juntas** which govern the Muslim world'.

Misuse and abuse
Especially in the aftermath of the 2005 bomb attacks on London, the significance of these arguments should not be underestimated. They place an indelible question-mark over the integrity of ministers who, it is alleged, continually allow a morally dubious **realpolitik** to shape a uniquely sensitive area of domestic law. Further, this objection is

reinforced by a third criticism which also calls into question the use law enforcers make of the powers they are given. One element of this is the use of stop and search powers (s. 44) to curtail political protest. Liberty has continually expressed its concern about this practice, the most notorious example of which was the use of 'blanket' stop and search powers against those protesting against the staging of the East London arms fair in 2003 (Liberty 2005). More recently, it has been alleged that these powers are being used disproportionately and unfairly against London's Muslim community. This emerged in light of a request from the **Independent Police Complaints Commission** that all instances where these powers are used be reported automatically to it (*The Guardian*, 25 January 2005). It is worth adding, though, that this allegation is hotly denied by the police, a point to which I shall return below.

The 'Ricin Conspiracy'
More troubling for police leaders is the way in which their use of anti-terror powers has been undermined by poor intelligence. The most dramatic and tragic example of this occurred on 21 July 2005 when what appears to have been a series of intelligence blunders led to the death of an innocent young Brazilian, Jean-Charles de Menezes, at Stockwell Underground station. However, it must not be forgotten that, only three months before, the so-called 'Ricin Conspiracy' trial collapsed when four of the five men accused of conspiring to manufacture and distribute ricin were acquitted. This immediately compelled the Crown Prosecution to drop a variety of other charges against them.

This episode demonstrates the inherent difficulties in bringing criminal investigations to a successful conclusion. For civil libertarians, however, it also highlights the way in which political pressures can affect the interpretation police officers can place on intelligence reports. In this respect, the crucial feature of the case was that the arrests of the accused occurred in February 2003, just as the US and UK governments were finalising their justifications for the war against Iraq. The then US Secretary of State, Colin Powell, deliberately referred to the arrests in a speech to the UN Security Council on 5 February in which he claimed that the men had al-Qaeda connections and had also received support from the Iraqi government.

While British ministers did not go quite so far, they certainly used the arrests to support their position on Iraq.[10] Subsequently, this led the celebrated investigative journalist Duncan Campbell (Campbell and Cowan 2005) to launch a sustained attack on the government's handling of the ricin plot. Campbell's analysis (he served as an expert witness for the defence) highlights how terribly thin the evidential base for the prosecution actually was, so much so that he leaves his readers with the distinct impression that 'not guilty' verdicts were more or less inevitable.

This point is taken up by another high-profile commentator, Simon Jenkins then of *The Times*, who wonders how 'a bunch of illegal immigrants and passport forgers, of whom thousands must be loose in Britain, were turned in the minds of the police and prosecuting authorities into criminal masterminds intent on murdering hundreds if not thousands of people?' (Jenkins 2005b). This obviously lends itself to the conclusion that the prosecution was politically motivated. While he rejects this, Jenkins hints that the highly charged political atmosphere did influence the officers involved. If so, it simply adds further evidence to those who question the reliability of anti-terror investigations.

Anti-terror principles and non-emergency laws
An increasingly important sub-theme to this debate is the manner in which certain legal principles associated with anti-terror laws have begun to appear elsewhere in the criminal justice system. One example of this emerged in the case of *R (Roberts)* v. *the Parole Board and Another* (2005) which we examined in Chapter 4. This hinged on the use of secret hearings and court-appointed special advocates to determine whether a notorious life-sentence prisoner should be released. The parallels between this and the procedures of POAC and SIAC were not lost on Mr Roberts' lawyer, who noted that his client was the first to experience the full force of practices designed originally to deal with emergency situations in a case where no emergency could be possibly said to exist.

More significantly, perhaps, a connection can be made between anti-terror laws and the Anti-Social Behaviour Order (ASBO). In an editorial published by *The Economist* (2005), it was argued that the outward growth of practices and principles associated with anti-terrorism legislation betrays an historic and deep-seated animosity among police officers to the criminal trial itself. As the leader writer points out, the legal system in the UK:

> is founded not on the assumption that everybody will behave with decency and restraint but on the rather more reliable conviction that most people, including the police, are capable of lying and many do so if it is to their advantage. Faced with two competing accounts of what one person has done to another, the courts normally give both of them a hard time.

The use of evidence which cannot be challenged, together with the reversal of the burden of proof, are hallmark features of anti-terror legislation. That they are helping to shape the law on anti-social behaviour is evident in the following:

•   The willingness to allow professional witness statements and hearsay evidence to be admitted in court.
•   The use of the civil law test – the balance of probabilities – to determine whether or not an order should be made. This is despite the fact that breach of an order can lead to a criminal conviction.

The result is that the police stand to achieve a favourable outcome without having to undergo the rigours of a criminal trial, a situation which is justified by that 'typically British assurance: our powers may be draconian, but decency and common sense will ensure that we don't overuse them'. However, as we saw in Chapter 5 and as the editorial itself asserts, the history of the ASBO does not fully support this position. The fact that procedures which first emerged to deal with some of the world's most dangerous men and women are now, albeit with fewer consequences, being used 'against crotchety old neighbours, prostitutes, beggars and mothers who argue with their children' is enough to make anyone a little uncomfortable.

The law and order society revisited

Why, then, do ministers continue to expose themselves to political criticism, not least when the way in which anti-terrorism laws are implemented exposes them to accusations of hypocrisy and double-standards? This is especially so when, according to prominent civil libertarians, tackling terrorism can be done using the ordinary criminal law allied to effective intelligence gathering (Chakrahbati 2005).

For the Left, the answer can once again be found in the structure of decision-making in Whitehall. In a later piece, Kettle (1996) argues that the law and order society dominates the history of anti-terrorism legislation, just as it does with covert surveillance. This began with the 1974 Act, which he dismisses as 'a political gesture, forced on a weak Labour government by the police and MI5 as part of a bigger agenda of their own devising', and has continued ever since. As a result, the overriding goal of 'these dark forces' (Jenkins 2005) – namely the elimination of political and legal restrictions on their work – drives forward the political agenda with little meaningful opposition from within Whitehall. Ministers are simply too fearful of the political consequences of not acting on their advice to consider a more measured response.

The ministerial response

How do ministers defend themselves against such accusations? As mentioned above, ministers have never denied that anti-terror laws are widely drawn. However, this is not the result of the authoritarian schemers and 'dark forces' which allegedly inhabit the Home Office. Rather, it is a response to terrorism itself. The central issue is this. The increasingly sophisticated yet diffuse nature of the terrorist threat means that law enforcement officers are compelled to act on intelligence which gives rise to strong suspicions but falls short of the evidential test used elsewhere in the criminal law. This is why, for example, the definition of terrorism itself is so broad. Equally, it explains why so many of the powers discussed above are designed to give the authorities maximum discretion, while shielding them from the normal processes of legal scrutiny. The peculiar nature of terrorism places huge and unusual barriers in the way of terrorist investigations. This is because obtaining evidence of involvement in terrorism is far harder than gaining the initial intelligence. This means that the authorities must be given the opportunity to act on their suspicions to an unusually high degree, even if this means that a case is not subsequently brought before the ordinary courts. Further, even where there is a reasonable chance of conviction, the costs – revealing sources, embarrassing foreign governments, disillusioning the public – might be too great. Successive Parliaments have recognised the fundamental truth of these assertions. In the last analysis, the extraordinary powers they created have survived because they have proved their worth, a point also recognised by the several reviewers who have commented on anti-terror statutes since 1984 (see below).

Mature reflection

The robust nature of the government's defence was particularly marked during the passage of the Anti-Terrorism, Crime and Security Act 2001. In a succession of speeches and newspaper articles, David Blunkett called for 'mature reflection' before condemning his proposals on human rights grounds. What he might have meant by this is summarised below.

- Even when new measures are rushed through Parliament, it does not follow that they have not been carefully considered. In the case of the ATCSA the Home Office trawled through the Terrorism Act for two months before bringing its proposals before MPs. As a result, it was able to present a detailed set of reforms at a time when a previously shocked House had been able to reflect on the events of 9/11.
- Critics of the legislation have something akin to a 'blind spot' when it comes to considering the difficulties faced by ministers. On the one hand, the latter have responsibilities to promote democratic values in keeping with Britain's political traditions. On the other, they are aware of the weight of public expectations that they will not put principle before security. In such circumstances, when they receive intelligence reports suggesting a threat, they have little alternative but to act on them. As Michael Howard – then Home Secretary – pointed out during the debate on the 1996 amendments to the old Prevention of Terrorism Act, ministers are not experts. To substitute their view for that of intelligence officers would be wholly irresponsible at a time of obvious danger.
- As a result of the intelligence component to anti-terrorism operations, ministers labour under the same handicap we saw in the previous chapter; that it takes a terrible event like the 7 July bombings before their critics are convinced that the threat is not

exaggerated. Other evidence – of plots frustrated or plans disrupted – simply cannot be brought before the public.

The Home Secretary's frustrations emerged during the Commons debate on 19 November 2001. Despairing of the inability 'of some to hold in their minds the gravity of what we are dealing with', he rubbished some of his opponents on the grounds that their greatest moral dilemma was posed by selecting alternative items from the shelves of supermarkets (White and Wintour 2001). In addition, and more importantly, he accused others of wilfully misinterpreting the nature and purpose of anti-terrorism law, largely through an excessive and unjustified reliance on jurisprudence (the philosophical issues

Box 7.7 Sir Ian Blair on the Terrorism Act

The accusation that police officers misuse their powers is strongly denied. As mentioned above, this became a highly topical issue early in 2005 as a result of complaints from Muslim organisations that their people were being subjected to excessive use of stop and search powers. This drew a passionate response from the Commissioner of the Metropolitan Police, Sir Ian Blair, who condemned the manner in which police operations are reported. A large part of Sir Ian's irritation stemmed from what he saw as 'headline chasing' by certain newspapers, notably *The Guardian*. The example he cited was a report which suggested that the number of stops on Muslims in London under the Terrorism Act had increased by 300 per cent in 2004. While technically an accurate figure, its representation in the press distorted reality by failing to mention that, in absolute terms, the number of stops had increased from two to a mere six. More importantly, Sir Ian pointed out that the secrecy which surrounds anti-terror policing prevents the police from demonstrating that, not only is the use of their powers moderate and proportionate to other aspects of policing, but that it produces results. To quote a second example, though the number of anti-terror arrests had risen precipitously to 700, this could be justified by the equally unprecedented number of those arrested who were subsequently charged: 254 in all. It was in this context that Sir Ian announced that he would be seeking approval from the Attorney General to lift some of the reporting restrictions on terror cases.

Source: Travis 2005.

underpinning legal debate) at the expense of government's obligations to do justice (Travis 2001). This is a critical argument since it once again goes to the heart of the executive's case. Ministers have grave responsibilities which far exceed those of their critics. For better or worse, they must have the discretion to discharge them, even when certain legal principles are compromised in the process.

Usage

The third set of arguments picks up on this last theme; simply because ministers have widely drawn powers at their disposal does not mean that they will be used inappropriately. Again, this reminds us that ministers place considerable emphasis on their own common sense, the openness of British politics and the resource implications of heavy-handed implementation as the most effective safeguards against abuse. This point is also recognised by Lord Carlile who notes that in a liberal democracy 'we are entitled to assume . . . there will be a sensible use of the discretion to prosecute' (Carlile 2005, para. 27). His Lordship adds that many people would regard as absurd the idea of prosecuting GM crop protestors under anti-terror laws. This would only discredit the law itself, while wasting valuable resources which should be used in much more serious cases.

That ministers accept this can be seen in the relatively low use of specific anti-terror measures. Taking proscription as our first example, it is noteworthy that of the thirty-nine organisations banned under Part II of the Terrorism Act, not one is classified as a domestic terrorist

Table 7.1 Arrests in Great Britain under the Terrorism Act, 2002–4

Year	arrests	Arrests in connection with domestic terrorism	Charged	Charged with terrorism offences	Charged with immigration offences
2002	193	15	74	38	42
2003	275	22	94	47	31
2004	162	9	40	19	30

Source: Reports on the Operation of the Terrorism Act 2000 for 2002–3 and 2004 (Annexes E and D)

group. In short, this measure has been used exclusively in respect of Northern Ireland and international terrorist groups.

Low usage is also apparent in a number of other areas. Though they give some credence to critics' views that terrorism laws are used for immigration purposes, the data in Table 7.1 would appear to confirm the government's claim that these laws are not used when other measures will suffice. As a result, most offences under the Act do not see any prosecutions, including the really controversial ones: ss. 12–13, s. 19 and s. 38B. Similarly, in 2004, only three seizures of terrorist cash were authorised and in all cases the monies taken were returned.

Safeguards and oversight

For defenders of the current arrangements, that these figures are as low as they are demonstrates the effectiveness of the various safeguards

Table 7.2 People charged with terrorism offences in Northern Ireland, 2002–4

Offence	2002	2003	2004	Total
s. 11 (membership)	4	34	9	47
s. 12 (support)	0	0	0	0
s. 13 (uniform)	0	0	0	0
s. 15 (fundraising)	9	6	2	17
s. 16 (use and possession)	0	0	0	0
s. 17 (funding)	0	0	2	2
s. 18 (money laundering)	0	0	0	0
s. 19 (disclosure)	0	0	0	0
s. 38B (information)	0	0	0	0
s. 54 (weapons training)	0	1	0	1
s. 56 (directing)	0	0	0	0
s. 57 (possession)	17	32	24	73
s. 58 (collection)	17	10	1	28
s. 103 (terrorist information)	6	5	1	12
Schedule 4 (contravention of restraint)	0	0	0	0
Total number of charges	53	89	39	181
Total number of people charged	38	62	26	126

Source: Reports on the Operation of the Terrorism Act 2000 for 2002–3 (Annex C) and 2004 (Annex B)

Table 7.3 Patterns of charging with terrorism offences in Great Britain, 2002–4

Offence	2002	2003	2004	Total
s. 11 (membership)	8	13	4	25
s. 12 (support)	0	0	0	0
s. 13 (uniform)	0	0	0	0
s. 15 (fundraising)	6	2	2	10
s. 16 (Use and possession)	0	3	0	3
s. 17 (funding)	0	2	4	6
s. 18 (money laundering)	6	0	1	7
s. 19 (disclosure)	0	0	0	0
s. 38B (information)	0	6	0	6
s. 54 (weapons training)	0	4	0	4
s. 56 (directing)	0	0	0	0
s. 57 (possession)	22	29	2	53
s. 58 (collection)	6	9	5	20
Total number of charges	48	68	19	135
Total number of people charged	38	47	19	104

Source: Reports on the Operation of the Terrorism Act 2000 for 2002–3 and 2004 (Annexes D and C)

which have been put in place. These exist at various levels. For example, it is notable just how many powers either demand authorisation from a judicial b▒▒▒▒▒▒▒ be appealed against. This issue was famously raised duri▒▒▒▒▒▒▒▒▒▒age of the Prevention of Terrorism Act 2005. However, m▒▒▒▒▒▒▒ght point out that it exists in many other areas:

- The Proscribed Organisations Appeals Commission can quash proscription orders.
- Court orders are needed to gain access to excluded and special procedure materials (for example, legal and journalistic documents) under Schedules 5 and 6 of the Terrorism Act and the monitoring of bank accounts.
- Most importantly, a system of judges now hears applications for extended detention under Schedule 8. Previously, the power to extend detention had been held by ministers.

While these examples are important, possibly the most important safeguard of all is, once again, the seniority and experience of the judges and police officers involved. For Lord Carlile (2005: para. 66) this is particularly evident in applications for release of excluded and special material. Noting that very few of these applications are ever turned down, he explains this with reference to the experience and knowledge of those involved. It is these who 'act as quality control mechanisms' and prevent abuse.

In turn, this brings us on to the role of the official reviewer himself. The government does point out that the use of the Act is subject to continuous review, the findings of which are published in an annual report. The work of the reviewer prevents ministers from making policy in a moral and legal vacuum. Moreover, the current reviewer, Lord Carlile, has highly impressive credentials for the post. With thirty-two years' experience as a criminal lawyer at his disposal, he has been able to accumulate extensive insight into the operation of the law which is, with the exception of his predecessors, probably unmatched. These facts, together with the unequivocal nature of his recommendations, makes it very difficult for ministers to ignore his reports. Indeed, the willingness of ministers and officials to act on his advice is a key feature of Lord Carlile's assessment of the law's wider legitimacy. Certainly, if they refuse to accept one of his proposals for change, they will have to marshall a very effective set of arguments. Of course, precisely the same point applies to those who, out of concern for civil liberties, question his willingness to properly tackle the government. Lord Carlile has made no secret of his view that, with certain exceptions, the legislation is both necessary and proportionate to the terrorist threat. Those who dispute this are obliged, therefore, to show how and why their insight or knowledge is so much greater than his.

Conclusion

This chapter has focused on some of the most topical and controversial elements of law and order policy in the UK. If it has done nothing else, it should have reinforced the notion that, at the heart of the debate over the relationship between the government's 'core' law enforcement tasks and the state of civil liberties lie contrasting theories of power and images of those who wield it.

From a civil libertarian perspective, the late Hugo Young's (2001a; 2001b) commentary on the passage of the ATCSA captures the essence of the case. The first of his many points is that the public should always treat ministerial statements to the effect that a new threat necessitates yet more powers with considerable scepticism. 'Arguments from security are like that. There's always another hypothesis to guard against. That's what justice ministers are in office to assert.' Secondly, these same 'justice ministers' invariably slide into the intellectual equivalent of partial-sightedness once exposed to the complexities of office. Soon, all they see are their own needs and those of the people with whom they enjoy the closest professional relationships. That this doesn't trouble them stems from an accompanying feature of the ministerial mindset. This is their self-image as people who take civil liberties so seriously that they refuse to see themselves, or their colleagues, as anything other than nobly benign. Helena Kennedy (2004) makes exactly the same point when she suggests that, because ministers believe themselves to be decent people, they reject any notion that the erosion of the legal *principles* by anti-terror laws can possibly threaten the lived reality of freedom in the UK. She adds that too often ministers come to see civil libertarians as peddlers of an outdated ideology, one which dates from an age 'when democracies were more fragile'.

By contrast, in a recent lecture the Director-General of MI5, Dame Elizabeth Manningham-Buller (2005), gave a very different account of anti-terror laws. In her view, and despite the scepticism of critics, the nature of terrorism is now so threatening that soon society will be compelled to recognise what expert opinion has known for some time: that highly regarded freedoms will have to be jettisoned in order to meet the level of threat. This suggests that the reforms discussed above are merely the start of a more profound reassessment of the relative value of fundamental liberties in Western democracies. Dame Elizabeth is especially keen to draw attention to the vulnerability of the rights of defendants to a fair hearing. Her view is that the normal rules of evidence will have to be replaced with more relaxed rules allowing significant infringements of personal liberty on the basis of uncorroborated intelligence reports. In other words, despite the evidence to the contrary, British citizens will have no choice but to trust in the professionalism and integrity of those they charge with the responsibility to protect them.

··

✅ **What you should have learnt from reading this chapter**

• An overview of anti-terror legislation in the United Kingdom.

• A detailed insight into the specific features of the Terrorism Act 2000 and associated legislation, together with the way in which these statutes threaten civil liberties.

• An awareness of why civil libertarians remain sceptical of the necessity and value of anti-terror statutes.

• Ministerial justifications for this body of law, especially in light of recent developments in global politics.

• The very different perspectives adopted by both sides of the political divide as they attempt to assess anti-terror legislation.

🔍 **Glossary of key terms**

Al-Qaeda ('the Group') A well-known, loosely connected international organisation founded by Osama bin-Laden. The ultimate aim of al-Qaeda is the re-creation of a single Islamic state. In the meantime, its supporters are pledged to remove all non-Muslims from Arabia, overthrow Islamic governments who they see as corrupted by Western influences and, inevitably, destroy the state of Israel.

Birmingham pub bombings On 21 November 1974, two city-centre pubs – the Mulberry Bush and the Tavern in the Town – were destroyed in a co-ordinated PIRA attack. The pub bombings, coming so soon after similar attacks in Woolwich and Guildford, changed political attitudes to Irish terrorism and paved the way for modern anti-terror laws. At the same time, however, they inadvertently exposed deep-seated deficiencies in the criminal justice process. Those people originally convicted for the atrocities – the Maguire Seven, the Guildford Four and the Birmingham Six – were all subsequently acquitted on appeal after some of the worst miscarriages of justice witnessed in English courts.

Guillotine motion A parliamentary device for restricting the time available to discuss a Bill or other item of business.

Independent Police Complaints Commission The body created to replace the much-criticised Police Complaints Authority. The IPCC has a variety of powers to monitor and supervise the investigation of complaints against police officers.

Jihad In Arabic, jihad literally means 'effort' undertaken on behalf of God and Islam. Its modern usage, however, refers to a holy war waged against non-Muslims.

Junta A term originating in Spain and Portugal in the seventeenth century describing a ruling group which seizes and retains political power by force.

Omagh Outrage In late August 1998, the Northern Irish town of Omagh was devastated by a bomb planted by the Real IRA, a splinter group that had broken from the PIRA in the aftermath of the Good Friday Agreement. The Real IRA's decision to attack Omagh was a desperate attempt to provoke a political crisis and derail the peace process. It remains the worst single atrocity committed during the Troubles.

Realpolitik A German term which refers to a system of politics based solely on practical considerations at the expense of ethical or philosophical ones.

Whistle-blower A person who reveals the wrongdoing of another. British government is particularly vulnerable to whistle-blowers who feel that divulging secrets is the only way they can bring to the public's attention unconstitutional behaviour. As the recent case of David Shayler demonstrates, these people often endure considerable hardship as a result of their decisions to speak out.

? Likely Examination Questions

Why has anti-terrorism legislation expanded so dramatically in recent years?

Do anti-terrorism laws tilt the balance of power too much in favour of government at the expense of individual liberty?

Helpful websites

www.cia.gov   The Central Intelligence Agency

www.fbi.gov   Federal Bureau of Investigation

www.gchq.gov.uk   General Communications Headquarters

www.met.police.uk   The Metropolitan Police

www.fco.gov.uk   The Secret Intelligence Service

www.mi5.gov.uk   The Security Service

www.met.police.uk/so/special_branch.htm   Special Branch

Suggestions for further reading

The websites listed above are all excellent for those who wish to find out more about anti-terror operations from the perspective of those who carry them out. They also explain why law enforcers believe the powers they possess are absolutely fundamental to national security. A highly readable account and one which offers a different perspective is Stephen Dorrill, *The Silent Conspiracy* (London: Heinemann), 1993, an

excellent history of MI5 and associated agencies and one which
covers material relevant to Chapter 6 as well as 7. It should go
without saying by now that both Ewing and Gearty (1990)
and Ewing and Dale-Risk (2004) also contain relevant chapters on
terrorism.

Notes

1. The previous year had seen emergency legislation passed to assist in policing operations in Northern Ireland.
2. The Anti-Terrorism, Crime and Security Act 2001 is the government's response to the attacks of 9/11. The Prevention of Terrorism Act 2005 was necessary because Part IV of this statute was ruled unlawful by the House of Lords (see Chapter 4).
3. A press release was issued to this effect on 30 October 1997.
4. At this point in time, this piece of legislation was the successor to its 1974 namesake.
5. Unsurprisingly given the complexity of the subject matter, the Act was a considerable piece of law-making. It contained 131 sections and sixteen schedules.
6. These are largely contained in the Proceeds of Crime Act 2002.
7. Lord Lloyd's objections had been based on democratic principle; that imposing such a wide-ranging obligation to inform has echoes of a police state and is incompatible with British tradition. One of the UK's leading experts on anti-terrorism law, Professor Clive Walker (2002: 108), agrees and draws our attention to the implications of this for family life.
8. The forerunner of the Terrorism Act 2000.
9. This was the defence successfully run by lawyers in a famous case known as *Kebilene*.
10. See, for example, the Prime Minister's televised appeal on 6 February 2003.

CHAPTER 8

After the Bombs

Contents

Overview

As this book was being written, the city of London was subject to a devastating series of bomb attacks. The loss of life on 7 July, while it did not compare to that experienced on 9/11 or even in Madrid, nonetheless caused understandable revulsion and no little fear. This was affirmed two weeks later, when sheer incompetence alone seems to have saved countless others from further heartache.

This chapter concludes this study by examining the main consequences of this desperate episode, in particular to see what light they shed on the topics we have studied. The Prime Minister, Mr Blair, has stated his view that 7/7 is a watershed in the constitutional history of the United Kingdom. But if it is true that the 'rules of the game' have now changed, what precisely have they changed to? More importantly, has anyone in Downing Street told the judiciary?

Key issues to be covered in this chapter

- The political dilemma faced by the government after the events of July 2005
- The 12-point anti-terror package announced by the Prime Minister
- The principal civil liberties issues to have emerged as a result of this
- The reaction of the civil liberties lobby and its ongoing concerns over the state of liberty in the UK

The July 2005 bombings and the Blair government

In so many different respects, the terror attacks on London were a political nightmare for the Prime Minister and his colleagues. Primarily, they have reopened (yet again) the debate on the wisdom of Britain's unequivocal support for US foreign policy in the Middle East and western Asia. Public doubts over Blair's stance are now so great that they are likely to dog his reputation long after he has left office. Then there is the question of the bombers themselves. The fact that they were young Britons raises yet more questions over the sustainability of **multiculturalism** as government's preferred solution to the problems of ethnicity and integration. This is particularly awkward for the Labour leadership. Multiculturalism was very much the creation of the Labour party when in office during the 1960s. Despite its alleged failings, many party members remain committed to it, something which extends even to the Prime Minister who has been unbending in his support for '**faith schools**'. Consequently, any admission that this policy has failed would be divisive and embarrassing in equal measure (White 2005).

A still more pressing question concerns the bombers' motivations: what did they possibly imagine the temporal gains their sacrifice might achieve? The grim realisation has now dawned that they probably did not expect to gain anything at all. These were not intellectually inadequate young men. They would have realised better than most that even their most tangible demands – the restoration of the **Caliphate** and the destruction of Israel – are things which, as the Prime Minister acknowledges, no sensible person could accept (*The Guardian*, 27 July 2005). Such a stance leaves politicians like Mr Blair utterly frustrated. His every instinct is to negotiate, to seek a settlement through quiet diplomacy. In this instance, however, this is utterly impossible.

In the long term, however, it is the ability of the bombers to strike so easily which will pose the government its biggest dilemma. The bottom line is this. The blameless, disturbingly orthodox lives led by the bombers meant that they never drew the attention of the police or the Security Service to their conspiracies. Despite the powers and resources granted them, the latter were virtually helpless to prevent the attacks from happening. In their defence, it should be noted that a similar problem confronted British law enforcers in the early years of the Troubles. Eventually, though, the **PIRA** leadership was successfully

confessions and long-term mental trauma, will no doubt weigh on the judicial mind.

The new rules on deportation
The government's ability to survive a legal challenge to extended detention for pre-trial suspects may well depend upon its willingness to offer certain concessions. The maximum period could be lowered to a month or possibly six weeks, while enhanced levels of judicial oversight could be built into any subsequent legislation.

By contrast, it is difficult to see what concessions could be offered that would persuade the judiciary to accept the new proposals in respect of deporting terrorist suspects to countries which practice torture. This is a long-running problem which, as we saw in the previous chapter, has already caused ministers considerable legal and political difficulties. What the government is now proposing is that a 'memorandum of understanding' signed between the UK and the recipient country will suffice to meet objections that deportations in such cases contravene the (unconditional) rights protected by Article 3. As Liberty point out in their initial response to this proposal, amending the Human Rights Act in respect of Article 3[1] will not be enough for this purpose. Ultimately, the government may have to withdraw from the Council of Europe altogether. This would be unprecedented. It would mean that one of the main architects of the European Convention and the first to ratify it, is no longer prepared to offer its protections to its residents when no other signatory is considering a similar move.

Box 8.2 Article 3 of the European Convention on Human Rights

'No one shall be subjected to torture or to inhuman or degrading treatment or punishment.'

The terms of Article 3 are stark. The reader will note that, unlike those Articles studied in Chapters 5 and 6, it does not include any qualifying conditions, nor does it allow governments to enter a derogation in order to suspend their obligations under it.

However, regardless of this, it would seem that ministers hope to persuade judges in the UK and Strasbourg to accept their word that the memoranda offer meaningful guarantees that deportees will not face torture. Early indications suggest that, despite the Prime Minister's bravura performance on 5 August, they are none too confident of their ability to do this (White 2005). His theme – that the 'rules of the game are changing' – was subsequently taken up by David Blunkett, returned briefly to the Cabinet as Work and Pensions Secretary. While Blair was away on holiday, Blunkett reopened his long-running feud with the judges that Parliament's will should be respected on this matter. If MPs and peers are happy to give ministers the discretion to determine when a memorandum is acceptable under the Human Rights Act, the judiciary should accept this (Travis 2005). It will be interesting to see whether or not calmer voices will have prevailed by the time any legislation has been drafted.

Kneejerk illiberalism

For civil libertarians, the tragic events of July 2005 simply confirm their worst suspicions over the integrity of the Blair government. For Andrew Rawnsley (2005) the plan was little more than a desperate bid to convince the public that the government is firmly in control. That Blair is prepared to jettison both constitutional tradition and the cross-party consensus in order to achieve this goal points in equal measure to his skill and failing as a democratic politician: that there is little in politics over which he is not prepared to negotiate. Accordingly, Rawnsley insists that some of the ideas included in the announcement of 5 August should be anathema to any true democrat. That Blair is prepared to consider them at all is a disturbing development, compounded by the fact that they are highly unlikely to work. The Director of Liberty, Shami Chakrahbati (2005), picks up this theme as follows:

- It is impossible for a democrat to compromise on torture since 'inhuman and degrading treatment . . . te abominations, which violate the inherent h turer and victim alike'. It follows that the merest risk of such treatment should stay the hand of any Home Secretary as he prepares to sign a deportation order, memoranda of understanding or no.

- The ▓▓▓▓▓▓ offence of 'condoning, glorifying or justifying ter▓▓▓▓▓▓ in the world is far too broad. In the first place, it ▓▓▓▓▓▓ sm of any regime, no matter how dictatorial or brutal. In the second, it does so for making statements which fall a long way short of direct incitement for others to commit acts of political violence.[2]
- Similarly, the idea of changing the law on proscription so that a peaceful organisation such as Hizb ut-Tahrir can be banned sets a precedent for the elimination of a wide range of political organisations or parties simply for holding to extreme positions.

The list of complaints could go on. Once again, it reminds us that, while most people accept the need for balance over such matters, there is very little consensus over where it might be struck. Strong doubts remain that, unless they can break free of the shackles of their own fears, ministers of all parties will continue to regard liberty as something which is indistinguishable from any other 'public good': a factor which must be always considered but not one worthy of unique political protection. This might be an inevitable feature of democratic politics in the age of fear. Whether or not there might emerge the political will to challenge it is far less certain.

....

✓ What you should have learnt from reading this chapter

- A basic understanding of the government's immediate plans to extend anti-terrorism laws in the UK.

- An appreciation that, unless the government changes course, further clashes between itself and the judiciary are inevitable.

- Insight into why the Prime Minister's announcement of 5 August has provoked genuine dismay among civil libertarians.

🔎 Glossary of key terms

Caliphate In the immediate aftermath of the Prophet Muhammad's death in 632 his followers agreed that one of their number should assume the title 'Caliph' and be recognised as the Prophet's successor: the chief civil and spiritual leader of all Muslims. For the followers of men such as Osama bin-Laden, the restoration of the Caliphate is an essential feature of their political programme. It would mean uniting Muslims under a single political entity; by implication, the most remarkable transformation of the global political landscape since the emergence of the Mongol Empire in the thirteenth and fourteenth centuries.

Faith schools A controversial development in English education, 'faith schools' recognise the demand among certain parents for greater flexibility in educational provision. Though the Prime Minister is a keen supporter, many in his party see such establishments as a retrograde step, especially in the education of young women and the promotion of tolerance.

Multiculturalism A strategy for the political integration of ethnic minorities based on two premises: official recognition of ethnic minorities by political authorities and an attempt to absorb leaders emerging from these groups into the political mainstream. Multiculturalism has always been much more popular among Labour and Liberal Democrat politicians than Conservatives.

PIRA An acronym for the Provisional Irish Republican Army (or 'Provos'), a body originally formed in the late 1960s among Catholics in Northern Ireland to protect themselves against attack from Protestants and the Protestant-dominated police force: the Royal Ulster Constabulary. The term 'Provisional' denotes the lack of formal legal status which can only be confirmed by an all-Ireland government. Unable to break the lines of communication and financing arrangements established by the PIRA leadership, the British government eventually decided to search for a political solution to the Northern Irish crisis.

Likely examination questions

Why is there so much political disagreement over the state of liberty in the UK?

In what ways do the various reactions to the London bombings of July 2005 reveal the lack of consensus over law and order policy?

Helpful Websites

www.hrw.org   Human Rights Watch

www.pmo.gov.uk   Prime Minister's Office

United Nations human rights reports can be accessed via www.un.org

Suggestions for further reading

The contemporaneous nature of these events makes the task of recommending further reading a little difficult. Those of you who wish to gain a better understanding of these complex debates really must consult the Prime Minister's website, along with those of the Home Office and Liberty. The *Guardian* newspaper's 'archive search' facility is also an excellent source of contemporary information, notably the various 'Special Reports' it periodically produces. All of these sites are referenced at the end of preceding chapters. Happy surfing.

Notes

1. Technically, Parliament could remove Article 3 from the list of rights protected in Schedule 1 of the Human Rights Act.
2. The Mayor of London, Ken Livingstone, has often pointed to the 'Mandela test' in such cases; the idea being that, if a proposed measure would have aided the apartheid regime in South Africa in its bid to destroy the African National Congress (ANC), he will not support it. If so, this proposal is likely to give Mr Livingstone considerable pause for thought.

References

Bailey, S. H. et al. (2002), *Smith, Bailey and Gunn on the Modern English Legal System*, London: Sweet and Maxwell.

Barnett, Hilaire (2004), *Constitutional and Administrative Law*, 5th edn, London: Cavendish.

Blackstone, Colin (2000), 'Thatcher "spied on ministers"', *The Guardian*, 25 February.

Bodi, Faisal (2000a), 'Draco would be proud', *The Guardian*, 16 August.

Bodi, Faisal (2000b), 'Britain's terrorism errors', *The Guardian*, 29 December.

Bradley, A. W. and Ewing, K. D. (2003), *Constitutional and Administrative Law*, Harlow: Longman.

Bright, Martin (2004), 'Are these all that stand between 11 untried detainees and their liberty?', *The Observer*, 19 December.

Campbell, Duncan and Cowan, Rosie (2005), 'Terror trail that led from Algeria to London', *The Guardian*, 14 April.

Carlile, Lord (2005), *Report of the Operation of the Terrorism Act 2000 for 2004*, London: HMSO.

Carvel, John (2005), 'Security fears over medical database', *The Guardian*, 30 June.

Chakrahbati, Shami (2005), 'The price of a chilling and counterproductive recipe', *The Guardian*, 8 August.

Clark, James (2000), 'Straw signs five bugging orders a day', *The Guardian*, 9 July.

Cohen, Nick (2004a), 'Goodnight freedom', *The Observer*, 9 May.

Cohen, Nick (2004b), 'There is no case for torture, ever', *The Observer*, 24 October.

Cohen, Nick (2004c), 'Marking your card', *The Observer*, 5 December.

Coxall, Bill, Robins, Lynton and Leach, Robert (2003), *Contemporary British Politics*, 4th edn, Basingstoke: Palgrave.

Dorrill, Stephen (1993), *The Silent Conspiracy*, London: Heinemann.

Dyer, Clare (2004), 'Selection of judges condemned as biased', *The Guardian*, 2 July.

Dyer, Clare (2005a), 'Judges speak out against erosion of independence by government', *The Guardian*, 26 April.

Dyer, Clare (2005b), 'Parole board can use terrorism powers, say law lords', *The Guardian*, 8 July.

Economist (2005), 'Taking Britain's liberties', *The Economist*, 5 February.

Ewing, Keith and Gearty, Conor (1990), *Freedom Under Thatcher*, Oxford: Oxford University Press.

Ewing, Keith and Gearty, Conor (2000), *The Struggle for Civil Liberties*, Oxford: Oxford University Press.

Ewing, Keith and Dale-Risk, Ken (2004), *Human Rights in Scotland*, Edinburgh: Thomson–W. Green.

Feldman, David (2000), *Civil Liberties and Human Rights in England and Wales*, Oxford: Oxford University Press.

Fenwick, Helen (2000), *Civil Rights*, Harlow: Longman.

Fignant, Cyrille (2004), 'Police Cooperation and the Area of Freedom, Security and Justice', in Neil Walker (ed.), *Europe's Area of Freedom, Security and Justice*, Oxford: Oxford University Press.

Gearty, Conor (1998), 'The Bill's a disgrace', *The Guardian*, 2 September.

Griffith, John (1997), *The Politics of the Judiciary*, Fontana: London.

Hattersley, Roy (2004), 'Justice and its enemies', *The Observer*, 14 March.

Ingle, Stephen (2000), *The British Party System*, London: Pinter.

Jenkins, Simon (2005a), 'Ministry of fear takes over', *The Times*, 28 January.

Jenkins, Simon (2005b), 'A sledgehammer for a nut', *The Times*, 15 April.

Jowell, Jeffrey (2003), 'Administrative Law', in Bogdanor, Vernon (ed.), *The British Constitution in the Twentieth Century*, Oxford: Oxford University Press.

Joyce, Peter (2002), *The Politics of Protest*, Basingstoke: Palgrave.

Kennedy, Helena (2004a), 'A good brand: is that all the Lord Chancellor is?', *The Times*, 24 February.

Kennedy, Helena (2004b), *Just Law*, London: Chatto and Windus.

Kettle, Martin (1983), 'The Drift to Law and Order', in Hall, Stuart and Jacques, Martin (eds), *The Politics of Thatcherism*, London: Lawrence and Wishart.

Kettle, Martin (1996), 'Cowardice in the face of the ruling class', *The Guardian*, 3 April.

Kirkham, Sophie (2005), 'Six arrested for defying protest ban', *The Guardian*, 8 August.

Liberty (2005a), The Right to Protest (www.liberty-human-rights.org.uk).

Liberty (2005b), *The Prime Minister's 12-Point Anti-Terror Package: Liberty's Initial Thoughts*, London: Liberty.

Lustgarten, Laurence and Leigh, Ian (1994), *In From the Cold*, Oxford: Clarendon.

Manning, Jonathan et al. (2004), *Blackstone's Guide to the Anti-Social Behaviour Act 2003*, Oxford: Oxford University Press.

Morrison, Alan (1996), 'Courts', in Alan B. Morrison (ed.), *Fundamentals of American Law*, Oxford: Oxford University Press.

Muir, Hugh (2005), 'No-go zone to encircle arms fair', *The Guardian*, 8 August.

Neuborne, Burt (1996), 'An Overview of the Bill of Rights', in Alan B. Morrison (ed.), *Fundamentals of American Law*, Oxford: Oxford University Press.

Norton-Taylor, Richard (1997), 'Rank and file caught in cold war paranoia', *The Guardian*, 26 August.

Pierce, Gareth (2005), 'A stampede against justice', *The Guardian*, 8 March.

Rawnsley, Andrew (2005), 'New Labour goes back to its old vices', *The Observer*, 14 August.

Reiner, Robert (2000), *The Politics of the Police*, Oxford: Oxford University Press.

Robertson, Geoffrey (1993), *Freedom, the Individual and the Law*, London: Penguin.

Rose, David (1996), *In the Name of the Law*, London: Jonathan Cape.

Scruton, Roger (2001), *The Meaning of Conservatism*, Basingstoke: Palgrave.

Singh, Robert (2002), 'Law and order', in Peele, Gillian et al. (eds), *Developments in American Politics 4*, Basingstoke: Palgrave.

Slapper, Gary and Kelly, David (2004), *The English Legal System*, London: Cavendish.

Stanley, Jay (2004), *The Surveillance-Industrial Complex*, New York: ACLU.

Stanley, Jay and Steinhardt, Barry (2003), *Bigger Monster, Weaker Chains*, New York: ACLU.

Stevens, Dallal (2004), *UK Asylum Law and Policy*, London: Sweet and Maxwell.

Straw, Jack (1998), 'My emergency Bill is because of Omagh. And foreign crimes', *The Guardian*, 2 September.

Travis, Alan (1999), 'Straw wants to curb liberal judges', *The Guardian*, 12 October.

Travis, Alan (2000), 'Courts fight shy of three strikes', *The Guardian*, 27 December.

Travis, Alan (2001), 'Blunkett unveils tougher laws on terrorism', *The Guardian*, 4 October.

Travis, Alan (2004), 'Wardens to issue fines for anti-social behaviour', *The Guardian*, 29 October.

Travis, Alan (2005), 'Blunkett warns judges over terror plans', *The Guardian*, 8 August.

Travis, Alan and Dyer, Clare (2000), 'Power shifts to the judges', *The Guardian*, 11 September.

Van Bueren, Geraldine (2004), 'The case for a social justice act – human rights for the poor', *The Times*, 9 November.

Waddington, David (1992), *Contemporary Issues in Public Disorder*, London: Routledge.

Wainwright, Martin (2005), 'Anti-war protester escapes asbo', *The Guardian*, 18 May.

Walker, Clive (2002), *Blackstone's Guide to the Anti-Terrorism Legislation*, Oxford: Oxford University Press.

Ward, Richard and Davies, Olwen (2004), *The Criminal Justice Act 2003*, Bristol: Jordans.

White, Michael and Wintour, Patrick (2001), 'MPs savage terror bill', *The Guardian*, 20 November.

White, Michael and Wintour, Patrick (2003), 'Old-fashioned committee provides a window on Whitehall's "ring of secrecy"', *The Guardian*, 11 September.

White, Michael (2005), 'Public mood has hardened over terror cases, Blair tells judges', *The Guardian*, 27 July.

White, Robin and Willock, Ian (1999), *The Scottish Legal System*, Edinburgh: Butterworths LexisNexis.

Yarbrough, Tinsley (2002), 'The Supreme Court and the Constitution', in Peele, Gillian et al. (eds), *Developments in American Politics 4*, Basingstoke: Palgrave.

Young, Hugo (1995), 'Umpires now turning into players', *The Guardian*, 9 May.

Young, Hugo (2001a), 'Blunkett holds liberty and the judges in contempt', *The Guardian*, 15 November.

Young, Hugo (2001b), 'Once lost, these freedoms will be impossible to restore', *The Guardian*, 11 December.

Zander, Michael (1998), 'UK Rights Come Home', *Politics Review*, April.

Index

Bold indicates that the term is defined

Conservative policy on, 110–13
Criminal Justice and Police Act
(2001), 115–16, 118, 121, 124, 129
Criminal Justice and Public Order
Act (1994), 112–15, 123–4
defence of, 127–31
Labour policy on, 113, 117, 123,
127–8, 129–31
Police Act (1996), 109
Protection from Harassment Act
(1997), 116, 119, 121
Public Order Act (1936), 108–9, 111
Public Order Act (1986), 109–12,
113–19, 124
see also ASBOs, Crime and Disorder
Act (1998)
public order policing, 107–9, 111–13,
124–6

R v. *Benjafield and Others*, 76
R v. *Brown*, 75, 76
R v. *Gough*, 63–4
R v. *Immigration Appeals Tribunal, ex parte
Shah*, 93
R v. *Secretary of State for the Home
Department, ex parte Kebilene*, 199
R v. *Secretary of State for the Home
Department, ex parte Lul Adan and
Others*, 94
R v. *Secretary of State for the Home
Department, ex parte Ruddock*, 139
R (Roberts) v. *the Parole Board*, 76, 197,
213
R (on the application of Q) v. *Secretary of
State for the Home Department*, 77,
94–5
Race Relations Act (1965), 8, 70
ratio decidendi, 43
raves, 114–15
*Re Bow Street Metropolitan Stipendiary
Magistrate ex parte Pinochet Ugarte*,
62–3
Reagan, President Ronald, 79, 80
Rehnquist, Chief Justice William,
61, 79, 81, 82, 83, 84

right to privacy, ch. 6; *see also*
investigatory powers
ring of secrecy, 136
Roberts, Chief Justice John, 81
rule of law
Dicey on, 7–8
and judicial independence, 45

Scalia, Justice Antonin, 61, 80
Scarman, Lord, 9, 13
Scotland Act (1998), 30–1, 56–7
Scottish Executive, 30, 31, 32, 57,
58–9, 150, 154, 156
Scottish Parliament, 26, 30–1
Security Service (MI5), 140, 141, 141,
143, 145, 146, 148, 149, 150, 152,
161, 162, **175**, 199, 200, 211
Sedley, Sir Stephen, 97
sentencing policy (UK), 85–90
September 11th attacks (9/11), 164,
167, 181, 188, 200
Shayler, David, 148
social and economic rights, 4–6
UN Covenant on Economic, Social
and Cultural Rights, 4
Special Immigration Appeals Tribunal,
197, 213
Spycatcher, 74
Stevens, Lord, 150
Straw, Jack, 87, 90, 94, 110, 117, 148,
153, 179, 195
Supreme Court (UK), 48, 50, 54–5, **65**,
99
Supreme Court (USA), **66**
accusations of political bias, 79–81
appointments to, 59–61, 79
protection of civil liberties, 6, 82–4
Supreme Court Act (1981) (UK), 48,
56

Taylor, Lord Chief Justice, 86
Thatcher, Baroness Margaret, 10, 14,
72, 74, 148, 160
Thomas, Justice Clarence, 61, 80
Thomas, Sir Swinton, 156, 157